Yes We Are!
The Living Body of Christ

By Father Jim Hogan

Helen

Thank you for your great service in calling forth God's "New Reality"

your brother in christ,

Jim Hogan

With a Foreword by Robert J. Egan, S.J.

"Yes We Are! The Living Body of Christ"

By Father Jim Hogan

ISBN 1-931291-76-4

Library of Congress Control Number: 2009928012

Published in the United States of America

First Edition

Publishing Consultant: Stoneydale Press Publishing Company,
523 Main Street, Stevensville, MT 59870 Phone: 406-777-2729
Email: stoneydale@montana.com

Additional copies of "Yes We Are! The Living Body of Christ"
may be obtained from:
> Father Jim Hogan
> 901 S. Higgins Ave. #301
> Missoula, MT 59801
> (406) 721-5090 jjhpadre@christthekingccm.org
> web.mac.com/fatherjimhogan

DEDICATION

In gratitude I dedicate these pages to
  Archbishop Raymond G. Hunthausen,
  coach, mentor, bishop and friend,

  and to you the reader and to men and women
  like you who know at least intuitively that we
  are the Living Body of Christ and are resolved
  to honor the vision of Pope John XXIII and
  the Second Vatican Council.

THANK YOU

• for the inspiring Foreword: Father Bob Egan, S.J.

• for reading this manuscript when it was still very long,
   and for offering your helpful criticisms:
        Sister Dorothy Feehan, BVM
        Kathleen Jackson
        Keith Thrailkill
        Joellen Estenson;

• for reading and helping me clarify my writing about the
   influence of St. Augustine and St. Thomas Aquinas:
        Bruce Bender   Mary Ann Gruba
        Tom Hagan   Jeremiah Sullivan
           Jamie Yule

• for the cover and other photos: Jim Streeter;

• for the cover design: Joe Boddy;

• and for professional direction and sound advice: Dale Burk.

TABLE OF CONTENTS

Also by Father Jim Hogan:

"REMOVE YOUR SHOES"

FOREWORD

John XXIII, HUMANAE SALUTUS #23
"Renew Your wonders in our time,
As though for a new Pentecost . . . . "

RESTARTING THE RENEWAL
By Robert J. Egan, S.J.

Catholicism is many things at once. It is a message – "glad tidings" of an event in human history in which God's truth has been revealed. It is a particular way of being human that results from a particular kind of inner transformation or conversion. It is at once a renewal movement, a faith community, and a religious institution – forms of symbolic action that give structure and intelligibility to the *communion* we Catholics share among ourselves and with the mystery of the Triune God.

Catholicism is also a system of symbols, a structure of ideas, a distinctive ethos, a redemptive counterculture. It is, as well, a messianic mission freely undertaken in history and society entrusted to us by God. And it is, at the same time, a living *tradition* received from our ancestors, made our own, and hopefully passed on to our descendants – though currently with considerable difficulty and frequent disappointment.

It is what Vatican II famously called "the People of God."

What we do about the church, how we decide to act in regard to it, depends very much on what, in our hearts, we *imagine* Catholicism to be and the specific judgments of truth and value we make about it. It isn't so much a "theory" about the church that matters most, as it is an *imagined* truth expressed in metaphors, images, stories, songs, and sacraments, and *practices* of different kinds as well: hymns of praise, acts of love, struggles for justice, and celebrations of beauty.

In his address at the beginning of the second session of Vatican II, Paul VI said: *"The Church is a mystery. It is a reality imbued with the hidden presence of God. It therefore lies within the very nature of the Church always to be open to new and greater exploration."*

If American Catholics took to heart one idea from Vatican II, it was that *they themselves* were the church: lay people as well as clergy, women as well as men, married people as well as single people. *All of us are the church:* we speak of the church most authentically when we speak in the first-person plural.

In 1965, that was an exciting realization. It inspired many Catholics to study their faith, to become more involved in parish life, to join social movements for peace or for the defense of human rights, and to seek jobs in church ministries and agencies. Throughout the church Catholics felt a renewed interest in spirituality, prayer and meditation, the classics of Christian mysticism, and the ministry of spiritual direction. It felt like the church was awakening from a long sleep.

In retrospect, it may seem strange that Catholics had forgotten this truth: that *all of us are the church.* But the important people in the church so often didn't look like us, didn't dress like us, didn't talk or think like us. They often spoke and acted as though they alone were the agents of the church's mission. And when we gathered for worship, it felt like something we had come to watch or hear, not like something we had come to do or pray. It *felt* as though "the church" were those others who spoke and acted at the Eucharist. In fact, they were speaking in the first person plural, but in a dead language most of us didn't understand.

Then something happened at the Second Vatican Council! Whatever the continuities with the preconciliar church – and of course there were many – Catholics experienced a seismic shift after the Council. Depending on who you were, and where you were, it might well have felt like a rupture in church history! *Catholicism now meant all of us,* and that's precisely what the liturgical changes kept telling us. It was *our* community, *our* mission, *our* tradition, *our* Eucharistic prayer, *our* worship. It was a time of new life in the church. It felt, as Pope John hoped it would, like a "new Pentecost."

Most Catholics expected the church to continue to change. They anticipated more participation and dialogue, more consultation and collegiality, and more mutuality and accountability. They anticipated more respect, more candor, more affection, more friendship. They dreamed of an adult church. It was hard for us to acknowledge that this wasn't happening, that the church was cutting off dialogue and resisting participation, that power and authority were becoming *more* centralized rather than *less*, that mutuality and accountability were being postponed and ignored.

Yet in these intervening years a shadow has surely fallen over us. Catholicism is no longer thriving here. By now we all should be able to acknowledge that something is wrong. In lots of ways we all were forced to improvise after the Council. There were no manuals, no maps, no old hands at the tasks we were facing. Some of us were hasty and careless in making changes; others were resentful and high-handed in resisting change. Mistakes were made on every side.

In the last two decades, the greatly broadened identification with the Church has begun to change. Now it seems to be changing even more rapidly. Some promises made at the Council were never kept. Some important advances have begun to be reversed. Bishops were appointed with little support from the local people. A large majority of Catholics disagreed with church leaders about several important issues, and were simply ignored.

As a result, many no longer feel at home in the church. What goes on in the church no longer seems to be about their own lives, their deepest worries, their real hopes, or their most cherished relationships. The attitudes expressed there have begun to seem strange to them, the language used has begun to sound anachronistic or pretentious. So far as they can tell, many leaders of their church seem not to care about their feelings of estrangement.

Especially among young adult Catholics, the church may seem not just wrong, but *morally* wrong – morally wrong about the rights and dignity of women properly understood, about the rights and dignity of gay and lesbian persons and the unqualified equality of those rights, about the ethical and theological critique of authoritarian social structures, and about the requirements of social justice, whether in the church or outside of it, and about the rights of all believers to practice a fully and honestly *inculturated* faith and to express reverence in ways intelligible and genuine in their own cultural contexts. For many Catholics and their friends and colleagues these failings, at the outset of the twenty-first century, have been discouraging – and even heart-breaking.

In a time of crisis, when our "loyalty" has been shaken and may seem to be deserved no longer, if we have "no voice," no place and time in which to tell the truth as best we can about our own experience, then the only option remaining for us may be to "exit." Many today are tempted simply to drift away from the church, with neither a curse nor a blessing upon it. But if the truth is that *we are* the church, then it isn't really possible to "drift away" from it! And in our culture, at this time in our history, that doesn't sound like something we need *any more of.*

Rather than resign ourselves to such a melancholy outcome, it behooves us all to think again what we are doing, to re-examine what we imagine Catholicism to be, and to set about a "new and greater exploration."

This eloquent, moving, and deeply thoughtful reflection – and reminiscence – by Fr. Jim Hogan can be a help and a model for all of us in this exploration. What we see in its pages is a vibrant local church, a faith community, with a gifted leader, an admired and respected elder. We need to become more mindful of what we're doing in the church, at the present time, of how it makes us feel, and of what these feelings bring to mind. I believe it's becoming urgent for us American Catholics to share our stories with one another, open-heartedly and truthfully, reflecting on the course of these recent decades, with all their conflict and confusion, and to listen and receive each other's stories in humble, thankful, prayerful, and discerning spirit.

It's only by telling our stories, and listening to each other's stories, that we'll be able to undertake a "communal discernment" within the church and to identify which movements among us – and within our hearts – are from the Holy Spirit, and which are in resistance to the Holy Spirit.

Yes We Are! The Living Body of Christ is a heartening example of what we need. Down to earth, full of concrete details, suffused with faith, in a particular place. And the account is a remembering, an _anamnesis_, _a bringing to mind and a keeping in mind_ of key events in a history of a people with God. But it's more than that. It's a prayerful reflection and ongoing interpretation rooted in faith – on these people and this history with God. We could call it: "doing theology from life." This is what all of God's People must learn how to do now. Then, with Fr. Hogan, we could rekindle our common hope that it will be possible for us to restart the Conciliar renewal.

[Father Robert Egan is a Jesuit priest and professor of theology at Gonzaga University in Spokane, Washington.]

PREFACE

A PERSONAL VERSE
"Tulips bloom, explosions of color, the rainbow rising up.
The painter's palette spilled.
More diverse, or less than we of human heart?

I am seventy-four years of age and have been an ordained Roman Catholic priest of the diocese of Helena for forty-eight years. In 2006 at the age of seventy-one, I entered Senior Status. Friends and acquaintances commented over and over again, "I bet you are busier now than you were before you retired." Some folks worry that my life will be boring with nothing to attract my interest. There certainly is far less demand on my time and energy. When folks hear I am trying to write a book, the same questions are always asked. "Why are you doing that?" "What is the book about?" Such questions help sharpen my focus and purpose.

Initially I engaged in writing this as a form of personal catharsis. Gradually my primary motivation evolved. Since entering Senior Status I continue listening to good Catholic folks who are confused and disturbed by the current situation within the Catholic Church. Now my purpose in writing this is to encourage folks like you to be persistent in maintaining the vision of the Second Vatican Council.

Since my ordination, I have been privileged to serve in parish ministry among people in Missoula, Montana, for forty years. Missoula is situated in a broad glacial valley. Snow-capped mountains, canyons and forests surround us. Two rivers flow through our valley. You may have read that wonderful book, *A River Runs Through It*. That's Missoula!

The Bitterroot is one of those rivers. Early in the morning an endless stream of headlights flow north into Missoula on Highway 93. That asphalt strip parallels the river. In late autumn and during the winter months when snow accumulates on the mountain peaks, a dense morning fog often rolls off the river across the fields and the highway. Visibility is diminished. Drivers fearing an accident slow to a crawl.

Today many of us in the Roman Catholic Church feel a spiritual fog now obscures our ability to see what it means to follow the way of Christ. We remain grateful for the Council's vision even while its bright promise seems to be diminishing as the twentieth century fades in our memory. If in some way the words and feelings expressed in this book reflect and are descriptive of your own, perhaps that will encourage you to persist in keeping the vision of the Council alive. We are the Living Body of Christ. Our shared task is to create a new expression of our Catholic culture while being actively engaged in the dominant culture in which we live.

That spiritual fog began to settle upon us in the years following the II Vatican Council. Initially some resisted the vision of the Council. We still hear voices from the halls of the Vatican sounding a call to retreat from that vision. Others welcomed the Council's call for renewal and today struggle with determination to pursue the Councils' vision.

This is not the first time in our history that divisiveness has threatened our communion. Read the *Acts of the Apostles* and the epistles of Paul. Our early ancestors struggled with the threat of division within the young church as a whole and in their local churches. Diversity has characterized the church throughout the centuries. It is our diversity that prompted me to write a poem including this verse,

Tulips bloom, explosions of color, the rainbow rising up.
The painter's palette spilled.
More diverse, or less than we of human heart?

Diversity among us is a gift. Unfortunately it increasingly seems to be a burden.

Writing these pages is a work born out of my love for the Roman Catholic Church. It could not be otherwise. This ancient household of faith has been my home since birth. It has been the source of inspiration, the source of my spiritual life, the guide for my passion and the arena in which my life work evolved. The church has shown me who I am, what it is to be a companion of the Risen Christ and it remains the object of my appreciation and gratitude. Perhaps this book will provide you some help in navigating through the confusion, perplexity and discouragement in our community today. I invite you to pull aside and read it.

The Jesuit priest Anthony de Mello offered advice I try to follow in my living. I try, "To dance my dance as well as I can. If others benefit from it fine. If not, too bad."[1] I hope you will benefit from my dance in the pages of this book.

We are church for others. We have work to do. It is the work of

Christ! In *The Pastoral Constitution on the Church In The Modern World,* the Council addressed the hopes and dreams of the human family and called all modern Christians to look at and understand the world in which we live.

The joy and hope, the grief and anxiety of the people of this age,
especially those who are poor or in any way afflicted, this is the
joy and hope, the grief and anxiety of the followers of Christ.[2]

"We read to be taken out of ourselves, to be drawn into another world which then returns us, wiser, to our own."[3] If you choose to read this book, I hope these pages will take you out of yourself, draw you into another place, and then return you to your own, somehow wiser and newly motivated to pursue the vision of John XXIII and the Second Vatican Council.

The wisdom of Mahatma Gandhi, that holy man from India, still applies today: "You must be the change you want to see in the world." We are the Living Body of Christ. That is the beacon of light I set before you. I hope that every time you extend your hands for the broken bread of his body and the poured wine of his blood, the *"Amen"* you speak will affirm your own truth. The Body of Christ! Amen! Yes, we are.

CHAPTER 1

THE GOSPEL OF JOHN:
"A voice cried out in the wilderness.
Make straight the path of the Lord."[1]

A SINGLE VOICE

As I began my second year in Senior Status, I enrolled in a continuing education program in the American College at the University of Louvain in Belgium. At the conclusion of the program I traveled to Assisi, Italy. My journey required two overnight stays in Rome where I unexpectedly heard a voice in the wilderness.

On the first morning in Rome, I met a Maryknoll priest at breakfast. He has served the church in Latin America these past twenty-five years and was just completing three months in a renewal program at the Vatican. He summarized his experience with the startling comment that "the age of Camelot has ended!" He told me that quip expressed the message he heard spoken repeatedly in the classrooms favored by the Roman Curia and at least by some American bishops. It was his impression that they have set themselves the objective of recapturing the model of church so familiar to us prior to the Second Vatican Council.

This missionary priest was undaunted by and unwilling to allow that oft-repeated declaration to dampen his spirit. His passion for the gospel ignited in his soul by that Council burns still. He was renewed and ready to return to his ministry among the victims of AIDS; renewed in his determination and commitment to continue the vision of the Second Vatican Council.

The passion in his soul and mine is a fire of gratitude ignited by our good fortune to be Catholics nurtured and inspired by that vision. The Council provided freedom to discover the Christ vision anew and awakened us to our responsibility to make life better for all people. That passion burns in my soul like the wildfires that so often consume the forests of Western Montana. They explode, leaping into the sky, rushing across the mountains and valley floors. Wildfires burn the accumulated forest debris and prepare the mountains and meadows for the next cycle of life to blossom. So it was with the Council.

On May 27, 1961, Joseph Michael Gilmore, then bishop of Helena, called forth seven men and ordained them. I was among them. Something totally unexpected was about to happen in my life. In those first years, I wore a cassock and collar and said Mass in Latin facing the wall. I preached sermons naively oblivious that the church had become a dark, dusty, even lifeless old mansion. Our imaginations were dulled by routine and memorization. We lacked vision and navel gazed while Vietnam and our own black ghettos burned. On the day of ordination neither my classmates nor I understood what it was to be baptized, to be priest, to be Catholic or even what it was to be church.

Then an old man became pope. He took the name John XXIII. He opened the windows and let the Spirit blow through the house we name church. He called the bishops of the world to gather with him in St. Peter's basilica. The Second Vatican Council was heralded as a New Pentecost and it was. It awakened us to the meaning of Baptism and Eucharist and a deeper awareness of the mystery of Christ. Christ became for us far more than an abstraction or pious idea. He is risen, alive and present among and in us as he promised. "Wherever two or three of you gather in my name, I am there with you."[2]

That Maryknoll priest I met over breakfast in Rome was a total stranger whose voice reminded me that no one is able to rush us forward into the past unless we allow them to do so. His voice reminded me of a challenge we share. The dominant culture in which we live is undergoing a transformation of historic proportion. It seems a great abyss has opened between individuals and communities. Bridges are needed that will enable us to reconnect.

Listen to Maya Angelou whose poetry is so full of wisdom. "When people show you who they are, believe them."[3] We show others who we are through our words. There is power in words. It is power capable of changing hearts and minds. Christ empowers us to be bridges, voices of hope calling both culture and church into God's unknown future. That future is filled with all the possibilities set before us by the One who creates and sustains us in the great web of life.

On the day of my ordination, neither Bishop Joseph Michael Gilmore nor I had any way of anticipating what it meant for him to lay his hands on my head and to anoint my hands with the holy chrism. If he had, perhaps he would have hesitated. If I had, I surely would have been far more eager and willing than I was on that spring morning when the litany of the saints was intoned over our bodies prostrate on the floor of the Cathedral of St. Helena. I scarcely understand the mystery even now.

That great abyss calls, and I ponder, wonder.
The roar comes pounding, and I, a mute echo, flee.
Mighty it comes, climbing, and I a single voice sing.
Beyond time it comes: the song of God.[4]

We live in the Communion of Saints. The Christ-life flows within and among us! That life is like the cool waters of an underground spring gushing up out of the ground in the high mountains of western Montana or Glacier National Park. It gushes up from deep within us. This Christ life within us is the foundation of our hope.

Recently in one of the small Catholic communities to which I belong, we found ourselves discussing words. Someone observed how common it has become for people to avoid serious conversation. There is much discord and confusion among us. It is hardly surprising that most of us have at least some subconscious fear that our words will instigate an argument. So often we seek the easy way and talk about being busy, the weather, or a recent sporting event.

There always is the risk of being misunderstood. In writing this book I embrace that risk mindful of the observation of the former president of the Czech Republic. "Words are capable of betraying us unless we are constantly circumspect about their use."[5] Loving always involves risk. Words are ambiguous but there is power in words beyond our ability to measure. No one need listen to them, but a transformation occurs both in those who speak them and in those who listen. As I try to be careful with my words, I am trusting you will be careful in reading and listening to them. My emotions are real and if these words are read with a prejudiced mind, they easily could result in harsh judgment and misunderstanding.

A young Irish woman, newly married to a man from Montana, moved to the United States. More specifically they moved to Butte, Montana, a town filled with rich Irish traditions and a colorful history to say the least. Her husband Joe had a job that occasionally required him to travel away from home. They found themselves a nice upstairs apartment. The neighbors were friendly and they began to establish a home for themselves.

Shortly after their arrival in town, Joe was away on business and his young bride had no alarm clock. With naive innocence and neighborly good intention, she went to her neighbor's apartment and rang the bell. She politely said: "My husband is away. Will you please ask your husband to come and knock me up about six tomorrow morning!" The neighbor was shocked and offended!

In that simple incident my friend discovered the power and the danger of words. Words do not always mean what we intend or think! A simple request in a remote village of Ireland has a far different meaning in Butte, Montana. Words can be bridges that connect people or walls that separate and divide us.

In 1984 our diocesan bishop assigned me to be pastor of a university parish. The educational level and diversity of that community posed a challenge to me as it would for anyone in such a position of leadership. In addition the parish still rumbled with the aftershocks and turmoil caused by a crisis a few years earlier.

As I prepared my first homily, trepidation flooded my soul. Distrust and anxiety were a shadow lurking behind hopeful anticipation. There was no doubt in my mind that the words of that first homily would determine far more than I could foresee. To assuage my own anxiety, I told the story of that young Irish bride in Butte asking that recently battered community to be kind, patient and listen to the meaning of my words. I asked them to trust me and try to understand the sincerity of the intention behind my words.

The community seemed to appreciate the connection. Not all, but most of those folks, honored that intention throughout my tenure there. So many graces came into my life while serving that community for twenty-two years. My soul was flooded with gratitude as I prepared my final homily. As I thanked the people for their kindness and love, I retold the same story. Some of the older members of the community recalled hearing it the first time.

There is power and danger inherent in words. Someone claims the average man or woman who lives to the age of seventy-five spends approximately one-fifth of his/her life talking. That was before we had mobile phones! The same researcher also claims that every day most of us participate in approximately thirty conversations and in the process speak twenty-five to thirty thousand words. That is enough to fill a fifty-page book in one day! In one year we speak enough words to fill 134 hundred-page books! Certainly the availability of mobile phones must multiply all of those numbers.

Words are like windows through which we allow others to look into our interior. The author of Sirach in the Hebrew Bible warns us. "The test of a person is in conversation."[6] Jesus of Nazareth also understood the power and the danger of words.

Words flow out of what fills the heart. Good people draw good things from their store of goodness; bad people draw bad things from their store of badness. So I tell you this, that for every unfounded word people utter they will answer....[7]

Throughout these pages my words will allow you to look into my heart and mind. May you hear words that serve as bridges to new insight and understanding; words that help us journey into our common future as companions of the Risen One.

Those of us who were alive in the 1960's surely remember the name Angelo Giuseppe Roncalli. We remember him fondly and with gratitude as Pope John XXIII. He lived long enough to get many things right. He understood that throughout the centuries the church was marked by variety and change. He also understood the church had become too secure, self-confident, even dormant like a pool of stagnant water in which nothing can live. As he said on his deathbed,

Those who have lived as long as I have ...were enabled to compare different cultures and traditions, and know that the moment has come to discern the signs of the times, to seize the opportunity and to look far ahead.[8]

He had the courage "to seize the opportunity and to look far ahead."

Prior to the Protestant Reformation in the 1600's, liturgical diversity characterized the Catholic world. There was never only one way of understanding the significance of Christ, or the meaning of church. During the four hundred year period following the Reformation, the Latin liturgy became the dominant, but never the exclusive manner of celebrating Mass. In similar fashion, one way of explaining the significance of Christ, and one understanding of the meaning of church gradually dominated and became the sole expression of our theology for four centuries. Few realized it, but even then those dominant theological opinions never excluded all other explanations or understandings within our Catholic tradition.

That historical period known as the Counter-Reformation sought to resist the influence of the reformation churches, and the modern world. We in the Catholic household of faith became prisoners, shackled by our own concepts, explanations, theologies and spiritualities. In 1868-70, the First Vatican Council met for ten months. That was nearly seventy years after the Lewis and Clark Expedition to the Northwest. That Council declared the doctrine of papal infallibility. The influence of that declaration spread gradually until the middle of the twentieth century. Once convinced of papal infallibility, the Catholic Church gradually developed into an extremely monolithic institution isolated from the larger world. That First Vatican Council sought to hold back the course of history by enforcing rigid obedience to the past. As a result most of us experienced the church as some sort of club with privileged memberships. We were comfortable with that illusion and oblivious to the fact that others saw the Roman Church as a museum housing the artifacts of an age dead and past, thus ignoring the insight of the German theologian Wolfgang Pannenberg that "religions die when their lights fail."[9]

Pope John XXIII read the signs of the times. He borrowed that phrase from Jesus in the gospel of Matthew.[10] He used it in reference to public contemporary happenings "that call our attention to a significant change that is taking place in the world."[11] John XXIII understood the situation of the world and the church when he was elected bishop of Rome. He understood that it was important and necessary for us, as for every generation, to recognize and try to understand the particular historical circumstances and cultural forces in which we are privileged to live. Those unique circumstances are the milieu, the world context in which the church is called to minister.

John XXIII understood that our given historical circumstance and all new developments within the human family are opportunities offered to the church. He recognized and appreciated the positive and the negative aspects of the historical moment in which he lived. He was ready to embrace the positive as part of the mission of the church. He also was willing to discover how the church could respond in an affirmative manner to the negative aspects of modernity. With this perspective he invited the bishops of the world into Council.

Through the Council John XXIII invited us to be church in new and fresh ways. He knew the light of Christ was entrusted to us in our baptism and we were to keep that light burning brightly for the sake of others. By convening the Council he led the way inviting us to look to our future, rather than to our past.

The optimistic realism of Pope John XXIII was contagious. It had an extraordinary impact within the church and also spread to those of other religious traditions or of no religious conviction whatsoever. While, at times, his successor Pope Paul VI was more timid in following John's lead, he also seemed to understand the significance of trying to respond to the signs of the times. He embraced the risk of trying to do so.

We have neither the right, nor the capability of judging the successors of John and Paul as bishops of Rome. However we do have the right and the responsibility to be critical with love of their decisions and directions. It is my reading of our present situation that those in the Vatican are trying to rush us forward into the past as quickly as they can.

The dominant culture in which we live is changing far more rapidly and extensively than has happened in any previous age. Technology is shrinking the distances between us. The economic, cultural, political and even theological debates that now occur on the world stage are the guideposts that indicate where we are heading as a people. They provide the road maps we must follow if we are to make the gospel relative to the next generations in this twenty-first century. The journal, *New Theology Review,* constantly reminds us to read the signs of the times in which we live.

It would be a gross error to say that our cross-generational experience of what it means to grow up Catholic in the United States is uniform. We find drastically differing experiences of what being Catholic means or meant, even within each generational group. There are still among us many of the pre-Vatican II generation. I am one of them. Our responses to the vision of the Council range from total rejection to unquestioning endorsement. The same range of response is also found in the generation of the Council. The post-Vatican II generation lacks the experience required to make an informed response to the Council. Yet within that generation there are some who embrace the vision of the Council, and others who yearn for the return of personal pious practices about which they have heard but which they never experienced. This amazing diversity is itself one of the more significant signs of the times in which we live.

Since our understanding of church and mission differ, it is quite natural that our diverse understandings easily lead us into serious disagreements about Catholic life, and our shared mission. Perhaps you agree with me that our task as church is to "make the world a just, peaceful and reconciled place in which everyone can grow up."[12] If you do agree, it is important that we always be mindful there are others among us who, for legitimate reasons, do not agree.

It certainly is not clear to me how our bishops or we as church could or should address the events and trends that comprise the signs of the times. Those signs are many and diverse. The challenge for us is to see "what positive good is to be drawn out of events which at first sight seem utterly negative."[13] I assume that given the leadership role our bishops have accepted among us, it is their responsibility to engage us, the baptized people of God, in mutual dialogue, and a spirit of collegiality. When we allow the Holy Spirit to guide, we discover our common direction as church.

Clearly efforts to rush us forward into the past have dampened the fires ignited by the Second Vatican Council. With determined, intentional effort, we can free ourselves of confusion and remain focused on humankind's shared future. That Maryknoll priest in Rome reminded me that a single voice is able to change the world. Your voice and mine are significant, especially if we remain conscious that we are the Living Body of Christ.

CHAPTER 2

OUR TASK

Cannon Beach in the state of Oregon is majestic in every season and all sorts of weather. Occasionally I make my annual spiritual retreat there. The long, white sand stretches far into the distance. Sea gulls are constant companions. Huge, monolithic rocks, carved by centuries of wave and wind, stand guard at strategic locations above the crashing surf. Winter there is amazing. The howling winds drown out the pounding surf. Monstrous logs piled like pickup sticks against the steep cliffs provide wonderful sheltered places for contemplative silence. Dressed warmly in waterproof gear I have sat for hours among those logs and rocks and the pounding surf. Springtime sun falls bright on the same beach, the surf is less wild and the same logs and rocks invite me to sit in silent prayer. Perhaps the same seagulls that served as winter retreat masters assume the task again in spring. It was on such a spring day this verse fell out of my pen.

Long strands of cream race ahead of the churning surf,
wild and free,
cotton balls left unpicked,
frothing white suds festoon the battered sands.

The world of nature that sustains us and imprints memories upon our senses is complex and multi-layered. Modern living, mimicking the "long strands of cream" and "the frothing white suds," leaves us feeling battered, like the grains of sand. Today there seems to be as many new challenges and opportunities as there are drops of water in the ocean. They contain a mixture of positive and negative elements.

If as Pope John XXIII stated, we who are church "are called to serve man; to defend above all and everywhere the rights of the human person,"[1] then this modern world in which we live opens new ways to appreciate the mystery of life and the reality of God. It also confronts us with an enormous task. We begin and end that task when we gather for Sunday Eucharist. In our Eucharistic celebrations we create places of solitude and silence. We listen to our own thoughts and to the still, small voice of God. This is a tremendous moment in an age of such extensive transformation and disruption. It is in our shared solitude and silence that it becomes possible for us to establish and nourish community with one another.

It is within the community that we can enable one another to understand and appreciate the meaning and implications of global family. It is within community that it becomes possible for us to bond with others and with God. A brief list of some positive and negative elements in these challenges and opportunities may help us clarify our task.

On the positive side we see that we are beginning to understand that global warming is real, and more of us are aware of possible solutions. Friends and family members are now safe to publicly claim they are gay or lesbian. Globalization could move us to the realization of "The Beloved Community" of Dr. Martin Luther King, Jr. It was his dream that we could build a community in which the dignity of every human being would be respected, and justice would assure the basic existential needs of all were met.

Contemporary science has gifted us with modern technology. Computers, the Internet, mobile phones and text messaging have become normal components of our lives. This technology has already transformed our world in positive and beneficial ways and is transforming the sort of human beings we are. In my home recently, eight of us were engaged in a spirited dinner conversation. One of the young mothers was repeatedly distracted and tinkering with her mobile phone. After dinner she informed us that throughout the meal she had been text messaging back and forth with her son.

When my mother was ninety years of age, she began using a mobile phone. It was a new world for her. Soon after learning how to use it, she was with a group of women in a home up Rattlesnake Canyon. I called her on her new phone. She asked with a puzzled tone in her voice, "How did you know where I am?" "In 2007, the number of cell-phone users surpassed 2.5 billion worldwide."[2]

These space-age devices are shrinking the planet on which we live. We have almost instantaneous access to friends and family on every continent. It is no longer necessary to make a trip to the library. All the information collected in human history is now literally at our fingertips. Rapid communication can help us understand and appreciate the meaning and implications of global family, inter-connected and interdependent.

On the negative side we witness the collapse of the traditional nuclear family. "The rate at which Catholics marry outside of the Catholic community is sky-rocketing."[3]

We face a major financial crisis. Unemployment is increasing. "On any given night, somewhere between eight hundred thousand and a million Americans are homeless."[4] That number is likely to increase. The middle class in our country is shrinking and perhaps could disappear.

It doesn't require a Ph.D. in macroeconomics to know that if the rich are getting richer by the minute, and the poor are getting poorer, there is something badly wrong.[5]

We gradually are beginning to feel the emotional, financial and social consequences of two wars.

Poverty causes unimaginable human suffering for those without clean water, nutritional food and minimal conditions of hygiene. Our domestic animals enjoy far better housing and food than millions of our brothers and sisters in countries like Haiti, the Congo or Darfur. They are imprisoned in economic systems from which it is impossible for them to escape. Commercial television appeals to and stimulates the mimetic desire of adults and children, fostering artificial needs and making us increasingly indifferent to the suffering of the poor. Immigration is creating new urban concentrations of people as national borders leak or collapse, and citizens demand harsh retaliation against immigrants.

The promotion of sleep and sex-enhancement medications and various painkillers also subtly promotes the use of street drugs. Stadiums and arenas where enormous crowds gather for sport spectacles provide a limited catharsis for some of our aggression. Perhaps they also contribute to the violence that is a growing problem in our own land and around the planet.

Gambling of all sorts has proliferated even here under the Big Sky. A recent issue of *The Week* magazine reports "our country now has more than five hundred casinos, which rake in at least fifty billion dollars a year." The same editorial notes that,

Gambling only seems like a painless way for governments to raise revenues. ... When a state legalizes casinos, it opens the door to thousands of ruined lives.[6]

25

Among the health problems that burden our nation are those directly linked to food. Obesity, anorexia and bulimia are the most publicized. Fast food chains are everywhere and busy. The consumption of soft drinks is at all time highs. Many children go to bed hungry while the sale of dietary aides and medications has become a thriving business.

Some express legitimate concern that all of our "Hi-tech gadgets seem to be creating a Culture of Distraction."[7] A 2004 survey by the University of California, Los Angeles, concludes that our young people are so wired they are less and less interested in or capable of one-to-one, face-to-face interaction. There is something out of sync when people are no longer able to be personally present to others. In home or office, in cars or on the sidewalk, folks are immersed in a sea of sound, preoccupied with their mobile phone or unable to turn away from their computer screen long enough to engage in a conversation.

For me the beginning of this 21st century is an exciting time to be alive. These challenges and opportunities, both positive and negative, can help us clarify our task as church. We are a community living out of the conviction that the Gracious Mystery we name God is leading us into our future. Perhaps our primary task, as church in this modern world, is to enable one another to understand and appreciate the meaning and implications of being a global family.

Most of us born and raised in western civilization were raised on a cosmology rooted in the creation narratives of the Hebrew book of Genesis. Those narratives address "the question of our relationship to nature and of where we fit into the big scheme of things."[8] The cosmology of Genesis imaged the universe as three-layered: earth, the heavens and the underworld. God resided above the heavens and we human lived on Earth. Many folks were unaware of that cosmology. Yet it influenced and shaped much of the theology we inherited.

Now, again with the majority of us unaware of it, a new cosmology is impacting and shaping contemporary theology. With increasing rapidity, the discoveries made by our modern physical sciences, like cosmology, are providing the sort of tools we need to carry out our task as church.

"Modern cosmology refers to a subfield of physics having to do with theories about the origin, evolutions, and present physical structure of the universe."[9]

This field of science is developing so rapidly because the Hubble telescope and other high-tech space probes have opened the door into the secrets of the cosmos and are transforming our understanding of the great immensity of space. We are offered new ways to see and think about the world and our place in the world. "Cosmology, rather than theology, is emerging as the queen of the sciences."[10]

We have very little appreciation or comprehension of what the words or concepts of modern cosmology mean. Yet they are beginning to influence our understanding of church and directing our task. This cosmos, the universe in which we live has been unfolding or emerging for some fifteen billion years. Michael Morwood, in his book *Tomorrow's Catholic* tells us,

Astronomers now estimate that there are more than three billion galaxies each with billions and billions of stars. In addition to our own sun, there are more than 200 billion stars in our galaxy, the Milky Way.[11]

Our planet Earth is a miniscule part of one solar system in that galaxy. We are not able to step out of our own solar system or galaxy to grasp the dimensions of our immediate home. Morwood suggests that we imagine,

A map of the United States. That map represents our galaxy, the Milky Way. Now still using that scale, place a postage stamp on the United States. That postage stamp represents our solar system, with the sun and planets. Even the smallest dot on that stamp is too large to represent our planet Earth.[12]

If you allow your imagination to play with his suggestion, you will begin to realize how insignificant Earth is within our galaxy, and how insignificant our own galaxy is within the cosmos. We have so much to learn! "There is not and never will be a complete and comprehensive scientific account of the universe that can be proved valid."[13] That is humbling but also gives encouragement to those of us seeking to understand and live within our modern world.

The editorial in a recent issue of *New Theology Review* offers a perspective well worth pondering:

The mystery of human existence unfolds against a backdrop as immense as the night sky. We worry about our own little star, never realizing how vast and limitless are the time and space allotted to us. The small and fleeting anxieties and sadnesses that fill our days, as large as they seem in the moment, are really small and fleeting.[14]

So we moderns are being led by the physical sciences to appreciate that all things and all peoples are far more interdependent and interrelated than we previously realized. "Nothing happens anywhere in the universe that does not affect everything, everywhere instantly."[15] Everything: galaxies, people, butterflies and mosquitoes all are connected. There is a deep web of relationships within all created beings that impacts and influences the whole of creation. From my perspective, modern science is simply describing the mystery of Christ. I think this new knowledge and understanding provides us the means to accomplish our task as church.

My own body feels and appears solid, as do the great boulders over which we climb on the mountains of western Montana. Modern physicists tell us that,

> *Like everything else, you, the boulders and I are composed of a whirl of subatomic particles, which relative to their size are as far apart as the planets in the solar system, so that to see us as we really are would be to see not a collection of individual bodies of varied size and shape, but a whole interdependent universe as vast and mysterious as the one we live in.*[16]

The Newtonian understanding of nature as a static machine has been replaced by a world full of surprises.

Our personal experiences often confirm these insights of modern physics. When things are "flowing" in our life, we often find a mysteriously "benevolent quality in the way all the bits of the jig-saw of our lives and actions, and the lives and actions of those around us, fit into a harmonious pattern."[17]

Meals are a sign of intimacy and love. Meals provide time and place for us to share our lives. When we sit around a table, taking part in the same food, we are bonded together. In our Eucharistic celebrations we invoke the Spirit of God over bread and wine. These are the visible, outward sign of the reality we name Eucharist. We break the bread and pour the cup to be shared, mindful the Risen One is present in and among us. In the sharing we become community.

For me this time in which we live is an exciting moment in history that both reminds and invites us to trust that the Spirit of God is leading us into our future. Many find the chaos of transition to be confusing. The Welsh priest and poet R.S. Thomas understood something of this when he wrote, "the temptation is to go back and flirt with the 'pale ghost of an earlier self'."[18] If we as church submit to that temptation, the important task for which we as church are responsible will be left unfinished. We can never go back. The past is past. The present is filled

28

with possibilities. Together we continue learning. Life at every stage of our development is about the same issue – trusting that the Spirit of God is guiding us. Because we really believe we are the Living Body of Christ, we have no option but to live with the same confidence expressed by the medieval mystic who wrote that, "All shall be well, and all shall be well, and all manner of things shall be well."[19]

CHAPTER 3

ANAIS NIN
"And the day came when the risk it took to remain tight inside the bud was more painful than the risk it took to blossom."

SOCIAL GLUE

One day while sitting on the banks of the Clark Fork River in Missoula, and musing about the great mystery of rivers, I wrote,

"We need something that keeps things together. Something that keeps things moving in the same direction, as gravity pulls the water in a stream down the mountain, or as an area of low pressure pulls the wind relentlessly in a particular direction. We need to have something that binds us together, something that keeps us moving in the right direction. If there is not, we will all eventually wander off and go our own way."

I previously noted the scale of innovation and change sweeping our world. The pace of that change is enormous and overwhelming to many. As technology shrinks our planet, many of the customs, traditions and social systems that provide stability seem to be disintegrating. Dramatic transitions shock our cultures like social earthquakes. The media report levels of stress and moral ambivalence that have never been higher. When folks feel isolated from reliable social contexts, they seek some sort of social glue, a means by which to identify or establish norms, rules and goals that will reestablish a feeling of security. The two most common and effective forms of social glue are religion and nationalism.

The root meaning of the word religion, *"religere"* in Latin, is to bind together. Our European ancestors who first came to the shores of North America had deep religious convictions. Religion is social glue but not always for everyone. The Puritan and Protestant traditions of those first settlers were the glue holding their communities together, assuring their identity and placing them over and against the native peoples. Those already living on this continent were deeply rooted in their own religion yet welcomed the Europeans, who immediately returned the favor by labeling their hosts heathen. When our Catholic ancestors began to arrive, they also were feared, and treated as less than American because they too were of a different religion.

Our situation in this 21st century is drastically different. The Catholic

31

Church is now the largest religious denomination in our nation and part of the social glue. Many currently holding office in state and local governments are Catholic. For good or bad, the extent of our presence and influence in the arts, education, science, health care, banking, the entertainment industry and the Pentagon is impressive.

Nationalism is the other most common and effective form of social glue. It is a modern phenomenon that originated in Europe, probably with or during the French Revolution in the late eighteenth century. Nationalism is an ideology that focuses on the nation to the exclusion of other ethnic, cultural or social groupings. In our century nationalism has become the most significant political and social force on our planet. It often is the root cause of violence between peoples. Flags and national anthems are typical symbols of nationalism.

Nationalism as we experience and know it today was born in our nation's Civil War. The period of our history from the surrender of the Confederacy at the Appomattox Courthouse until the end of the Second World War was like our national adolescence. Since the end of that war nationalism has ridden a rising tidal wave of enthusiasm among us. When it is about something larger than the personal self, nationalism is a good quality. It is far less than good when it becomes a disguised form of self-veneration.

Patriotism commonly is defined as love of and/or devotion to one's country. It is a virtue and not synonymous with nationalism. It is not about wearing a national flag in the lapel of one's suit coat. It is about love and loyalty to one's country. There are two forms of patriotism and they are very different. Geiko Muller-Fahrenhold is a scholar who claims to be "German by birth and American by disposition." In his book *America's Battle for God*, he reminds us that, "uncritical love of country is an invitation to blithe morality, just as loveless criticism is an invitation to cynical moralizing."[1]

Authentic patriotism is a virtue to be desired and fostered by all. It is never afraid of the truth. It is the sort of love for one's nation that frees and inspires citizens to critically analyze both policies and people when basic constitutional principles and values are ignored or violated for whatever reason. Citizens are patriotic when they assume responsibility for their fellow citizens. Among other things, true patriotism includes paying one's fair share of taxes; being informed about political candidates; voting in elections; keeping streets clean and the environment safe.

False patriotism is less than virtuous. It makes boisterous, illusionary claims and weakens us as people. "My country, right or wrong, my country still" is a statement that ignores or denies all the ethical and moral values that are foundation stones for a healthy nation. This so called patriotism is unwilling to question national policy or behavior. Ultimately such an attitude is an expression of weakness and insecurity rather than strength.

A few years ago, Robert Bellah coined the phrase "civil religion."[2] Since ancient times, civil religion has been the means by which individuals or groups gained political power.

In the second chapter of his book *Hawaii,* James A. Michener tells a tale that dramatically illustrates the role of civil religion. His fictional account is located in Bora Bora and the surrounding islands one thousand years before Europeans arrived. A high priest with political ambition introduced a new god to the islanders. This new god was hungry for human sacrifice. By clever manipulation the high priest disrupts the social structure of Bora Bora, unseats the powerful king and assumes dictatorial political power.

As Ancient Rome became an empire, civil religion was an essential component, the glue holding the empire together. When Constantine ruled the Roman Empire, he understood this. As the presence and number of those who followed the way of Jesus increased, Constantine legitimatized Christianity as the official religion of the state in order to unify his empire and hold it together. And so civil religion has been the social glue of empires since humans can remember.

We are citizens of and in an empire. Our nation is known internationally as the United States of America. Today our nation initiates policies intended to spread our cultural and economic control over other peoples. Our eight hundred plus military bases are located in every hemisphere and on every continent, including barely known island nations. When our policies and actions are empirical, then surely we are an empire.

Constitutionally the United States of America is a secular republic. Most of our fellow citizens presume we are a Christian nation because so many of us go to church. The founders of our nation, especially Thomas Jefferson coined and adopted the doctrine of the separation of church and state to protect religious freedom. This is a treasured element of our national life. That doctrine was never intended to prevent the church from engaging the state in debate but to prevent the state from interfering in matters of the church. It has functioned well, but throughout our history and still today, there has been the gradual but steady development of another form of religion that is not separate from the state. It is the phenomenon that Robert Bellah labeled civil religion and today it serves well as the social glue maintaining our empire. As Constantine did in the 4th century, so the leaders of our empire have abducted the religions brought to this continent by our ancestors and transformed them into the civil religion of our empire.

This civil religion draws heavily on Christian images and symbols and includes references to Judaism, Islam, and other religious traditions. It is rooted in sacred documents like *The Declaration of Independence* and the *Constitution*. It gathers us at holy places, such as the Tomb of the Unknown Soldier; the Washington, Jefferson, Lincoln and Roosevelt monuments; the Civil War battlefields and statues on courthouse lawns. It gathers us for holidays (spell that "holydays") such as the Fourth of July, a secularized Halloween, Thanksgiving, Xmas, New Year's and Presidents' Day. Memorial Day honors the American soldiers at Gettysburg where President Lincoln, in his famous speech, linked the death of those soldiers with Christ's death. In many cities St. Patrick's Day is now part of the civil religion as it has been stripped of anything about "the saint" and draws people to parades and pubs. The day set aside to honor Dr. M. L. King, Jr., attracts little attention, perhaps because it has such deep connections to the gospel of Jesus. The national anthem is the sacred song with which enormous crowds celebrate national identity united around the flag that has become the equivalent of the cross for Christians.

This eclectic assortment of religious symbolism has made it easy for the majority of our citizens, even those professing the creed or tenants of Judaism, Christianity or Islam to embrace this civil religion. They do so unconsciously, even when it denies the principles or values of their own tradition. Fewer of our citizens, including many who are Catholic, gather for rituals rooted in the life of Jesus, while more and more gather for rituals of national identity honoring the military and those who serve the nation.

A careful examination of our national response to the destruction of the World Trade Center demonstrates that civil religion has a far more significant influence upon our national life than any of the major religious communities. In his book to which I referred earlier, Muller-Fahrenhold reminds us, "A striking example of America's civil religion was on display in the 'worship service' at the National Cathedral in

Washington, D.C., on September 16, 2001."[3] In that service the leaders of various religious traditions were involved. The President of the United States spoke from the pulpit!! Unwittingly many of our fellow citizens turned to him as the high priest of America's civil religion. Christ was mentioned to confirm our destiny as a chosen people but at the same time the teaching and model of Jesus were ignored or blatantly denied. Christ was relegated to the role of being a national icon.

Recent presidents, even prior to the election of George W. Bush, have boldly adopted civil religion as their most effective instrument in shaping both our domestic and foreign policies. Examine their rhetoric. Presidents customarily close their public addresses with the seemingly innocuous phrase, God bless America. That now is such a part of our tradition that no one ever questions it. Those of my generation may remember that moving speech in which President Kennedy challenged us to "go forth to lead the land we love, asking God's blessing and help, knowing that here on earth, God's work must truly be our own."[4] Those are moving and powerful words. Personally I treasure his statement, but conditionally. It is unclear what he meant by the word God. He may have meant what we who seek to follow the way of Jesus mean when speaking that name. However in speaking that name as the president of the United States, his meaning may have been entirely different.

As in all previous empires, the merging of religion and nationalism into a civil religion has ripple effects. I suspect the powerful impact of civil religion on our national imagination helps to explain the rapid emergence of religious fundamentalism. The term identifying fundamentalism first appeared in the nineteen twenties. At that time it was applied to Protestant movements in the United States that interpreted the Bible in a strict, literal sense. We all need an environment of stability that helps us develop our own personal identity and define our purpose for living. If one has a simplistic worldview, innovation and novelty easily threaten personal or social identity. The consequence is fear. Fear awakens a need for clear, simple and absolute assurances of truth, meaning and purpose. Religious fundamentalism offers certainty, authority and absolute truth by paternalistic spokesmen who easily appropriate enormous influence and become defenders of doctrinal orthodoxy. "It tends to affirm that a ready-made plan for secular realities can be drawn directly from a religious message."[5] In this way fundamentalism completes the blending of religion and nationalism. There are churches in our land today in which the American flag holds a place of honor in the sanctuary, subtly implying a union of church and state; eroding the distinction between the two, and reducing the possibility of authentic presence of one to the other.

The election of George W. Bush "would not have been possible without the financial and political support of Christian fundamentalists."[6] In a time of severe economic hardship, President Franklin D. Roosevelt said to this nation, "there is nothing to fear except fear itself." Eight years ago another president appealed to the fundamentalist spirit in our nation and instituted levels of threat and color-coded security alerts to remind us we must be afraid.

In John's gospel Jesus defined himself as "the light of the world."[7] He empowered people to do what he was doing and he remains among us today doing the same. In Matthew's gospel Jesus tells us,

You are light for the world. A city built on a hilltop cannot be hidden. No one lights a lamp to put it under a tub; they put it on a lamp-stand where it shines for everyone in the house. In the same way your light must shine in people's sight.[8]

That is our task. To be Catholic is to be open, inclusive and tolerant of the different. We cannot be Catholic and narrow minded, ideological, intolerant or exclusive. "In a fundamentalist's house there is only one room."[9] At least in the best tradition of our Catholic house there are rooms for everyone.

Civil religion and fundamentalist religion are characteristics of the dominant culture in which we live. We know the world is good and to be honored, and most of us are very comfortable with our nation's civil religion. Right now, the blossoms that will explode on our trees next spring remain tight in the bud waiting for warmer, sunny days. It always feels safer to keep our minds and hearts closed tightly, unwilling to criticize that with which we are familiar. But the day has come when the risk it takes to remain closed is more painful than the risk it takes to blossom. We cannot ignore the realities of the dominant culture and still honor our deepest truth as the Living Body of Christ. We are people given a task. The sooner we blossom, the better our world will be.

CHAPTER 4

PSALM 8
"I look up at your heavens made by your fingers,
At the moon and stars set in place.
Ah, what is man that you should spare a thought for him,
the son of man that you should care for him?"

MOUNT ST. HELENS

It was May in the year nineteen-eighty. Volcanic ash fell upon us like snowflakes in a winter storm. The blue sky over Western Montana grew dark. Within hours six inches of ash accumulated on the ground in my hometown of Missoula. That layer of ash literally forced us to remain indoors for a week. On Saturday we were preparing to cancel the weekend liturgies in all our parishes. Then the rain came, torrential rain. Many of us burst out into our yards and danced in the rain to celebrate the cleansing and release from our confinement.

Before that Sunday in May 1980, few who live outside the southwestern corner of the state of Washington ever heard of Mount St. Helens. Today it is a National Monument and major tourist attraction supervised by the U.S.D.A. Forest Service.

Apparently anticipating an eruption, scientists had been monitoring this snow-capped volcano for some time. Warnings were posted but most folks did not take them too seriously. The last eruption had occurred just five years before the Lewis and Clark Expedition passed through this country in the 19th century. Harry Truman, the elderly caretaker at Spirit Lake Lodge just below the volcano, refused to leave the lodge. He was convinced that any eruption would be minor and never reach as far as Spirit Lake.

Mount St. Helens lay dormant until May 18,1980. On that Sunday morning, repeated earthquakes shocked the area. When it happened, the eruption not only blew away much of the mountain but it radically changed 230 square miles of forest, river valleys and lakes. Spirit Lake

Lodge was buried under mudslides and ash.

When the eruption occurred I was with a group of high school students on the southern shores of Flathead Lake in western Montana. Mountains surround this crystal clear lake. It is twenty-five miles long, fifteen miles across at the widest point and in places it is more than four hundred feet deep. The water is clear and, at least for those of us born and raised in Montana, a delightful place to swim in the warm months of summers. The secluded and quiet location at the end of Indian Bay was an ideal place for this final experience through which those students were preparing themselves to celebrate the sacrament of Confirmation. They were a typical group of young Catholic high school students. Their participation was enthusiastic and contagious. The memory of the snow-capped peaks of the Mission Mountains as we drove along them that spring day still lingers in my heart. The sky was blue and life seemed stable and secure.

None of us had heard any news about the eruption of the volcano. After dinner we sat and sang songs around a campfire under the brilliant, star spangled night sky of Montana. I was wearing contact lenses and seldom if ever experienced headaches. It seemed that darkness came upon the lake early. Misty, fog-like swirls drifted through the trees and along the lakeshore. The young man playing a guitar suddenly stopped. His guitar was covered with something powdery. Then others began to complain about dust on their clothing or in their hair. We went into the small cabin. My head throbbed and the whites of my eyeballs were bright red! We flipped on the television and learned that Mt. St. Helens had erupted. That which appeared to be evening mist rising off the lake was ash from that volcano three states and hundreds of miles west of us.

On several occasions since that eruption I have stood on Johnson Ridge overlooking Mount St. Helens in southwestern Washington State. On the most recent visit the sky was cobalt blue. The valley below and the mountain above were still stained with the dull gray of ash and mudflows that devastated the area twenty-nine years ago. Plumes of smoke and steam were rising from the lava dome rebuilding the mountain.

It was easy to connect the scene before us with life as we have experienced it in the Catholic Church in the last half of the twentieth century. There are tremendous unseen forces operating below the surface of this planet. As those forces accumulate or release their energy, Earth shakes and volcanoes erupt. In such ways the surface of our planet is trans-formed. Old landmarks change. Forests disappear and new lakes are born. The vegetation is obliterated but soon blossoms again with new vitality. We who are Catholic people have chosen to believe in the existence of an ultimate, loving, creating, Gracious Mystery, far more and greater than ourselves. We name that Gracious Mystery God. We believe this Gracious Mystery is present in and throughout all of creation. This Creating God is the unseen source of the tremendous physical and spiritual power, energy and creativity slumbering in all of creation and in each and every person.

When I was ordained a Roman Catholic priest the Catholic Church was much like Mount St. Helens prior to the eruption of 1980. The rock solid appearance of our Catholic culture was deceptive. Jesus and I piety, connected and interwoven with Marian devotion, assured us all was well. We were Catholic and filled with certainty about the ultimate questions. We were confident that if we kept the rules laid out by the hierarchy, we would go to heaven, or as we then said, we would save our souls.

None of us expected to find our lives shaken up and dislocated by the eruption of a spiritual volcano. None of us expected that the tremendous spiritual power and energy slumbering within us was about to erupt, and like Mount St. Helens, awaken us and transform our spiritual landscape with new dreams and visions. The Second Vatican Council was about to change and transform so many of our traditions. We naively assumed Jesus established them. We presumed they would forever be the same.

The cultural practices that surrounded the First Communion Day for our children illustrate this. As in all parishes at that time, children in the second grade were prepared as a group to make their first confession and to receive Holy Communion for the first time. Ordinarily that was on a spring morning in May, often on Mother's Day.

All the little boys were dressed in a white suit, white shirt, and tie and white shoes. The little girls wore a white dress, white veil, white shoes, white gloves and a white purse. Sometimes a special sash was placed around the arm. Most children had a First Communion book, the size of a deck of cards, hard and shiny, containing the prayers they were expected to say. Sometimes white rosary beads completed the dress.

The children were accompanied to Sunday Mass by their smiling, proud parents. When fifty or sixty little ones, dressed in this manner, processed into the parish church, a rush of pride and joy filled parental hearts. At the appropriate time these little ones came forward with folded hands and downcast eyes, extended their tongue and the priest placed the host on their tongue.

The combination of anticipation and fear was tangible. Anxiety about how to walk, where to kneel or breaking the communion fast was not uncommon. I remember my own first communion well. I wish I could say I remember it because of my awareness of Christ's presence in the sacrament. I, like most children of that age, was anxious to do things properly. The Ursuline sisters in our school were wonderful women and good teachers. They had instructed us well. "Never touch the host with your fingers!" "Don't chew the host and swallow it as quickly as possible!" "Return to your pew, kneel and pray!"

No one had bothered to mention what we were to do if the host stuck to the roof of the mouth. That is what I remember most! The priest placed the Sacrament on my tongue, almost immediately, the host stuck to the roof of my mouth. As I returned to my pew, hands folded, eyes downcast, my mind was filled with panic. "What should I do?" "Could I loosen the host with my tongue or was that forbidden?" "Would it dissolve or simply remain stuck there?" Needless to say that moment cannot be classified as one of the most prayerful of my life.

In the mid-1960's, Barbara, a mother of a six-year old, came to the parish office wanting to discuss her concerns about her first grade daughter, Theresa. The pastor of this large parish was a wonderful, humble and good man from Ireland. He also was the Vicar-General of our diocese.

Barbara came to discuss her concern about Theresa's behavior at communion time. Theresa obediently remained in the pew when her parents went forward to receive Communion. Then when Barbara returned to the pew, her daughter insisted on hugging and kissing her "because she had just received Jesus!" Barbara was seeking a course of action and asked if Theresa could be allowed to receive Holy Communion now, a year earlier than the rest of her class.

The conversation took several weeks. Eventually all agreed it was a mistake to make the child wait. She was ready. This was a significant departure from a long established custom, so we invited the parish to an evening discussion about parish policies concerning First Communion.

Of course nearly every interested parent came and nearly filled the church. It seated 1,200 people. The principal of the grade school, then in full religious habit, and I in cassock explained our decision and the reason behind it. Each child develops at his/her own pace. Parents are the primary educators of their children and are the ones most able to determine the faith development of their own children. The parish staff was in agreement that respect for the individual growth of each child meant we would invite children to begin receiving Holy Communion whenever parents decided their child was ready. This could be individually or in small groups who were ready at the same time. The practice of white suits and dresses would continue, but the large communion class in the spring would be discontinued.

After presenting all the reasons for the decision, the parents were invited and encouraged to share their thoughts and feelings. Many rose to their feet. Some were confused and asked for clarification of reasons and possibilities. Most were enthusiastic and supported the idea. Some rejected it entirely. I will always remember one professional man. He stood to voice his objections. He was a pious and good Catholic husband and father. With emotion in his voice he asked us, "How can you change a tradition that goes back to Jesus himself?"

That question has been asked repeatedly following the various changes initiated by the Second Vatican Council. Pious practices, customs and devotions developed in different ethnic areas or as a result of various historical events. Gradually they became widely accepted. Most of those practices, customs or devotions had developed without any clear connection to the gospel. Eventually many were considered essential to Catholic life. The image of a dormant and inactive volcano is an appropriate description of the situation within the Catholic Church at that time in our history.

Those of us ordained as priests prior to the Council were trained in a very pious, individualistic piety. We in turn trained the laity in the same piety. For many reasons, we forgot that Christianity is, above all, a social religion. The modern notion that it is a private matter, something you do in your spare time and in the privacy of your home is nonsense. The core tenet of Christianity is that we should love God and our neighbor as ourselves.[1]

There was little foundation in the gospels for so much of the Catholic culture we all took for granted. It focused on self and personal salvation. There was no social awareness in that piety and our preaching never called the faithful to reach out to the poor or to work for justice.

I look back on the manner in which I celebrated Mass in those pre-counciliar days. I observed the rubrics with total respect and precision. Saying Mass was a very powerful experience for me. It was a Jesus and me sort of prayer. It was only later that the theology given to us by the Second Vatican Council awakened and drew me into a far more significant understanding and appreciation of the Mass.

Now these many years later it seems apparent that our decision allowing parents to determine when their child is prepared and ready to begin receiving Holy Communion was significant for many reasons. The gospel imperative for us to love God and to love our neighbor as ourselves is

A revolutionary concept. It urges us to come to terms with ourselves, to accept ourselves with all of our strengths and weaknesses, to like ourselves. This is no easy achievement in a world that preaches dissatisfaction from every corner.[2]

That decision about First Communion was a revolutionary step for many Catholics. Parents began to think of self in a more positive and wholesome manner. That one little step was born of the theology behind the liturgical and catechetical renewal mandated by the Second Vatican Council. All of us, ordained and laity, were offered a far more significant understanding and appreciation of the Mass. In the process we were freed to embrace a new but ancient way of understanding ourselves as baptized people, to accept who we are, to recognize what we have, and to channel our energies into helping others.

Prior to the Council the laity stood, sat, knelt, bowed and struck their breasts at the designated moments signaled by the ringing of bells. Most had little or no appreciation of why they did these things and little appreciation of the Mass as prayer. The majority prayed the rosary while the priest said Mass. Others simply endured the obligation, arrived late and departed immediately after communion, feeling their obligation had been fulfilled. It was all part of being Catholic.

Thus it was that we who treasured our Catholic culture were like an inactive volcano. We, the Living Body of Christ slept. Like Harry Truman, the elderly caretaker of Spirit Lake Lodge, most of us felt secure, safe and comfortable in a culture we were confident would never change. Then fifty years ago, the entirely unexpected happened. Pope John XXIII announced his intention to convene all the bishops of the world in what has come to be known as the Second Vatican Council. It transformed the Catholic Church, released the spiritual energy that had been dormant within us for so long, and set a vision of spiritual renewal before us that continues guiding us into our future. Our Catholic culture will never be the same again. Anyone under the age of fifty is unable to appreciate the importance of that transformation or vision. Although scholars now say it was the most significant religious event in the 20th century, many under that age do not even know what we mean when we refer to the II Vatican Council.

In some intuitive way, Pope John seemed to understand that,

"The death of a culture begins when its normative institutions fail to communicate ideals in ways that remain inwardly compelling, first of all to the cultural elites themselves."[3]

I think that observation by a social theorist, published after the Council closed, confirms the importance of the Council. When I was ordained the ideals of the gospel were no longer being communicated in a manner that was inwardly compelling. Most of us were motivated by fear more than love. Rules had replaced faith. Religion was far removed from the realities of normal, ordinary life. Our knowledge of scripture was far less than adequate. Our sacrament life was impersonal, without meaning, and generally perceived as magic more than mystery. I think it safe to say that our Catholic culture had died and was not yet buried, or it was in the process of dying. John XXIII was bold in making a decision to do something about our situation.

A few months before beginning to write this manuscript, I had an experience that for me was serendipitous. The experience reverberates in my mind as the principle metaphor guiding and shaping all I am trying to convey in these pages. That serendipitous experience occurred in the Ace hardware store on East Broadway Street in Missoula, Montana. It happened shortly after we had received an official liturgical document known as *The General Instruction of the Roman Missal.* In popular parlance, perhaps with a certain degree of sarcasm, the document is commonly referred to with the acronym *G.I.R.M.* This document was issued to revise the already revised liturgy of the Second Vatican Council.

A young male clerk in the Ace hardware store was very helpful and accommodating in helping me select a gift for a friend. The item was not on display, so the young clerk took a box off the shelf and offered to remove the item from its packaging. I objected since the photo on the box was not exactly the sort of thing that my friend had described. The clerk assured me that did not matter and it was no problem. So ignoring my objections he carefully and gently removed Styrofoam, plastic bags and cardboard inserts designed to protect the contents. Finally he removed the item itself. He was not surprised or disturbed by my less than enthusiastic response. He recognized this was not the item for which I was searching.

You may agree that one of the great mysteries in life is how an object is placed in a cardboard box with all that protects it. If you ever stood by a clerk as s/he tried to repackage an item, then you know how totally helpless I felt at that moment. It quickly became apparent that we ordinary mortals do not have the skill to put the item and all that protects it back into the box as it was originally packaged. No matter how he positioned the box or arranged the Styrofoam, the various plastic bags and the cardboard inserts, the item was simply too large for the box. It seemed foolish to make suggestions so I refrained. Then my laughter began, the sort of belly laughter that endangered my life as a young altar boy. The clerk's frustration mounted along with his determination. The muscles of my stomach tightened but I could no longer contain my impulse to laugh so I muttered a thank you, excused myself, and fled the scene.

A few minutes later, while sitting along the banks of the Clark Fork River, my laughter exploded. I found the incident so funny because I can remember many times when I have tried to do the same thing. It may appear simple to return items to the packages in which they were delivered. Even with great care, the Styrofoam, the plastic bags and the cardboard inserts made of linerboard get bent out of shape. Eventually the box is stretched beyond its limits and the laws that govern such things lead to a bursting of the seams. Or worse, if the item contained by the box is fragile, the enterprise may result in the destruction of the item itself.

That experience is reminiscent of Jesus' teaching about putting new wine into old wine skins. I share it here as a metaphor that aptly illustrates the dynamic behind the growing confusion and frustration within our Catholic household of faith today.

A box labeled The Catholic Church was opened by a great historical event called the Second Vatican Council. The Christ mystery, the core gospel values and ideals that are the essence of living the Christ life were the treasured items contained in the box. The Catholic culture may be understood as the various packing materials around those treasured items. Instead of Styrofoam, plastic bags and cardboard inserts made of linerboard, there were all the traditions and customs by which our Catholic identity was established and maintained.

Surely John XXIII must have understood that opening the box and removing all the contents was a fragile undertaking. Certainly a few others understood this. From the day he announced the Council and ever since, some within the halls of the Vatican and some local bishops were filled with fear the contents would be destroyed. They never understood the Council's vision and never accepted Pope John's invitation to open the windows and allow the Holy Spirit to move freely among us. Still today there are bishops and laity who never accepted, even rejected the Council's invitation to spiritual renewal. They have been unwavering in their intention to put it all back into the box. That is an impossible task but they continue to try. The packing and the box have been stretched beyond their limits and in accord with the laws that govern such things, the seams are bursting. The Catholic household of faith is being damaged in the process. It is never wise to put new wine into old wineskins. The Church can never again be as it was before the box was opened.

There is little to be gained by lamenting that the dominant culture in which we live has moved far from God. Jesus understood this. The dominant culture in which he lived, as the dominant culture in which we live, was burdened by injustice and violence. His mission is the mission or task for which we who are church exist. The gospel invites us to the task of Jesus himself. Carefully examine how he lived and his teaching. His life was dedicated to empowering people to live God's new reality. His parables speak of God as the one source of hope for healing the sickness of human existence. It is only in God that we will rediscover the vision capable of inspiring us to respond in a positive and creative manner to the moral dilemmas that confront us. Jesus modeled for us and throughout his public life spoke about the reign of God. Some recent scholars help us to understand what he meant when he spoke of God's new reality.

If we put that concept into contemporary language it may sound something like this. Each and all of us are called and sent to live God's new reality. Jesus was fully human because he was so open to that Gracious Mystery we name God and because he lived in total harmony with God. We experience God in and through the compassion, kindness, unconditional love and power of nonviolence so evident in him. As and when our own spirit and life style is more authentically like that of Jesus, we become more fully human as he was. As the numbers of those becoming more fully human increase, so the concentric circles of love (Holy Spirit) spreading outward from Christ grow in intensity. As that happens, God's new reality becomes more evident in our world. We have been empowered by the Holy Spirit to live as Jesus did and sent to announce God's new reality to others, using words only when words are needed.

So now, two thousand years later, the long story of our human family gives testimony that we children of Adam and Eve, brothers and sisters of Cain are certainly not yet fully children of God. Memories of the Holocaust and Hiroshima cast a long shadow. We heard little or no moral outrage as our un-relinquished thirst for revenge crushed the peoples of Afghanistan and Iraq. Once again we are confronted by the startling truth spoken by Mahatma Gandhi so many years ago. His experience of Christians led him to describe the church as,

"A first class human tragedy. That peoples of the earth who claim to believe in the message of Jesus whom they describe as the Prince of Peace, show little of that belief in actual practice."[4]

Today we are a nation of people, nominally followers of Christ, who allow our political officials to convince us that our very existence depends on our willingness to be a household of fear and violence. When we fail to learn from our past, we repeat it. The words of Gandhi continue to haunt us! They will continue to haunt us until we finally appreciate what it means to be Living Body of Christ.

The Second Vatican Council recognized that liturgy is the basis and fountain of spiritual renewal. The manner in which Eucharist is celebrated shapes the church. The church than influences the larger cultures in which we live. God's new reality announced by Jesus is manifested primarily where human life and the environment are respected. The Second Vatican Council had the clear intention of awakening and provoking us to engage in concrete efforts for peace and justice. That was the goal when it called for the renewal and reform of the liturgy. Catholic liturgy is true to itself only when it leads the baptized assembly to action on behalf of justice and peace.

There are grand old neighborhoods in this city where I live. The great maple trees that line the streets stand tall, fresh with buds in spring, brilliant green in summer, crisp gold in autumn, and barren in winter. In every season these giants transform our streets and neighborhoods. Large, sometimes weather-worn houses are interspersed among the trees, reminiscent of a monopoly game. Such historic mansions, like the trees surrounding them, are graceful reminders of the abundant heritage we share as a river city nestled in the mountains of western Montana.

Most of those grand old mansions continue to be occupied, some with grace and dignity, others draped with neglect. A few unattended leaks in the ceiling or plumbing can swiftly transform any of those beautiful homes into old, abandoned derelicts. If cracks in cement foundations and peeling paint on exterior walls are neglected, it is only a matter of time until their beauty and charm fades and they become symbols of death rather than life.

In recent years, a few entrepreneurs or private owners have invested time and money in one or the other of the houses that seemed forgotten. There is magic in the restoring, remodeling and refurbishing of such houses. It is like the warm and bright light of the July sun rising up upon us from behind Mount Sentinel. Because of their work, within a few months, streets, neighborhoods, even the very character of our city feels the warmth and charm of a forgotten and forlorn facade. Because of their efforts, shared pride in our river city is renewed and we are reminded we live in a special place.

Occasionally there are other owners who apparently lack appreciation for our rich heritage and the long hours and creative skills that designed and built the grand old mansions of our city. They are people of good will who are proud of this city in which we are neighbors, but sometimes that good will and intention are insufficient. It is a terrible loss when a grand old mansion is demolished and removed because we are unable to recognize and appreciate the beauty in a forgotten, neglected and forlorn facade.

Like many visitors to our city, I marvel at these houses as I drive or bicycle past them. They trigger my imagination and I find myself musing about life, Catholic life and Catholic liturgy. The Catholic household of faith is a grand old mansion. It has been my home since birth. It is an ancient house of grace in which so many good and holy people have been nurtured. Within this grand old mansion there are many levels and many rooms peopled with a widely diverse assortment of residents. We all share the same address but often not the same language. Some of us have lived in this mansion since our birth, while others moved in more recently. Some of us recognize the need for repairs and renovation. These understand and appreciate the process of renewal and have been willing to tolerate the confusion and chaos.

Pope John XXIII used the Italian word *"aggiornamento"* when he summoned the bishops of the world to meet with him. He used that word in calling us to spiritual renewal. He was asking us to allow the Holy Spirit to bring fresh new life into the church. He was a leader who viewed the world as filled with possibility. With great foresight he was enabling all of us to be Catholic in more than name and to influence our nation and world in positive ways.

There are some in our grand old mansion who for whatever reason, neither understand nor appreciate the process of renewal. They are uncomfortable with any sort of change and prefer things be left as they were. From the beginning or perhaps as the process of *aggiornamento* continued, they were or became increasingly unhappy. That is no surprise since it was a long time since repairs or maintenance had been done on this old house we call church. The renovations were to be extensive and take time.

As typical of any group of people sharing the same residence, we often have some serious disagreements. In such a large and ancient mansion with so many residents, it is impossible for everyone to be happy all of the time. It seems that wherever Catholic folk engage in conversation we hear the same stories repeated over and over again expressing concern that the process of renewal is stalled, delayed or simply being reversed. There is a widespread sense of disillusion among us about the situation in which we now find ourselves. All of us care about our home, our common residence. None of us want to see the beauty and charm of this grand old mansion fade or to see it demolished and removed.

The social structure of the apostolic church was egalitarian and free of legalisms and class distinctions. It was free of the class separations and purity laws that excluded and marginalized people. Jesus brought together an entirely new kind of community rooted in the mystery of God as love. In this new community there was room for lepers, tax collectors and Samaritans. All were equal partners, brothers and sisters in Christ. No one was dominant or superior. No one was subordinate or inferior. The church was the living sacrament of Christ in the world, the Living Body of Christ.

Then as the church grew and extended into new cultural situations, we were divided into clergy and laity. The laity were treated as second-class citizens.

Exclusion returned with the reinstitution of a 'Christian' priesthood, along with a revived 'holiness code' – consecrated altars and consecrated men and women and 'consecrated fingers' with the exclusion of the laity (especially women) from altars, from secret conclaves, from decision making, from control of the believer's money. The 'rood screen' separating clergy from laity was a great barrier in the Middle Ages and it survived for a long time in the 'communion railing'.[5]

In the document *Lumen Gentium,* the Council clearly acknowledged that the church is not limited to and does not belong exclusively to the clergy. The gap between clergy and laity began to be bridged and healed. The process of *aggiornamento* began and continues still.

Many among us who are comfortable with the clergy-centered church of our past, while accepting the teachings of the Second Vatican Council, deplore many of the things that happened since the Council. They feel like many of us did when we first entered the world of computers, printers, fax machines or media centers. It seems inevitable that all the wiring gets criss-crossed and tangled. Many like myself do not have the sort of well-developed skills needed to handle all of this technology with ease. When I see that mess of wires, I become uncomfortable. It seems the same happened to some within our household of faith. Once the box was opened, the items removed and the process of renewal initiated, the wires slowly, inevitably got criss-crossed and tangled.

As the years of renewal moved forward, the anticipated changes that affirm and develop the insights of the Council's *Pastoral Constitution on the Church* have taken roots in many communities. In spite of that, recent liturgical directives and adjustments emanating from the Vatican are clear. They send a signal announcing it is time to place the clergy back up on a high pedestal! It is natural that some welcome this trend. However those of a more egalitarian mind-set wholeheartedly embraced the teaching of the Council. Such communities lament the possible return of the clergy centered model.

Gary Wills speaks for them in his book, *What Jesus Meant.* He describes our situation today with this observation:

Jesus did not work miracles for their own sake and rebukes those who ask him to do so. His miracles are targeted to teach lessons about the heavenly reign he brings with him, and one of the main lessons is that people should not be separated into classes of the clean and the unclean, the worthy and the unworthy, the respectable and the un-respectable. He has told his followers that they are privileged, since they enter into a new intimacy with the Father.....[6]

Current efforts to restore and strengthen a clergy centered model of church leave many of us feeling frustrated or confused. If that has been your experience, perhaps it is time simply to recall the vision of church set before us by the Council. Wit, persistence and mutual encouragement are required of us today. There is no adequate answer to the commonly voiced question – "why are these things happening?" Rather then burning our energy struggling with such questions, it may be far more beneficial to remember that the work of God's Spirit cannot be stopped or turned back. Movement from a clerically dominated to a more egalitarian church is a monumental task and will occur slowly. The membership of the Catholic Church is enormous, perhaps numbering one billion members. The institutional structures of the Catholic Church are extremely complex. We are experiencing the sort of inertia that characterizes any social body of such size.

Rather than being discouraged, marvel at the extent to which reform and renewal has occurred in such a relatively brief time! It has been an amazing historical event. When I am inclined to feel frustrated or discouraged because the renewal seems stalled, I find the words of wisdom people like Ralph Waldo Emerson encouraging. "What lies behind and what lies before us are tiny matters compared to what lies within us."

In all of this I find the metaphor of the box helpful. For the purpose of throwing open the windows to allow the Spirit of Christ to move freely among us, a great historical event called the Second Vatican Council opened the box. That box contained our Catholic culture and all the parts and pieces determined necessary for what Pope John XXIII called *aggiornamento,* spiritual renewal, the replacing of all that had grown stale, with fresh new life. Pope John XXIII had great foresight when he summoned the bishops of the world to meet together. Apparently he hoped that in doing so he was creating the possibility for all of us to be Catholic in more than name and to influence our nation and world in positive ways. *Aggiornamento.* The word contains great potential. It was a long time since repairs or upkeep had been done. The renovations were to be extensive and take time.

It is said that repetition is the mother of learning. We who are residents dwelling in this grand old mansion have a task to do. We also are responsible for the maintenance of the mansion. I encourage you to be persistent in your commitment to restore our home with new vigor and vitality. We are church, the Living Body of Christ. It is our responsibility to move forward into the future. The Spirit of God is directing and leading us along the way.

There is a gift in living where the seasons change with such dramatic effect. As the leaves fall and accumulate on the ground, we here in Missoula are aware winter is coming. Already snow is accumulating on the peaks that surround us and will soon descend into the valley. Then a few months later spring will surprise us with new bursts of life and the cycle continues. Learn from the seasons and from each new morning as it introduces a day filled with new possibilities. The Holy Spirit is with us, guiding us and leading us in ways we cannot anticipate. In spite of efforts to put everything back into the box, the renewal called for by John XXIII eventually will succeed.

CHAPTER 5

WENDELL BERRY
"It may be that when we no longer know what to do,
we have come to our real work."

BACK AROUND and PUSH

I was born and grew up in Anaconda, a small town in western Montana. One of the largest copper mining companies in the world operated a smelter in Anaconda. The rich copper, silver, lead and zinc deposits were extracted from the deep underground mines in our sister city, Butte. These were transported by our own world-class railroad to the smelter in Anaconda for processing. The original plan for The Butte, Anaconda and Pacific Railroad was to provide a rail link from Butte to Seattle. The track was laid as far as Georgetown Lake, twenty-five miles west of Anaconda, and that became the terminus of the line. Locals commonly referred to this rail system as the "B. A. & P." which then was fondly nicknamed, "The Back Around and Push." After a brief recall of Catholic life prior to the II Vatican Council, I will return to the "B. A. & P." Railroad.

We were proud of Anaconda for many reasons. Certainly the most unusual source of our pride was the tallest smokestack in the world. It remains standing today on the mountainside high above the smelter-site on the east end of town. That smelter provided employment for most of our fathers and for many of us as we worked our way through college.

We also were equally proud of our Catholic heritage. The city of Anaconda was and remains predominantly Catholic. We were born Catholic. Most of us were raised in Catholic homes and schools. On Sundays the stores were closed and on Good Friday all the stores in town closed from noon until three o'clock. As children and young adults we were like goldfish in a bowl, swimming in a safe, yet closely monitored Catholic environment.

Most of us did not understand the external rituals that surrounded us. In spite of that, we treasured them as part of our social, cultural identity. They filled us with a sense of mystery and splendor, and occasionally provided fits of laughter for those of us who had the opportunity to serve as altar boys. Perhaps it was because those rituals often occasioned such laughter that they were a significant part of the religious cultural that held us together like glue. If you don't understand what I mean, then surely you were never a pre-Vatican II altar boy.

There were distinguishing marks that clearly identified us as Catholic and connected us, even with the Catholic kids in the public schools. We all signed ourselves with the cross and attended Mass.

Sunday Mass was a major event. We all knew it was a mortal sin to miss Mass on Sunday. We dressed up in our good clothes and crowded into our parish churches. Devotion to Mary brought us to Tuesday night novena. We abstained from meat on Friday and lined up for confession on Saturday afternoons following the matinee at the Bluebird Theater. Our parish church was in the center of town and another parish was located at the east end, near the copper smelter that provided our economic sustenance. Even on the street it was easy to pick out those who were Catholic. We learned at a young age to sign ourselves with the cross whenever we passed the doors of the church.

There often was a great deal of comedy when we gathered on Sundays. It was not planned comedy but easily and quickly recognized and appreciated. We entered the parish church with a reverential attitude, in silence, dipping our fingers into the holy water dish. For some, the gesture of signing self with the cross was so hurried it gave the impression of swatting flies. Each of us rendered our own personal version of a genuflection that occasionally looked like the individual tripped and fell to the floor.

Every pew was filled at every Sunday Mass. We sat, stood and knelt at the proper times following our little black Missal. The priest stood facing the altar, back turned to us, reciting the Latin prayers. Some priests spoke the words carefully, perhaps with understanding. Some raced through the rite, far more quickly than we could read the English translation. Part of the unspoken comedy was our own futile effort to race through the prayers as swiftly as possible, then skipping pages to catch up with the priest. The culture was so intense that no one ever questioned how the priest could say all those Latin prayers as swiftly as he did.

It was only after my ordination that I really began to understand how they did it. The second parish to which I was assigned was large and so too was the spirit of community among the people. We had turned the altar around so that Mass was celebrated with the priest facing the people as directed by the Second Vatican Council. We had been preparing a large group of people to enter the church. We were explaining the Mass and had asked these people to attend Mass together.

So it happened that twenty-five of them sat in the front pews on a Sunday morning when our pastor, Monsignor Denis Patrick Meade said the Mass. He was Irish born, thoroughly a man of the church, a delightful, lovable and somewhat impish man. After the Mass we invited the group of twenty-five to join us in the basement of the rectory for a discussion about the Mass.

After their experience in the church, folks were curious and asked many good questions. Then someone wanted to know "what was Monsignor mixing?" The questioner was not satisfied when told he was not mixing anything! He persisted noting that several times during the Mass it was apparent that Monsignor was mixing something on the altar. The questioner wanted to know what it was.

Then a light went on in the brain! In the liturgy at that time, there were three separate prayers during which the priest was directed to make the sign of the cross with his right hand, three times over the bread, three times over the wine, and three times over both bread and wine together. The Monsignor was capable of saying Mass as swiftly as anyone and those signs of the cross had became a blurred swinging of his hand over the bread and the wine. To those unfamiliar with the Mass (and probably to many who were born and raised Catholic), the manner in which he made those signs of the cross gave the appearance of mixing something on the altar.

As altar servers, young boys were privileged to share a special world beyond the communion rail. We were closer than anyone to the altar and to the priest and of course dressed in a black cassock and white surplus. The combination reinforced "S-ter's" instruction that the responsibilities entrusted to us were serious. "S-ter" was a commonly slurred manner of speaking of the Catholic nuns or Sisters who taught us in school. They were charged with teaching us the Latin responses and the rituals of being an altar boy. We never doubted the seriousness of the task. But we were young boys and some situations were so humorous, our stomachs nearly burst in our effort to restrain our laughter.

We memorized the Latin prayers without comprehension, and the bows and gestures that accompanied those prayers. It was a slow, tedious process. Once we began serving at the altar we gradually realized it was impossible for the priest to enunciate the Latin words properly with such speed. The Catholic nun who trained us was no longer close enough to hear our performance. So we often imitated the priests and the older altar boys with our own creative methods of skipping, slurring and truncating the Latin into jumbled, mumbled sentences that got the job done while inserting the proper gestures at the appropriate time.

After we learned the Latin prayers and the proper movements and gestures, we wore the cassock and surplus and sat next to the priest in the sanctuary. That situation was ideal for unrehearsed comedy.

A biretta is the special hat that was part of the vestment worn by the priest in days past. He wore the biretta while walking to or from the altar and whenever he sat during the Mass. It was made of black satin with cardboard liners to maintain the proper shape and topped with a fluffy pom-pom. On more than one occasion one of us whose responsibility it was to hand the biretta to the priest, failed to move quickly enough. When the priest sat, the squishing sound was far more than twelve year olds could contain. Somehow we tightened up our stomach muscles, storing up the bellyaches for some other occasion when supervision was not so near.

It required a special touch to present the water and wine, to wash and dry the priest's hands properly, to ring the bells at the appropriate moment and to handle the incense bowl and thurible. It required repeated practice to master the proper bows, to know when to strike one's breast and how to genuflect correctly.

Normally moving the book, known as the Missal, from one side of the altar to the other was uneventful and routine. Occasionally for some reason the routine varied. One day while serving the early morning Mass at 6:00 a.m. I was involved in a collision that should have broken the priest's fingers. He was a large, strong Frenchman and at the time pastor of a small rural parish in Philipsburg, Montana. His manner was brusque, his motions swift, and we felt he was intimidating. At the normal, customary moment, I ascended the steps to remove the missal with the large brass bookstand on which it rested. I turned to descend the steps. As I did so, the priest swiftly turned back to the book

56

and clobbered the brass bookstand with his hand. The look on his face caused my serving partner to leave the sanctuary, seeking a closed door behind which he could release his laughter.

Altar boy stories worth retelling are beyond the capacity of any one person to remember, and far beyond the ability of most to imagine. There was the red-haired, freckled altar boy who devised a creative way to light the candles on the v-shaped candelabra. He extended the wick on the lighter six inches or so and managed to ignite the highly starched altar clothes. Imagine if you can, the total and absolute look of surprise on the face of the priest standing at the coffin during a funeral when he took firm hold of the thurible chain from the altar boy who had inadvertently allowed the chain to rest for awhile on the red hot charcoal within the brazier. Legend has it that pastor's reflexes were so sharp he inadvertently threw the thurible to the far end of the church.

Those who served in church choirs had their own comic experiences. A dear friend has trained many church choirs and other singing groups. Years ago she was a young teacher in my hometown. At that time there were two morning Masses in our parish church. They always were High Masses meaning the priest sang many of the prayers requiring a vocalist in the choir loft to sing the responses.

It happened that the organist-singer for the eight o'clock weekday Mass was incapacitated. Our local pastor, Father Joseph Schulte, called this young music teacher and asked her to play the organ and sing at that Mass until the regular organist could return. Barbara declined, insisting she did not know how to play the organ. Our mild mannered pastor insisted she could do it. So after learning a few stops on the organ, she submitted to his insistence.

In that era it was customary for one of the assistant pastors to be available in the confessional during the Mass. All was going well for Barbara. Then one morning a close friend was with her in the choir loft. The Mass had started when this temporary organist-singer, decided she wanted to go downstairs to go to confession. Barbara asked her friend to cover for a few minutes and sing the responses. Her friend refused and firmly said, she would not do it! Barbara ignored her protestations, left the choir loft, descended the stairs and went to the confessionals. In our parish church, the priest sat in a small cubicle covered by green drapery. There was a small cubicle to his left and another to his right. Each also was covered by green drapery. Those going to confession slipped into the cubicle and waited for the priest to push the sliding door aside, the signal to begin one's confession.

After waiting for a moment or two, Barbara, the temporary organist, pulled aside the drape and entered the confessional. As she knelt waiting her turn, she heard Father Schulte who was saying the Mass, sing in Latin, *"Do-min-us vo-bis-cum….."* She listened. There was no response! Her friend had failed her! So she pushed the curtain aside, leaned out into the church, and sang the response, *"Et cum spir-itu tu-o….."*, as if that were the normal manner of doing things! If the Tridentine Latin Mass provided anything, it certainly provided many opportunities for laughter.

Church laws reached far beyond the doors of the church prompting peals of laughter in unexpected places. Saturday nights provided multiple opportunities for adolescent imagination to probe this Catholic culture. Following a dance at our local Catholic high school, we would gather at The Arctic Circle for ice cream and milkshakes, or at Bill's Drive-In for burgers and fries. As the hour of midnight approached, those who intended to receive communion at Sunday Mass would begin to watch the clock. At that time the laws of the church were drilled into our heads. Anyone intending to receive Holy Communion was required to maintain a Eucharistic fast. The fast began at midnight and required that no foods or liquids could be consumed until after communion. Even a glass of water was not allowed after midnight.

It was a popular diversion for Catholic adolescent minds to pose questions about major issues to the priests and sisters entrusted with passing on the intricacies of Catholic culture. Among the favorite questions would be, "if I accidentally swallow toothpaste, can I still receive Holy Communion?"

The determination of the exact moment when the Eucharistic fast was to begin also stimulated complex questions. My hometown, Anaconda, is located on the western edge of the Mountain Time zone. Among the more technical, casuistic questions asked were premised on the physical location of our city. Our adolescent creativity rationalized that the Eucharistic fast began only at twenty-two minutes after midnight. I don't remember how we arrived at the idea but we applied the same reasoning to argue that when Daylight Saving Time was in effect, we could eat or drink until 1:22 a.m. Note the precision!

In spite of the efforts of Pope Pius X encouraging frequent reception of Holy Communion, the Eucharistic fast was an obstacle. The majority of Catholics seldom received Communion unless they were attending a very early morning Mass. Eventually developments after the Council reduced the law requiring the Eucharistic Fast to one hour before reception of the Sacrament. Today the reception of Communion during Eucharistic celebrations is the norm and those who do not approach the Table are the exception.

The Eucharistic fast was a source of anxiety for many of our young souls. Perhaps an even greater source of anxiety for nearly all of us was the practice of weekly confession. Once we made our first confession, our normal Saturday routine was well established. Ordinarily we attended the afternoon matinee at the Bluebird Theater. Then on the way home we stopped in St. Paul's Church for confession before returning home for dinner.

The practice of weekly confession began in the first grade when we were schooled for our First Confession. This is a custom that still lingers on in some parishes and there are many today who still insist our children must go to confession before receiving Holy Communion for the first time. It was never clear to me forty plus years ago, nor is it clear today, why parents or pastors think six or seven year olds have sinned in some way that separates them from God.

Recall for a moment my brief description of the confessionals in my home parish church. We entered the confessional by pulling aside the dark, velvety green curtains. We then knelt on a hard, wooden kneeler in the dark, waiting for the sliding, wooden door to open. The priest sat on the other side of the screen and would alternate between the penitents on his left and then his right. My early years as an assistant pastor made me aware that many of our customs at that time reduced the sacrament to the fulfillment of an obligatory but meaningless ritual.

The first two parishes to which I was assigned had parish schools. During the first week of every month, the other assistant pastor and myself were assigned confession duty. This meant that on the first Monday, Tuesday, Wednesday and Thursday of every month, we were to sit in the confessionals every morning from eight to noon, and again after lunch from one until three thirty. The students were brought to the church and were expected to go to confession.

A numbing stream of children poured through the confessionals. Each child repeated nearly the same words over and over and over again throughout the morning, and then again throughout the afternoon. Listing one or two insignificant matters of disobedience or misbehavior followed their well rehearsed "bless me Father for I have sinned." One after the other they would come, beginning with the first or second graders until the entire student body and we had endured the process. As they waited in line along the wall of the church, most probably believed that somehow they were bad.

We sat in the confessionals in black cassocks, struggling to remain awake. We tried to respond to each child in a warm and caring manner. Most of the time we wondered why we should pray the words of absolution over these little ones, God's innocents. They confessed, but nothing that could be classified as sin. We did the penance!

Our Catholic heritage is a gift for which I am deeply grateful. My own imagination, thinking and view of the world are Catholic. I remain proud of being Catholic, even now, when deeply disappointed and saddened by the circumstance in which we find our household of faith.

When a long-time friend, now among the senior attorneys in our city, heard my comment about trying to write a book, he asked what the book was about. He refuses to admit that Catholic culture, as we knew it, is dead or dying although his own children no longer cross the threshold into our parish churches. In response to his question I said, "I feared that Catholic liturgy is in danger of dying." He looked puzzled by my response and pressed me to explain why.

On the previous weekend we both had participated in the liturgy of Pentecost in one of our rural parishes. My friend was sitting behind me during that liturgy. He was present but not actively engaged. In response to his question, I asked what that particular celebration meant for him. He responded, "it was good, but I really prefer the Latin." I readily admit that our efforts over nearly four decades to help him and others to understand and appreciate the vision of the Second Vatican Council were generally ineffective. Perhaps that is because well educated professional people like my friend simply never accepted their own responsibility to improve their own understanding of the Mass and all it means to be Catholic. It did not surprise me that he could not understand why that particular liturgy was not a good experience for me. In my personal journal I found a description of how I remember my experience of pastoral ministry in those early years after ordination:

I have lived a pretty standard-brand existence, typical of many diocesan priests in pastoral ministry. As the country struggled with political corruption during Watergate, as the church struggled between reform and resistance, as one society drowned in affluence and others sank further into poverty, I went blithely

60

on, basically unaware. I said my prayers and did my work. It was all good work, all well-meaning and right-hearted. But it also was safe, secure, satisfying and totally self-centered.

The bright promise of the Second Vatican Council called us out of that small, Catholic world. For many of us that bright promise of the Council seems to be fading as we near the end of the first decade in the 21st century. It is apparent that some among us still cling to those elements of our Catholic culture that others have discarded. That reminds me of the rail system on which the rich ore from the Butte mines was transported to the Anaconda smelter. It was referred to as the "B. A. & P." We called it "The Back Around and Push."

I understand nostalgia. Like many of my peers I am grateful for the foundation and nourishment of our Catholic culture as I experienced it. I also appreciate why some folks think it is time to turn the vision of the Second Vatican Council around, and push. However, as my own understanding of what it means for us to be the Living Body of Christ has matured, I realized our primary responsibility, as church is to call forth God's new reality today and in the future, not the past. Doing so requires us to develop and shape a new Catholic culture suitable to the task.

CHAPTER 6

SHUSAKU ENDO ("THE SEA AND POISON")
"When you sail, don't pull up the anchor weeping.
Be a man, do it laughing."

JOHN'S COUNCIL

Sailing in a small boat is one of those physically demanding activities that forced me to learn about myself. Interacting with wind, water and boat does not come easily. As I acquired the skill it taught me how to cope with my own limitations and how to respond to situations or circumstances beyond my ability to influence. I think of those occasions when all goes well and we in the boat are in harmony with wind and water, as mystical experiences.

When Charlie Brooke first invited me to go sailing with him, I jumped at the opportunity. It turned out to be a bright, warm day on Flathead Lake in western Montana. The wind was perfect for sailing. His 21-foot Thistle was an open-cockpit boat built for racing. During the previous winter I had classroom instruction about the theory of sailing. The classes had been helpful. Charlie gave me a brief summary of the mechanics of sailing; we climbed aboard his Thistle and set off with the brisk wind. The exhilaration welling up within me was suddenly replaced with anxiety and panic as Charlie slid forward on his seat and told me to take the tiller. We were keeled over in the wind and the water was rushing along the gunnels. I was afraid to move lest we capsize. Perhaps many in our household of faith experienced a similar confusion of emotion in those years when the renewal called for by John's Council were being implemented on the local level.

Before my day of sailing ended, the panic was replaced with a degree of confidence. I was able to maintain a course and negotiate the turns without capsizing. From that moment onward there was a yearning in my soul to sail. It has not been like that for all of us in the Catholic household of faith. As I invite you into this chapter, I think of it somewhat as the adventure of sailing. I will return to that metaphor again.

Surely if Pope John XXIII were still among us today, I suspect he would agree that his decision to gather the church in an ecumenical council has been justified by the fact that the Council freed so many of us affirm our own deepest truth. YES! We Are The Living Body of Christ!

There are truths the church has always taught and about which the New Testament is clear. There has never been any dispute among us that Christ came to bring all reality into union with God. St. Paul described our experience with the poetic image of creation groaning with birth pains. Our world is in process, evolving, and we along with it. For those of us who are Christians, Christ is the center of that process. We believe that in Christ we discover we are part of something far greater than ourselves. We are united with Christ and in Christ we are united with one another.

Our tradition is clear. All the baptized are members of Christ's body. Read the biblical texts closely. At least implicitly these texts acknowledge that everyone, everyone is part of Christ's body. It is not my intention to offend those who do not claim the name. Yet I believe that is the mystery of Christ. St. Ambrose urged his community to recognize themselves as the Living Body of Christ. He pleaded with them to live in such a manner that folks would recognize Christ in them. The word *"amen"* means yes and St. Augustine expected the *"amen"* spoken when receiving communion to be a word of truth.

In the written gospels it seems that Jesus understood his ministry in terms of setting people free. His mission, his life, death and resurrection were not about changing God's mind or winning back God's friendship. He came among us to change our minds and hearts and to help us wake up to the mystery of our own life. His expressed, consistent intention was singular. He came to bring us into intimate union with God as participants in the divine life. We do so as we become fully human.

We who name ourselves church believe we are called and sent to continue the work of Jesus of Nazareth. We have established certain institutional structures to help us maintain the vision of the gospel and continue Christ's work. The most visible expression of those institutional structures is seen in the ministries of pope, bishops and priests. They call us together for the celebration of the Eucharistic liturgy.

Since our origins, there have been occasions when concern about our common life has motivated those in leadership positions to gather for the purpose of addressing theological or pastoral concerns common to all. These gatherings are called ecumenical councils. In these official gatherings, our leaders and representatives "assist in the process of decision making within the Church."[1] "Ecumenical councils are supreme exercises of the collegial authority of bishops."[2]

Current church law specifies that only the Bishop of Rome (Pope) can convoke an ecumenical council.

According to the Roman Catholic Code of Canon Law, an ecumenical council is an assembly of bishops and other specified persons, convoked and presided over by the pope for the purpose of formulating decisions concerning the Catholic faith and discipline, which decisions require papal confirmation.[3]

It further specifies in canon #336 that,

The college of bishops exercises with the pope the highest and most perfect form of oversight over the whole Church and that is in an ecumenical council.[4]

A most fundamental conviction of our Catholic life is that, "according to the promise of Jesus, "the Holy Spirit operates in the Church … and is at work … in an ecumenical council."[5] An ecumenical council is the highest teaching authority of the church. On this basis,

An ecumenical council may claim a special binding authority, even though its decrees and definitions are incomplete, fragmentary human words.[6]

Pope John XXIII first announced his intention to call an ecumenical council on July 25, 1959. He convoked the Second Vatican Council on December 25, 1961,[7] and asked the bishops of the world assembled in Rome to share his vision. It was the largest gathering of Catholic bishops in history. John was an amazing man and his vision touched the heart of all peoples. He underscored the positive opportunities of the Council and saw it as a fertile opportunity to work toward the unity of humankind. He spoke to our world convinced that speaking truth to one another would unite us and charity would be our common law.

"Such councils represent the universal church and demand absolute obedience."[8] Because we believe and trust that the Holy Spirit guides and directs us as Church, we expect the resolutions of a council to be decided "in unanimity and with a spiritual consensus."[9] That does not exclude the probability of controversy. John's Council was marked by controversy and consensus. In every session a minority group of bishops were consistent in their opposition to the direction taken by the Council. Their concerns affected the integrity of the Council documents.

In spite of that, John's Council was like a fresh springtime. The dormancy of a long winter was set aside. Theologians, liturgists and scripture scholars collaborated with bishops. Most bishops returned home from the Council and invited us to rediscover what it is to be Church and to embrace our discovery. This set in motion an explosive period of change within the church that reverberated outward into the secular world. It was felt in the movements of liberation awakened among peoples on all continents.

John XXIII's purpose in convening this Council was unique. "Unlike many previous councils, Vatican II had not been called to combat heresy or to deal with some serious threat to the unity of the Church."[10] In his opening address to the council, he said,

> *The council's goal was to eradicate the seeds of discord and to promote peace and the unity of all humankind, not to repeat traditional doctrinal formulations or to condemn errors.*[11]

John XXIII set before us the concept of *aggiornamento*. As I mentioned earlier, the Italian word *aggiornamento* means, "to make things ready for today, today's needs, today's times, today's people."[12] More than twenty-six hundred bishops from all over the world gathered for four separate sessions in Rome to do that.

Of the twenty-one general councils of the Church, this was the largest and most universal. That alone underscores the importance of the work and the vision set forth by the bishops in this historic gathering. It still is regarded by many as "the most significant religious event since the sixteenth century Reformation and certainly as the most important of the twentieth century."[13] The documents of the Council were rooted in scripture and incorporated the research and insight of the best theologians and scripture scholars among us. They call us to be the Living Body of Christ, the light of Christ to the world. They are linked by that magnetic phrase *aggiornamento*, the implications of which were far more extensive and deeper than simply rearranging the furniture in our liturgical spaces and praying together in a language that we understood. Our bishops reminded us we are not simply observers or consumers. We are church, the visible expression of the Living Body of

66

Christ.

I mentioned earlier that the renewal inaugurated by John's Council was like the eruption of a long dormant volcano. Here in the United States, many of our bishops returned after each session of the Council with a new appreciation of what it is for us to be church and for them to be bishops. Many of them, not all for sure, but most were infused with a determination to help us appreciate and adopt what they had discovered and learned together in the Council. That is the inspiration of the Holy Spirit.

The Council met in Vatican City, Italy, from 1962 through 1965. Ordinary people first experienced *aggiornamento* in their pews on Sunday mornings. Bishops and pastors who understood the Council prepared their people for that moment. Unfortunately such preparation was not universal. Without an understanding of the historical, biblical and theological reasoning behind the Council documents, the folks in the pews experienced *aggiornamento* as calling for external changes. It should have been no surprise that reactions were mixed. It is still not a surprise that so much resistance to the challenge of renewal lingers on.

For the majority of us prior to the Council, the word church meant bishops, priests and Sunday Mass. Being an active Catholic referred to those of us who attended Mass on Sunday. We were confident that what happened in the Tridentine Mass did not happen anywhere else. Without Mass there is no church! For most Catholic people in those pre-conciliar days, knowledge and understanding of our faith was minimal at best.

The council occurred and deeply significant changes were mandated in the rubrics and the spirit of the Mass. These changes impacted our experience of being church and our own self-understanding as Catholics. The reformed liturgy became in fact both sign and symbol of all the Council sought to achieve with *aggiornamento*.

In nineteen sixty-nine Pope Paul VI promulgated the final liturgical reform mandated by the Council's *Constitution on the Sacred Liturgy*. That document reminded us that the Mass is the source and summit of Christian life. It called and continues calling us to be well disposed to the reform. It challenges us to learn what we are doing in liturgy and to actively participate as the people of God, as the Living Body of Christ. This document restored the Eucharist as an action to be engaged in by the entire church rather than a static object of devotion or theatrical performance. Among the most significant paragraphs in the documents published by the Council is this:

*The church earnestly desires that all the faithful be led to that
full, conscious, and active participation in liturgical celebrations
called for by the very nature of the liturgy. Such participation by
the Christian people ... is their right and duty by reason of their
baptism. In the reform and promotion of the liturgy, this full and
active participation by all the people is the aim to be considered
before all else. For it is the primary and indispensable source
from which the faithful are to derive the true Christian spirit.*[14]

The Council envisioned the renewal of the liturgy as the foundation
for a genuine reform and renewal of the entire church. The liturgy of
Vatican Two "embodies the values of the Council in many ways."[15] The
changes were not some newly devised and frivolous adjustments seeking
to make the Mass relevant. The Council was guiding us to retrieve the
spirit and the style of the Mass as it was in the earliest centuries.

Liturgical reform is not a new phenomenon. The liturgy is the
prayer of a living community. Change is inevitable in a living body. Each
century of the church has been marked by liturgical change. Sometimes
it was happenstance and random. More often, and especially since the
fourth and fifth centuries, it has been directed by legitimately established
authority. By the seventh century, Augustine's profound appreciation of
Eucharist as both source and symbol of Christ's life in us had been lost.
That may have been due to the development of an excessively large
body of clergy/presbyters which led to a proliferation of Masses offered
for personal devotion and/or special intentions. The personal piety of
that development was expressed in church architecture. Small chapels,
each with their own altar, lined the walls of churches. These provided
space for many priests to say Mass simultaneously at different altars.

This practice simply disregarded the rubrics requiring that a
community of people be present standing around the priest and eventually
became known as the low Mass spoken by a priest in whispered tones.
The passivity of the faithful increased until they simply came to hear
Mass being said by the priest. This custom persisted into the years
immediately following my own ordination. Every priest was expected to
say Mass every day, and we did so, often with only a single altar server
present. Breaking out of that custom was an enormous challenge.

In the late nineteen-sixties, five of us from the diocese of Helena
arranged a ski trip to Aspen, Colorado. The local parish in Aspen made
good practical use of their building that had been a parish school. The

68

empty, unused classrooms were converted into bedrooms. The parish welcomed visiting priests to stay there for two dollars a night and that included showers and the use of a kitchen. It also provided us the opportunity to say Mass every day. There were a number of side altars in the church. On the first morning we arose early, vested in turn, each saying Mass and serving for one another until all of us had finished.

A similar group of priests from Chicago also were staying in the building. On the first morning we noticed the Chicago priests did not observe the custom of individual Masses in the side chapels. At that time articles in various theological and liturgical journals reported the Council was expected to revive the custom of con-celebration of Mass. The Chicago priests had a pastorally progressive Cardinal-Archbishop. They were far ahead of the American church in many areas. Con-celebration of Mass was clearly one of those areas.

That night we were tired by the physical exertion of a great day of skiing. We shared our stories of a day on the slopes but soon were absorbed in a conversation about the concept of con-celebration. The next morning my companions decided to join the Chicago priests. The only exception was myself. I wanted to say my Mass and fortunately those with me were willing to tolerate my resistance. By the third day I joined them and in the process experienced the beginning of the end of the individualistic piety in which all of us had been trained. I also was introduced to a new understanding and appreciation of liturgy as the prayer of the church in which we together become newly aware of ourselves as the Living Body of Christ.

During the first four centuries all who assembled for liturgy received Communion under both forms with hands extended. Gradually the faithful felt unworthy to receive and the frequency of reception declined. Eventually a Council of the church in 1215 established the requirement that remains in church law today that the faithful had to receive Communion at least once a year during Easter time. Realize what that says! You must receive Communion at least once a year! That single law is an extraordinary expression of how badly the liturgy needed to be reformed. The meaning of Eucharist was forgotten. The spirit of the liturgy had fallen into a slumber.

Those developments and changes in the medieval period had a profoundly significant impact on our self-understanding as church. We are baptized and called to be the Living Body of Christ. The Eucharist offered and consumed nurtures and nourishes the Christ life within us.

Without the fullness of Eucharist, a shallow focus on individual, personal union with Christ emerged. Vestiges of that continue today in those who receive Communion, return to their place, kneel and bury their face in their hands.

The birthing of liturgical reform first occurred in Europe in the early years of the twentieth century. Several Benedictine monasteries became models of Gregorian chant. They were the wellspring of a renewed appreciation for long forgotten elements and dimensions of the liturgy. That reform movement gradually spread and the Benedictines soon brought the scholarly work behind it to the United States.

In a recent Commonweal magazine, Bernard Prusak comments,

From the second to the fourth centuries, the Eucharist, presided over by the bishop or by the presbyter who represented him, was a celebration in which the entire assembly of the faithful actively participated. The very word ecclesia meant the assembly of faithful who, as Augustine declared, became what they received, the Body of Christ.[16]

Those first engaged in laying the scholarly foundation for liturgical renewal treasured those words of St. Augustine. Their enthusiasm was fired by the recovery of Augustine's insight that the church is the Living Body of Christ. This became the foundational principle and remains the organizing measure of liturgical renewal set forth by the Council and guiding us today.

The liturgy of Vatican II calls all the baptized to a renewed appreciation of our self-understanding as the Living Body of Christ. The living, Risen Christ, gathers us, not just to influence us, inform us, or cause us to think. The Risen One gathers us around a table to feed us with his life and to transform us. That is what Eucharist is about. We are a community brought together to become what we eat and drink, the Living Body of Christ.

The Council restored the significance of both Eucharist and Word. A new lectionary was developed and we now enjoy a broader exposure to the Scriptures. A three-year cycle brings texts from the Hebrew bible, the New Testament letters and the gospels into our liturgical assemblies. We gather on Sunday for the Word that recalls the mighty acts of God among us. As we listen, we are reminded of who God is and what God has done and is doing. Then we have reason to offer thanks and praise when we celebrate Eucharist.

Recent controversy about the translations of Scripture has been distracting. Our current lectionary is a clear improvement over pre-counciliar Missals but inadequate in its structure. The texts generally are read out of context. For example in the current three-year cycle, one short passage from the letter to Philemon is read on one Sunday and it is completely out of context. Many of the texts were edited for the sake of brevity. My pastoral experience leads me to the conviction we need a new and total revision of the current Sunday Lectionary, providing continuous and unedited readings of both gospels and letters. It is through the lectionary that the majority of the church hears the gospel.

Now since the liturgy is proclaimed and prayed in our own language, we are able to understand and fully participate. The gestures and actions have been simplified and become meaningful. We sing with glad hearts and stand for the Eucharistic Prayer, mindful that we are a priestly people, the Living Body of Christ. Women and men are welcomed into a diverse array of liturgical ministries. Communion under both forms has become the norm.

All of this was in response to the Council's insistence that,

It is through the liturgy, especially, that the faithful are enabled to express their lives and manifest to others the mystery of Christ and the real nature of the true church.[17]

The Council retrieved an the theological insight of St. Ignatius of Antioch who taught,

The principal manifestation of the church consists in the full active participation of all God's holy people in the same liturgical celebrations, especially in the same Eucharist, in one prayer, at one altar, at which the bishop presides, surrounded by his college of priests and by his ministers.[18]

When John XXIII announced the Council, it was like calling us to lift the anchor and set sail. When forced to do so, some pulled up the anchor weeping. At the time of the Council, the diocese of Helena, the church in which I was ordained and continue to minister, was blest with an extraordinary bishop. He empowered us to pull up the anchor laughing. When he returned from each session of the Council he provided the leadership and enthusiasm that enabled our diocesan presbyterate to understand the invitation of Pope John XXIII. He enabled us to appreciate the vision set before us by the Catholic bishops of the world. He gathered us to listen to respected theologians and scripture scholars. He led us in discussion of the Council documents and we prayed together.

When parish leaders were informed, they provided their communities with scriptural, theological, psychological, and emotional reasons for the external changes. In such parishes renewal erupted with the force of Mount St. Helens. People began to appreciate it was time for us, the people of God, the Living Body of Christ to awaken to our own reality. Many among us did. Liturgical assemblies became joyful gatherings of prayer and celebration of the Risen Christ. The scriptures were proclaimed in a manner that made it clear we are sent to make a difference in the world. Eucharistic celebrations awakened us to our own deepest truth that we are the Living Body of Christ! Justice and peace moved to the front of our agendas. Pastoral Councils channeled the creative leadership of the entire community. Other Christian communities were touched and affected. Responsible observers claim the secular world was touched and affected as well. Suddenly our eyes were turned to the future rather than to the past. We were filled with confidence that in Christ the world could and would be renewed.

In response to the vision of the Council most communities of Religious Women in the United States realized their need for education in scripture and theology. They committed their resources to that work. Their apostolic ministries expanded and deepened. They remain an ideal for all of what it means to take John's Council seriously.

If the Second Vatican Council was clearly a new springtime in the church as many of us claimed with enthusiasm, then it certainly is valid to ask, what happened? If the Council's vision was so wonderful, why do we seem to be living in this fog of confusion and frustration?

Unfortunately some bishops who participated in the Council and many parish priests never appreciated the reasons why Pope John XXIII set us on a course of *aggiornamento*. They never understood the Council's vision and the implications of that vision. Even worse, there were some bishops who found the council threatening and disapproved of the entire process. They are the ones who pulled up the anchor but did so weeping.

This division among the bishops in the Council eventually resulted in Council documents containing contradictory messages. The core of those documents express and develop the vision of John XXIII and his call to *aggiornamento*. However in an effort to gain consent and support for the objectives of the Council, various compromises were made seeking to appease the prophets of doom. Those compromises are contained in the Council documents. This provided a base or rationale for two versions or interpretations of the Council. Each claims to be faithful to John's vision. Thus we find ourselves in the situation in which both John Paul II and Benedict XVI justify their determination to put everything back in the box.

In the post-conciliar period those bishops who never understood and disapproved of the Council failed to provide education for the priests and people of their local church. Trained to be obedient and unquestioning, there were those among us who did what they were told without questioning and without understanding. Certainly that is a factor contributing to the confusion and conflicts we experience today. When parishes only did what they were told to do without any understanding of the reasons, renewal also erupted with the force of Mount St. Helens. In such parishes the call to renewal caused disruption and devastation that reverberates still today. Such parishes welcome the Vatican's efforts to put everything back into the box.

In retrospect it is obvious that not everyone was suited for the task of implementing the vision of the council. Most parish priests are dedicated and obedient men. Many, perhaps most, did not understand what they were being asked to do. If they were unable to help the laity understand what they were being asking to do, external conformity became the norm. Dysfunction became the reality. The changes were implemented without adequate education or explanation of the historical, biblical or theological reasons for the changes. Altars were turned around. Latin was replaced with English. Singing became an integral part of our Sunday Assemblies. Laymen and women proclaimed the scriptures, distributed communion, and became members of pastoral councils.

In too many situations, discontent and or resistance of one form or another persists to this day. As recently as the summer of 2007, I visited a parish in which good Catholic people remain disturbed and upset by the things the Council set in motion. When questioned about the reasons for the changes, it is apparent that these folks and the priests who minister among them have no awareness of the reasons.

There also were other bishops who appreciated the reasons and understood the vision but were themselves not equipped and therefore were unable to teach and equip their parish priests with the tools needed for effective social change. When parish priests did not understand the "why" or the vision, neither did the community in which they ministered. Those parish priests were placed in the awkward situation of creating significant social change without the ability to provide the inner transformation required to sustain it. We see the consequences today.

In his wisdom it seems that Pope John XXIII foresaw all of this and addressed it in his opening speech that set the tone and the agenda for the council. He said he was,

Tired of listening to the negative tones of his advisors. Though burning with zeal, they are not endowed with very much sense of discretion or measure. These believe that our modern times, compared to past ages in the Church, are somehow worse, they behave as though they had learned nothing from history.[19]

Those are strong remarks. Then Pope John went further and said, "We feel that we must disagree with these prophets of doom, who are always forecasting disaster as though the end of the world were at hand."[20]

There are many prophets of doom within the church today as there were among the bishops in the Council. Some were peers of Pope John XXIII. Cardinal Ottavianni, the prefect of the Holy Office, Cardinal Larraona, the prefect of the Sacred Congregation of Rites, and Cardinal Siri were the most visible leaders of those in the Vatican Curia who considered the Council a mistake and the consequences a disaster. Their conviction and adamant resistance to the Council's vision persists among a minority of Catholic people and continues to be a lobby within the Catholic Church.

Mother Angelica and her Eternal Word Television Network are the most visible expression of that lobby in our country. They serve a supportive role to that segment of the Catholic population that has and continues to resist the Council's vision. Many Catholics, especially among our youth, are unaware of the implications of the programs viewed on that channel. It is likely that those who embrace the sort of pre-Vatican II mentality so evident in the programming of *EWTN* have been instrumental in gaining permission for the restoration of the Latin Tridentine Mass as an alternative to the liturgy called for by the Council.

If our experiences today fill us with disappointment, perhaps it is good to recall the wisdom of John XXIII, for there are prophets of doom among us today. Some are those for whom rubrics are more compelling than prayer. Some are disciples of canon law, more than disciples of scripture. Some simply lack adequate training and the natural skills of leadership. They are unequipped for their primary ministerial responsibilities and contribute to the cloud of misunderstanding in which we find ourselves.

A young Dominican priest by the name of John J. Markey relates that he is "among the first of a generation raised and educated entirely in a post-Vatican II context." With apparent appreciation for this he shares with us that "my life, education, and journey of faith have paralleled that of the Church since Vatican II."[21] He wrote a wonderful little book subtitled *The Theology of the Council's Constitutions of the Church.*

In his introduction Markey states, "by any estimation the Second Vatican Council was overwhelmingly successful."[22] To substantiate this claim he wrote a lengthy paragraph. I find it helpful to summarize his reasons in a numerical manner:

1. The worldwide membership of the Church has increased dramatically since the Council and now approaches one billion people.

2. The Church has opened relationships and friendly dialogues with almost every Christian denomination and world religion, yielding genuinely fruitful results in many surprising and hopeful ways.

3. There are more people ministering in the Church and behalf of the Church today than at any previous time in history.

4. The dramatic and unprecedented growth in lay participation at all levels in the life of the Church surely serves as a primary indication of the guidance of the Holy Spirit on the Council and its aftermath.

5. The Church both local and universal now finds herself more deeply involved in the lives of people in ways that would have been unthinkable or much more limited before the Council, (i.e., social service, political advocacy, health services, education, care for refugees, mediation for peace, defense of human rights and social justice, spiritual guidance and direction, etc.).[23]

Those who live in areas rocked by earthquakes know that aftershocks commonly follow the seismic activity. The years immediately following the Council were filled with aftershocks. A certain amount of confusion was inevitable as we tried to understand and then implement the teaching of the Council fathers. Much of that continues and we still find ourselves in that period of aftershocks. Then to complicate things, many set the Council documents aside. We have been wandering in a situation of increasing confusion ever since.

None of us set aside the documentation or directions when we purchase a computer, new software or a mobile phone. They come with a directions manual and most of us read and study the manuals and refer to them when malfunctions occur. If we ignore the directions, computer, software, or mobile phone will not function properly. Pope John XXIII set a vision before us. He

Underscored the positive purposes and opportunities of the Council; namely to work toward the unity of humankind so that the earthly city may be brought to the resemblances of that heavenly city where truth reigns and charity is the law.[24]

If a long series of mistakes burden us today, it is good to remember that our bishops are good men. They have been conditioned to consider their first responsibility is obedience to the Bishop of Rome. They look to Rome for answers and meet with their brother bishops without any meaningful discussion with the larger family. They reach conclusions based on their limited perceptions and shaped by curial officials in the Vatican. As a result they set out to correct their mistakes of the past by creating new mistakes and compounding our problems.

Today they recognize our household of faith is burdened with serious problems that result in confusion and frustration. They see the problems but, generally isolated from local churches, they fail to understand the spiritual significance behind those problems. It is apparent to any observer, including our bishops, that in the majority of our faith communities across this land, renewal began but too often in too many places has remained superficial. In many parishes the liturgical life of our household of faith is not prayerful and the preaching in our assemblies is inadequate. Scapegoats have been plenty. There is nothing gained by adding to the list. It is a fact that the renewal has faltered. In many cases it was inevitable that would happen. Even when those charged with the responsibility to instruct, form and inspire us with the vision of the Council have done so effectively, liturgy and life in many parishes still remains superficial.

I think that one significant reason for this is the architectural design of our church buildings. Most of these buildings were designed and built as theaters to accommodate the Tridentine liturgy. They simply prohibit the celebration of liturgy as envisioned by the Council. They presume a passive audience focused on a stage and neither invite nor promote interaction or engagement. It is physically impossible for the gathered assembly to experience itself as the living Body of Christ. The presumption has been that it is sufficient to make some physical adaptations of existing space. The removal of communion railings is important. Rearranging ambo, altar and Presider's chair was important. Such changes were significant but inadequate for the space remains the same. The liturgy of the Council cannot be experienced for it presumes a gathering of the people around Ambo and Table. It presumes space in which genuine participation and interaction is not only possible, but expected. A long marble altar, on a platform raised above the Assembly who are in rows stretching all the way to the back of the church building creates neither an experience of nor a visual sense of community. If the space is like a theater where people sit to watch, they will remain passive rather than participate.

Mass facing the people is not theater. There is a hidden life in those of us who gather with Christ. It is the Christ life and it is important that those gathered look across to one another and see the face of Christ. In this sort of space all feel spiritually united in the one prayer for which they are gathered.

We who gather around our bishops have a responsibility to help them be in touch with our experience and our needs. In each diocese, the bishop is the primary presider for Eucharist and the primary homilist. If there is no avenue available by which you and your community can speak to your bishop, be creative and establish a way. It is our responsibility to express our needs, frustrations and hopes in such a manner that our bishops can provide the leadership we need. Talk to your bishop and express your concerns, your hopes and your support.

Most of us born and raised Catholic, and many who joined us along the way, know there is something deep down within us about being Catholic that neither time nor neglect can diminish. We also know and treasure the institutional dimension of our Catholic life, the liturgy, and the hierarchy. Today the grand old mansions of our city have become symbolic for me of that institutional dimension of Catholic life. Much of our heritage retains the amazing grace and dignity we always have treasured. Some of it suffers from neglect. Some of it faces the possibility of irreparable deterioration. Some of it is beyond repair.

The Second Vatican Council set a dream in motion. It set a vision before us. We have the opportunity to regain our identity as the Living Body of Christ. It will take time but that vision will be realized if we remain committed to the vision. It is easy to be negative or discouraged and to throw up our hands and abandon the vision. That is not an adequate response for the Living Body of Christ.

After many years of sailing on Flathead Lake, several of us towed a 23-foot Clipper Marine sailboat to the San Juan Islands off the coast of Washington state. We spent two weeks sailing among those beautiful islands. The winds, the tides and the currents tested our skill and ability to set and maintain a course. Every leg of that journey engaged us in new challenges and on the several days when our skills were inadequate, we found ourselves anchored in some unanticipated harbor. One day under a clear, bright sky, our progress was steady when the wind died. The strong tidal current began to move us backwards. There was little we could do but go with the tide. We kept the sails trimmed and the rudder in the water. When the wind returned, we reset our course and reached our destination.

Developing the ability to sail efficiently requires the mastery of some skills that are basic for living a good life. At times the best we can do is keep the sails trimmed and the rudder in the water, waiting, trusting the wind will resume. I recall my sailing experiences often today when there is so much confusion within our Catholic household of faith. Perseverance requires focus and great inner resolve. I believe that the Holy Spirit, so manifest in the Council, is guiding us still. I continue trusting, and hope you do as well, that the wind will return. "I keep going; on the long path." The Hebrew prophet Habakkuk spoke words that are so appropriate for our time. He said, "the vision still has its time, presses on to fulfillment, and will not disappoint; if it delays wait for it, it will surely come."[25] There is some good in everything. Look for it. Above all be persistent in pursuing the Council's vision and don't let momentary reversals discourage you.

CHAPTER 7

EPICTETUS
"The key is to keep company only with people who uplift you,
whose presence calls forth your best."

TWO GIANTS

In the liturgical seasons of Advent and Lent, I often try to integrate a poetic verse or refrain into my homilies as a catalyst to break open the scriptures. In 2001 I used the refrain of a poem by Leonard Cohen. His poem, *How the Light Gets In*, attracted my mind and heart like a magnet. It seemed to do the same for many helping them to enter more deeply into the mystery we call Christ. I am writing this in 2008 and as we approached Advent this year, someone asked for the refrain from that poem.

> *Ring the bells that still can ring.*
> *Forget your perfect offering.*
> *There's a crack in everything.*
> *That's how the light gets in.*[1]

You may remember the joyful, exhilarating bells that rang throughout the Catholic Church following the Second Vatican Council. I do. They sounded a great awakening among us, a great rebirth. If today the ringing of those bells seem diminished or silenced, the poet reminds us to "ring the bells that still can ring," confident the bells that we ring do make a great difference.

Each of us brings hope into our world in a variety of ways. We are never perfect but do what we can, remembering things are not always as they seem. When you look in your mirror, recognize all that you offer to our world, and offer it as best you can. "Forget your perfect offering." The poet also reminds us, "There's a crack in everything."

Kairos is a Greek word that for me identifies those unique moments of grace in which God touches us, and we are never the same again. *Kairos* moments are like cracks. "That's how the light gets in." For many of us within the Catholic household of faith, the II Vatican Council was a *kairos* moment, a crack through which the light got in.

The Catholic University of Louvain in Belgium is one of the oldest universities in Europe and its academic tradition in theology is highly respected. Since its early origins Louvain has made significant contributions to the development of Catholic thought. I mentioned previously that in 2007 I was fortunate to spend several weeks of summer study at Louvain. Professors from various schools or disciplines provided the daily lectures that were both stimulating and informative. Roaming the streets, sitting in beer halls and visiting the lecture halls and churches of Louvain established a connection with our past. The short exposure to that environment was like a crack through which the light poured in once again. That light provided a new perspective from which to consider the post-counciliar conflicts and tensions that cause confusion within the church today. The light coming through that crack, like the morning sun over the Bitterroot River, slightly diminished the fog. I began to appreciate in new ways some of the causes for this situation in which we feel ourselves trapped. In this chapter I will try to explain what I mean.

Catholics of my generation struggled with the teaching that babies who die without baptism are excluded forever from heaven and are destined for an undifferentiated place of natural happiness called Limbo. Such thinking is a natural spin-off of the doctrine of original sin.

According to a theologian at Notre Dame, "Original Sin is the situation in which every human being finds him or herself."[2] While a doctrine of universal or original sin might be implied in some writings of St. Paul, the concept "does not figure prominently in the earliest Christian writings outside the New Testament."[3] It is no surprise there was no uniform agreement about the concept in the early church.

The doctrine of original sin received its fullest and most enduring development "in the writings of St. Augustine of Hippo."[4] He "identified 'original sin' with concupiscence, the yearning for self gratification in humans that turns them away from God."[5] Thus he linked original sin with "the human person's spontaneous desire for material and sensual satisfaction."[6] This teaching of St. Augustine dominated Catholic theology.

While the theological traditions of the Catholic Church are diverse, rich and life giving, most of us were shaped and formed by a single theology rooted in the doctrine of original sin. Fear, guilt and unworthiness are woven into the heavy shadow that follows too many of us. In addition most of us also are burdened by atonement theology with its narrow emphasis on sin and redemption. It is easy to fall into the swamp of thinking how bad we are.

In the most common and popular understanding, the story of creation is the story of human sin that alienated humankind from the Creator. In response to our alienated situation, atonement theology teaches Jesus appeased God's anger by becoming the scapegoat. As our substitute he took our sins upon himself. By his death on the cross he made amends for the offense of our sins. In this popular understanding of Christ's death and resurrection, his suffering and death were over-emphasized. We saw this distortion in Mel Gibson's atrocious movie, *The Passion of The Christ*. As the cross became the central element in Catholic theology and devotional piety, the resurrection of Jesus lost its significance as it was reduced to a proof of his divinity.

I find it helpful to identify how we arrived at such a situation. Christianity was born of the Hebrew religious tradition. The God of the Hebrew bible was dynamic and relational. In the Hebrew worldview, God changes; reality and truth change. The Hebrew and early Christian traditions accepted change and transition as normal. Gradually Christianity separated from and developed apart from Judaism. As it spread around the Mediterranean basin, the gospel was brought into intellectual tension with the Greek philosophical traditions inherited by the Romans. The ancient Greeks disputed the nature of reality and truth. For some Greeks like Plato, "the sensible world of experience is a limited imitation of, and participation in, a higher world of ideas."[7] This ideal world is stable and permanent. Plato and later traditions of Greek philosophy perceived all reality and truth as absolute, unchanging and permanent.

The influence of Plato and other Greek philosophers eventually led to the development of what scholars refer to as classical consciousness. According to Timothy G. McCarthy,

Classical consciousness comprised a universal and abstract way of knowing that was fundamentally applicable in all times and circumstances. It highlighted traditional ways, unchanging institutions, hierarchical rule and authority figures. The real was

a fixed order that was objective, unchanging, universal, and abstract. The ideal person was the wise person or sage.[8]

This Greco-Roman philosophical tradition was distinctly different from that of the Judeo-Christian tradition. Gradually the two interacted as great rivers do when they converge. The Christians introduced the gospel to the Romans by adopting Greek philosophical concepts familiar to the Romans. The Judeo-Christian conviction that God, reality and truth are fluid was reshaped by those Greek philosophical concepts.

There is no doubt that St. Augustine was a major influence on the church as an institution. Prior to and during his ministry as Bishop of Hippo in North Africa, Augustine engaged in various theological controversies. These controversies contributed to and shaped his theological thinking. If it is true that we become the very thing against which we fight, it appears that happened to Augustine.

A dualistic form of thinking arose within the early Christian communities known as Manichaeism. It is based on the teaching of a Persian by the name of Mani. He claimed to have received a commission to preach the definitive teaching of Zoroaster, Buddha and Jesus. He rejected the books of the Hebrew Bible and considered himself a follower of Jesus.

Mani and his disciples were radical dualists. They saw the world as governed by two opposite divine powers: the god of light or goodness and the god of darkness or evil. These two were in constant tension. This dualism provided Mani and his followers a satisfying explanation of evil. He taught that history was marked by the attempts of darkness (Satan or the devil) to conquer the world. The world was the creation of the powers of evil. All material creation, including the body, is evil. Procreation is evil. This meant that we human beings are caught up in a life-long struggle between these two divine forces. Since all matter is evil, we need to purify ourselves of our sins by living a strict ascetical life. If we allow darkness to conquer us we will never reach the light. Eventually "the church condemned Manichaeism as heretical because it contradicts the Christian doctrine of a benevolent creation."[9]

Even so, this religion was very influential in the Middle East at the time of St. Augustine. For some time he himself was an adherent of Manichaeism. Although he later wrote various anti-Manichean works including *The Confessions*, traces and shadows of dualism infiltrated his theology. While Augustine spoke of Satan in sermons and prayers, he declared that Satan does not exist as an independent being.

82

In his post-Manichean years, Augustine emphasized the goodness of the material world, the body, and procreation. He did not locate moral evil as an external force but attributed it to individuals freely choosing to turn away from God. Even so the influence of the Manichean tradition persisted in his thinking and finds subtle expression in the severity and negativity of his theology.

The Donatists were another group who claimed to be followers of Jesus. Augustine also engaged them in dispute. The Donatists were inclined to view the world through narrow and restrictive lenses. They were rigorists holding that the church must be a church of saints, not sinners. Because of serious conflicts within the church during a period of successive persecutions, the Donatists insisted that Christians who had caved in to persecution were no longer fit to occupy positions of leadership in the Church. They insisted that sacraments were valid only if the minister of the sacrament was free of serious sin.

In response to the Donatists, Augustine embraced a very pastoral attitude that eventually was adopted as the orthodox position of the Roman church. He argued that the validity of any sacrament does not depend on the holiness of the minister. In his effort to counteract the teaching of the Donatists, Augustine argued it was the office of priest, not his personal character that assured the validity of the sacraments.

The third controversy that influenced Augustine involved a Celtic monk named Pelagius. Pelagianism, as it was named, provided the stimulus for Augustine's development of the concept of original sin, as we know that concept today. Pelagius acknowledged our ability to choose separates us from all other creatures. Because of our free will, we humans have the capacity to do that which is good and have an inherent inclination to choose the good rather than evil. Pelagius and his followers argued that in theory a human person may live without sin and does not need any additional grace from God to live a good life. By implication this suggested that newborn infants did not need to be baptized.

In response to Pelagius and his followers, Augustine took the position that the sin of Adam is "passed on to all of us through the lust involved in procreation."[10] According to Augustine, "Human life has been corrupted by sin" and "so devastated by original sin that it could not handle God's revelation."[11] His pessimistic view of human nature and freedom concluded that because of original sin, while we humans are free, we are inclined to chose sin or to do evil. We are able to love but can do so only with divine assistance. We cannot reach moral perfection on our own. Our need for the grace of God is absolute and without it we humans are incapable of choosing and doing the good.

It is out of such theological disputes that St. Augustine's teaching on original sin developed. His teaching also was a factor influencing the later development of atonement theology and the emergence of the concepts of sin and redemption as dominant images within the Church. Augustine argued that since human nature was corrupted by the original sin of Adam and Eve, individuals were simply incapable of achieving salvation by their own efforts.

That conflict between Pelagius and Augustine continues to reverberate in the church today. Parents still seek baptism for their newly born fearing that if their infant die without baptism, s/he will be excluded forever from heaven and destined for an undifferentiated place of natural happiness called Limbo. It is likely that St. Augustine simply said they were condemned to hell and later theologians softened his teaching. His strong focus and emphasis was on God and last judgment.

In the fourth century Augustine introduced a form of neo-Platonism into Christian thinking. This mingling of traditions eventually led to the church's perception that reality and truth, especially revealed truth is absolute, permanent, and unchanging. Because of St. Augustine, Christian theology was transformed, shaped by and became deeply identified with classical consciousness. Thus we see the ongoing influence of St. Augustine in Catholic theology and teaching prior to the II Vatican Council.

Faith was a central virtue in the development of St. Augustine's theology. For him faith primarily was intellectual assent to dogma, expressed in keeping rules. Living in Christ meant dying to one's sinful nature. Human beings are perceived as sinners in need of redemption in order to escape the fires of hell. It is quite logical that more and more emphasis is placed on sin. That was the tradition of my youth in which my spirituality was formed. It conveyed a negative view of the world and matter.

I came away from the University of Louvain with the impression that the Second Vatican Council sought to restore a theological balance within the church. At the beginning of the twentieth century, Pope Leo XIII revived Catholic scholarship and sought ways for the Church to be open to the contemporary world. He promoted a revival of the philosophical/theological work of St. Thomas Aquinas. Pope John XXIII was a beneficiary of those efforts.

In the thirteenth century, Thomas Aquinas emerged as a theologian with a fresh appreciation of the gospel. While he had enormous respect for St. Augustine, he was open to the world beyond the walls of the church. His intellectual curiosity and deep life of contemplative prayer led him to seek for truth in whatever sources were available to him, whether discovered by reason or though revelation. He developed an entirely new theological methodology by using the findings of science and philosophy to present the gospel in a systematic and meaningful manner. His work is deeply rooted in scripture, but he also rediscovered the philosophy of Aristotle. He assimilated that philosophy into his theological constructs as well as Christian, Jewish, Islamic and various pagan or pre-Christian sources.

The focus and foundation for the development of Aquinas' theological perspective, is God's pure love creating and gracing us with enormous possibilities of goodness. His theology is very positive. He taught that "human beings are created images of God's intelligence and goodness."[12] Humans are intellectual, have free will, and are the source of their own actions. As images of God we are free agents of choice. His work came to be known as scholasticism.

For St. Thomas Aquinas, faith is concerned with human flourishing. Living in Christ is far more about virtue and freedom than sin. In reclaiming the theological perspective of Aquinas, the Second Vatican Council gave renewed expression to our human longing for the good, the true and the beautiful, emphasizing the basic goodness of human life.

Thus Aquinas differed from the Augustinian theologians of his time. He was open to the world and rather than simply appealing to authority he viewed the created world as inherently and essentially good. By extension this included the human body and all of the characteristics and functions of the physical body. He also rejected Augustine's identification of original sin with disordered concupiscence. Aquinas argues that God desires to be known and loved by us and is always present. Redemption is not some sort of rescue operation. God is integrally present in us and throughout all of creation.

Thomas Aquinas was convinced that the astounding love of God is revealed in Jesus of Nazareth. He was convinced that the Risen Christ was and is among us to reveal the intrinsic meaning of our lives. "The whole point of his coming was to bring an abundance to people's lives by his very presence."[13] He revealed the meaning of our shared humanity. He made known to us the enormous graced possibility of every life. God yearns to be experienced and known in every human life.

The theology of Pope John XXIII was strongly influenced by Aquinas and open to the world beyond the walls of the church. We see this in his call for the bishops of the world to learn from and address the signs of the times in which we live. The Council heard that invitation and responded. This directional change created a tension within the church that contributes to the fog in which we find ourselves today.

As the church emerged from the MiddleAges the world changed. The scientific revolution began in the fifteenth century. We know the names and history of people like Copernicus and Galileo. That revolution opened a new way of viewing or appreciating the world, space and time. For more than a century, this new worldview continued to develop from various diverse streams of philosophical and scientific thought. Scholars today refer to it as historical consciousness. Timothy McCarthy is my source again. He identifies historical consciousness in this way:

Tradition and authority were subsumed under freedom, equality, dialogue, community, and democracy. Instead of underscoring the objective, unchanging, universal and abstract, people concentrated on the subjective, changeable, particular, and practical. The ideal person was the free, autonomous, and rational individual.[14]

New philosophical traditions continued to emerge in the sixteenth and seventeenth centuries. They emphasized subjectivism and claimed reality and truth are not absolute and unchangeable as previously thought but are determined by the human mind. Luther and the reform churches brought all of this to a point of crisis for the church.

The church perceived such developments as a threat to the unchangable truth of divine revelation and withdrew further and further from society. The Council of Trent was convened in the middle of the sixteenth century in reaction to the reformers and other perceived threats. That Council affirmed and defended the absolute, permanent and unchangeable character of revealed truth,

This is how Augustinian thought became the dominant theology and the common spirituality of the Church. Augustine's pessimism perceived the world and human nature in a negative manner focused on sin and the afterlife. Rules and laws replaced faith and love. This led to negative attitudes about human sexuality and an exaggerated emphasis on sexual mores that persists in the hierarchical church today. The Council of Trent adopted a fortress mentality. The church closed the doors and windows and locked itself in a self-imposed medieval exile. Theology was reduced to a collection of sterile doctrines used to refute various movements that challenged church authority.

Additional developments like the industrial revolution in the eighteenth century shaped the modern world we inhabit today. Significant political and social changes occurred in the nineteenth and twentieth centuries. All of these intensified and solidified the church's fortress mentality adopted at Trent. In their effort to protect the church from the winds of change, theology became increasingly negative and irrelevant to those developments.

That fortress mentality is evident in the history of those elected to be Bishop of Rome (i.e. pope) in the last two centuries. Angelo Roncalli was an exception. The cardinals knew he was well read and educated but when they elected him Bishop of Rome, they were surprised to discover he was an unanticipated visionary. He recognized significant events that were impacting and shaping society. He understood the classical world and consciousness in which the church had lived for so long was being swept aside. Classical consciousness was being replaced by historical consciousness and the negative response of the church to the modern world needed correction.

As Pope John XXIII, Angelo Roncalli asked the bishops in his council to set aside the baggage collected by the institution for nearly five hundred years. He asked them to embrace his vision of *aggiornamento*. That vision involved a spiritual reform and renewal within the church that would prepare and enable us to re-engage the larger world in which we live. The direction set by Pope John when he summoned the bishops was in harmony with the new world-view that had emerged through the work of modern philosophy and science. He spoke of the council as opening the doors and the windows to allow the Spirit of God to breathe among and renew us. He knew and understood the theological methodology and the openness to the world that characterized the theology and worldview of Aquinas and thus looked at recent historical developments through a different lens than that of his predecessors at the Vatican.

John saw all of these developments of the modern world as signs of the times. For him they "were special signs of the presence of God in history that required the attention of Christians."[15] With the optimism characteristic of Thomas Aquinas, Pope John reminded the cardinals and the Vatican Curia,

> *Consult not your fears but your hopes and your dreams. Think not about your frustrations, but about your unfulfilled potential. Concern yourself not with what you tried and failed in, but with what it is still possible for you to do.[16]*

He understood it was only in being open to developments taking place in history that the gospel can contribute in positive ways to the life of both church and humanity.

Pope John was a wise man and recognized that some cardinals in the Vatican and some diocesan bishops were opposed to the direction he had set. They, and today those who continue their efforts to halt or reverse the renewal called for by the Council, were schooled and trained in the thinking of Augustine. They have a,

> *Pessimistic view of the signs and needs of the times. They believe the church is still in a stage of siege against a sinful world; that Christ is the light of a world that is pervaded with darkness, and that Catholics should be known for their life of prayer, humility, and obedience to the church's authority and tradition.[17]*

They were and are clinging to all the elements contained in classical consciousness. Those who embrace this theological perspective are convinced Church doctrine is set and unchanging. In their perspective an institution like the church cannot change because Jesus established its very structure with the pope and bishops at the apex, and they have been given the authority to teach and safeguard the truth.

Those within the Council who appreciated the vision of John XXIII responded to his invitation for us to respect the work and insights of modern philosophy and science. They, and those who continue their efforts today, also were schooled or influenced by the thinking of Thomas Aquinas. For them it was and is apparent that change is an inevitable characteristic of God's creation and of all institutions. Even the church changes and needs to change. They embraced the historical consciousness developed by modern science.

> *They see the church as a communion or sacrament of Christ, who is the servant of the world, and believe that Catholics should take responsibility for the life and mission of the church and be involved in the transformation of society.[18]*

This model of church is clearly that of the New Testament. In this model the ordained have a ministry of service, and authority rests within the entire community. The impact of the council document *Gaudium et Spes* was perhaps more significant than the Council's mandate for renewing the liturgy. *Gaudium et Spes made* it clear that,

> *The church is a prophet of Christ's message of liberation and must confront society the way Jesus confronted the evils of his society, especially patriarchialism, violence, and greed.*[19]

I realize this is a very brief and rapid sketch of this very complex topic. I share these thoughts because they helped me as I struggle to find our direction in this spiritual fog in which we wander. Before sharing these thoughts with you I submitted them to a highly respected professor of history in our diocesan college.[20] He enthusiastically confirmed the impressions I am sharing here. His affirmation broadened that crack I discovered in Louvain. The light from that crack helped me understand the tremendous ongoing struggle within the church since John Paul II became the bishop of Rome. He and his successor both are Augustinians in their theological thinking and thus consider it necessary to reform the reform undertaken by the Council.

Cardinal Joseph Ratzinger, now Pope Benedict XVI, was a theological expert at the II Vatican Council. As the vision of John XXIII began to unfold, Ratzinger gradually aligned himself with those in the Vatican whom John saw as prophets of doom. They were not opposed to renewal but understood it from a different perspective. For them renewal meant a return to the teaching of theologians like St. Augustine. For Ratzinger the Council was an effort to lead us into the future by going back to St. Augustine.

The vision of Pope John XXIII sought to update the church and move us into the future by directly engaging the modern world. This openness to and positive embrace of the modern world are characteristics of the theology of St. Thomas Aquinas. The updating embraced by the Council is deeply rooted in the gospels. It recognizes the signs of the times set the agenda to be addressed by the church.

It seems to me the theology of Aquinas reflects the gospel of John. "The disciples were filled with joy at seeing the Lord."[22] It is our faith conviction that the Gracious Mystery we name God moves freely within creation and is the source of our longing for God. Our existence and being are divine gifts shared with us by a loving God. The Risen Christ "breathed on them and said, 'receive the Holy Spirit'."[23] The Holy Spirit is breathed upon us enabling us to break out of all the restricting and limiting images and concepts that denigrate human life. The Holy Spirit empowers and makes abundant life possible for all.

The influence of Augustinian and Thomistic theology were the root sources for the tensions within the Council. *The Encyclopedia of Catholicism* states that many of,

> *The modern biblical, patristic, systematic, and pastoral theologies affirmed by the II Vatican Council were rooted in Aquinas's historical openness and positive depiction of God and humans.*[21]

If the light gets in through a crack, then for me the crack was my renewed awareness of the tension between the theologies of Augustine and Aquinas. That tension is evident in our current ecclesial experience. The theological traditions of the Catholic Church are rich and diverse. This diversity is a gift when understood and respected. Lack of such understanding and a dogmatic insistence on the validity of one tradition over the other has created the confusion and conflict in the church today.

I write this hoping it may encourage you to be persistent in honoring the words of Pope John XXIII quoted earlier.

> *Consult not your fears but your hopes and your dreams. Think not about your frustrations, but about your unfulfilled potential. Concern yourself not with what you tried and failed in, but with what it is still possible for you to do.*[24]

Maybe you also will find encouragement in the words of the poet.

> *Ring the bells that still can ring.*
> *Forget your perfect offering.*
> *There's a crack in everything.*
> *That's how the light gets in.* (Leonard Cohen)

Life is filled with cracks, with *kairos* moments. The bells that we ring do make a great difference! Keep ringing your bell! Eventually they will stop trying to put everything back into the box.

CHAPTER 8

PAUL TO THE GALATIANS
"Christ set us free, so that we would remain free.
Stand firm, then, and do not let yourselves
be fastened again to the yoke of slavery."[1]

HARRY POTTER and JESUS

Perhaps the most magnetic if not most far-reaching event in these first years of the twenty-first century was the birth of Harry Potter. On the day the first novel reached the booksellers, Harry Potter became an instantaneous success. Millions of fans worldwide rushed the booksellers and devoured the huge tomes. Most of those fans were young, but not all. Harry, Hermione and the other delightful young people in this series of novels are interwoven in sinister plots between the powers of good and evil. Together they fight to save our world from sinister forces of evil. Isn't that amazing? That almost sounds descriptive of the real world in which we live.

Many themes are hidden below the surface of the narratives. Behind the plots and throughout the narrative there is the overriding attraction of magic. Apparently that theme of magic and sorcery is why the Vatican and various fundamentalist Christian groups condemned Harry Potter and his friends. Ironically for many of our young adults, maybe even for their parents, the wagging finger of the Vatican may seem like the magic wand used by Harry's adversaries.

In some way all of us who are attracted by Harry Potter are charmed by his wizard's wand and the power of secret words. Some would claim these novels are very Catholic for they consistently imply there is more to life than immediately available to our physical senses. These creative works of fiction extol the virtue of friendship over and over. In a variety of ways they propose that the most powerful magic available to all is self-sacrificing love, agape.

Most of us who struggle to follow Jesus of Nazareth certainly agree. Unconditional love is the only power capable of resisting forces of evil and saving the world. Not everyone agrees but it certainly seems to me there is some sort of connection, not equivalence, but a connection between Harry Potter and Jesus of Nazareth. The most significant difference is that the Harry Potter series is about magic, whereas Jesus of Nazareth is about mystery.

We who embrace the Catholic tradition are a liturgical church. The Mass is a formalized gathering in and through which we celebrate our ordinary Christian life on Sundays. On Sunday we also celebrate the rites of passages by which we move through the various stages of our human experience.

The earliest reference to Christians gathering to remember Christ is found in the Acts of the Apostles. There it is referred to as the breaking of the bread. While still influenced by the prayer of the Hebrew community and while the language of the people was still Greek, this meal that we call the Mass became known as *Eucharistia* or giving thanks.

The New Testament asserts that during a final meal with his companions, Jesus broke bread with them and said, "Do this in memory of me." The Roman Mass is a complex of prayers and ceremonies developed around that action and those words. In the Mass we do as Jesus commanded in memory of him. That is the core of what the Church does when gathered around the altar/table to celebrate the Mass.

At liturgy the participants not only pray what they believe, but they perform that belief in symbolic and meaningful ways so that they may encounter God active in their lives and enter into the economy of salvation, making them God's people.[2]

Liturgy is authentic only when the participants are personally engaged, only when the Assembly, which always includes the presider, engages in the celebration in such a manner that all know the Risen Christ is in and among those gathered. Such experience is transformative and awakens a new desire to live and act more like Christ.

Weston Priory is a small community of Benedictine monks located at the edge of the Green Mountain National Forest in central Vermont. They have embodied the vision and spirit of the Council in their life and ministry. Their routine of life revolves around community prayer. They gather four times on weekdays and five on weekends to join their hearts and voices in song and silent contemplation. Their community prayer than moves outward in commitment to seek justice and peace in and for our world.

I became familiar with the music of Weston Priory more than thirty years ago. People instantly appreciated it in our parish liturgical celebrations. Vermont is a long distance from Montana. I always hoped that someday I would visit the Priory for my annual retreat. My move to senior status made that possible. In my time among the brothers, their celebrations of prayer and Eucharist confirmed my earlier impression that they truly are a community of faith. I have celebrated liturgy with many monastic communities. The Eucharist celebrated in the Weston community stands as an exceptional model. It was a deeply meaningful experience of Christ among us. Those of us gathered with the brothers departed with a new awareness that Yes! We Are The Living Body of Christ.

From the time of the apostolic church Eucharist was celebrated in memory of the Risen One. Initially the manner in which communities celebrated was fluid. Gradually the pattern defining the norm became more and more established. Scholars attempt to identify and understand the many stages of historical development in the Mass. That is a complex task. The change of language from Greek to Latin occurred when Greek ceased to be the language of the Christian community. Eventually uniformity was established and was known as the Roman Rite of the Mass.

A body of rules and regulations that govern our liturgical prayer establishes that uniformity. Those rules and regulations are found in various Roman liturgical books. The primary of these is the Sacramentary used for the celebration of Eucharist. Small red annotations known as rubrics are interspersed throughout the prayers in the Sacramentary. "These are called 'rubrics,' from the Latin *'ruber'* meaning red. They give direction to the manner in which something is to be done"[3] during the liturgy. The rubrics set the format of the Mass and also determine the use of variable prayers and scripture texts. Liturgy celebrated according to the rubrics can appear to be magic ritual or it can open us to celebrate mystery. The

Value or worth of ritual or rubrics is measured in the success or failure of the ritual or rubric to move those engaged with it from the public and external forms to the internal level of personal faith and love.[4]

Many of the gestures, signs or symbols in Catholic liturgy are archaic baggage of a by-gone era. Few if any know why a few drops of water are mixed with the wine. Few if any know why a piece of the consecrated bread is dropped into the chalice of consecrated wine. Few if any know why the priest bows, genuflects or speaks prayers inaudibly at various moments during the Mass. Few if any know why the presider washes his hands at the altar/table.

It is the task of Catholic liturgy to awaken those gathered to the presence and mystery of Christ. If the meaning of bows, genuflections, actions and inaudible prayers spoken by the presider is ambiguous, they are not life giving. Ambiguity conditions those who attend liturgy to do so in a passive manner, simply fulfilling their obligation. "Eucharist should express and celebrate the joys and sorrows, the hopes, dreams and problems, the needs and commitments of the gathered community."[5]

The words of the apostle Paul remind us of the danger of basing our faith on slavish adherence to laws and rules. He reminded the church of Galatia, "Christ set us free, so that we would remain free. Stand firm, then, and do not let yourselves be fastened again to the yoke of slavery."[6] A legalistic approach to life always seems easier and simpler than the uncertainty of freedom.

Prior to the Council the ordained were expected to obey every rule and rubric in the missal. Rome was the norm. Even faith communities in remote places like Darby, Montana, were expected to adhere to that norm. That was ideal in theory. In the days of the Tridentine Mass, I seldom attended Mass in which the presider obeyed every rule and rubric in the missal. He may have tried to do so but few succeeded.

The Council summoned us to a more mature approach to liturgy. As we gradually recognized that adherence to rubrics alone is not life giving, our liturgical celebrations exploded with life. So did our faith communities.

It would be irresponsible to simply ignore all the rules and rubrics and just do whatever we wish. It is also irresponsible, however, to simply adopt changes or policies based on mere obedience without prudent consideration of the effects on the liturgical life of the community.[7]

For Eucharistic liturgy to mean anything to the people gathered, the words spoken and the body movements of the presider and the community must enable those assembled to experience the presence of the Risen One in and among them. In the liturgy we celebrate the Lord's

94

promise to be among us whenever even just two or three of us gather.

The fundamental presence of the risen Christ is in the people of faith. Even the presence we experience in the Eucharistic consecration of bread and wine is presence to the assembled people in proportion to their faith.[8]

We believe that through word proclaimed, the Risen One makes himself known to us. We believe that through bread broken and wine poured and shared, the Risen One makes himself known to us. We believe that through the intimacy of table fellowship, the Risen One makes himself known to us. In Eucharist we learn we are the Living Body of Christ.

Liturgy is the work of the people, an action in which all of us are involved with the Risen One. It is obvious then that liturgy celebrated in parish churches is and must differ significantly from the manner in which liturgy is celebrated in monastic communities or Episcopal cathedrals. If bodily gestures and posture do not awaken us to his presence and to the communion among us, they are like rusty symbols. Body language that is ambiguous or not intelligible fails to speak clearly. The issue is not about being medieval or traditional. If we cling to signs and symbols that spoke to one age but no longer speak to our own, we unconsciously make idols of them.

Now back to the connection, not equivalence, but connection between Harry Potter and Jesus of Nazareth. According to Wikipedia and other sources, magic refers to various practices involving established rituals and words. In this way both magic and religion are similar. Most practitioners of magic are convinced their spells do produce the intended effect. If you say "abracadabra" correctly, the spell always works!

Prior to the II Vatican Council, the manner in which various rubrics of the Mass were acted out often created the impression of magic. The language of the Mass was Latin. It was unintelligible to most listeners. It was spoken or sung swiftly and accompanied by many gestures hidden by the priest's body turned facing the wall. There were genuflections, candles burning and bells ringing at various times. Often when the bells were rung, those present bowed and struck their breast. All of this inadvertently created the impression that the priest was engaged in some sort of magical activity.

The seminaries charged with preparing candidates for ordination as Catholic priests did the best they could. Their efforts were conditioned by the time and cultural environment in which they worked. The spiritual formation of diocesan priests imitated that offered in monasteries for those called to the monastic life. The theological education was shallow, more apologetic than evangelical, and circumscribed by fear of modernism.

During our years of study, we were assigned to serve the Mass of faculty members in the early morning hours. In retrospect it is apparent to me now that our professor of dogmatic theology suffered from an extreme form of scrupulosity. His scrupulosity was more than apparent when he was saying Mass. Remember, this was in the days of the Latin Mass. The formation process was intent upon forming us into conformist and obedient priests. Certain words and actions were considered absolutely essential for the Mass or sacraments to be valid. Those words were drilled into our minds and hearts. That portion of the Eucharistic Prayer often and unfortunately still referred to, as the consecration, was totally distorted. We were told repeatedly that the exact words of the consecration must be spoken with clarity and precision, in Latin. It was imperative that the words over the bread: *"Hoc est enim corpus meum"*—(This is my body) and the words over the cup of wine: *"Hic est enim calix sanguinis meum."*—(This is the cup of my blood) be spoken without deviation or mispronunciation.

This insistence on precision is an incubator in which the illness of scrupulosity nestles like an embryo in the womb. It did precisely that for this particular professor. When he came to the words of consecration, he would lean over the host held between his thumbs and forefingers, and breathing slowly onto the host, his eyes skipping back and forth from the missal to the host, he <u>slowly</u>, <u>distinctly</u> and <u>repeatedly</u> would speak the words, *"hoc est enim corpus meum"* until he finished the entire phrase. In a similar fashion he would hold the chalice, breathe into it, eyes skipping back and forth from missal to chalice, while <u>slowly</u>, <u>distinctly</u> and <u>repeatedly</u> speaking the words, *"hic est enim calix sanguinis meum"* until he finished the entire phrase. This good man was burdened by and lived with scrupulosity -- the enormous anxiety of doing it incorrectly. To anyone watching, it would seem he was engaged in some sort of magic ritual. Say the words and – presto – the result is achieved!

As we grew up and lived in the Catholic culture, most of us never noticed the dry rot and peeling paint that were the realistic condition of our Catholic house. A complex clerical culture was the foundation of hierarchical splendor and power. Clericalism obscured our gospel roots and isolated us from the good news we are privileged to share and sent to live. In a clerical culture only designated individuals can do special things, like turn the bread and wine into the Body and Blood of Christ. That is easily perceived as something magical.

Recently I asked a younger priest in our diocese why his voice and demeanor change so dramatically when he presides at liturgy and why he is so rigid about observing the rubrics of the liturgy. "The Mass is the same everywhere," he said. "The presider should not make a difference. So when I vest, I leave me in the sacristy." I wondered to myself: If the presider does not make a difference, why do thousands of folks put forth so much effort and spend so much money to be at a Mass in which the Bishop of Rome (pope) is the presider? And why is it that when a pastor's term of office has expired and the bishop transfers him to another parish community, the transition to a new presider is so difficult for so many? The truth is the presider does make a difference.

This attitude that the presider does not make a difference is totally unrealistic. I think it provides an escape route for those who do not know how to communicate or lead people in prayer. It also easily leads to the very disastrous opinion that "liturgy is just a fixed formula and it is simply a matter of getting through it as fast and efficiently as possible."[9] That is nice in theory. The Presider's voice, style and demeanor always make a difference, a considerable difference. Style significantly determines the manner and depth of participation by the Assembly.

No two celebrations of Eucharist are the same. That is true regardless of how scrupulously the presider observes the rubrics. This is inevitable because the celebrating communities are always different. The enormous range of experiences typical of everyone's week change us, and effect how we participate in liturgy.

Luke Timothy Johnson is a professor of New Testament at the Candler School of Theology at Emory University. He offers some helpful insights about the Catholic Church based on his observation of what he describes as typical Catholic parishes. He makes a distinction between two kinds of pastors. I think the distinction he makes is another way of stating the influence of the liturgical presider.

The first label he applies is that of the sanctuary pastor. This pastor symbolizes the institutional church, clericalism and the tendency to be autocratic and controlling. It is a model in which ordination is given antecedent to baptism. This pastor adheres closely to the rubrics without any appreciation of how the liturgy is experienced by the assembly.

The second label is the vestibule pastor. This pastor symbolizes church as community in which all are engaged and actively participate in all levels of parish life. It is a model in which baptism is given antecedent to ordination. This pastor freely adjusts the rubrics according to the expressed needs of the assembly.

Visit the parish of the sanctuary pastor and you see that "in the sanctuary everything is orderly and correct."[10] In professor Johnson's opinion this reflects hierarchical concern with doctrine, morality, authority, procedure and rubric. Visit the parish of the vestibule pastor and you see that "in the vestibule another religious world thrives."[11] It very often is cluttered and messy. It reflects the faith life of the parish community or more pointedly, of the Living Body of Christ.

I know pastors who are well educated and in varying degrees are enthusiastic about some of the new liturgical rubrics. Perhaps Luke Timothy Johnson would label them sanctuary pastors. The great danger for them is that the ordinary folks do not live in the sanctuary.

The first of those rubrics is the recently mandated bows. The sanctuary pastor values profound bows after the words of institution spoken over the bread and then the cup, and of course when folks approach to receive Holy Communion. My own opinion is that the disarray produced by this practice is ludicrous and counter-productive. One of the most significant and simple rubrics inserted into the liturgy by the II Vatican Council is the explicit affirmation – "AMEN," in response to the words "the Body of Christ" and "the Blood of Christ." This response is so appropriate that it quickly became the uniform practice after being introduced. When a person receives communion with respect, that one word is a profound expression of faith. It means yes, I believe this is the Body of Christ; yes, I believe this is the Blood of Christ. By implication it also means yes, I believe this is the life of Christ offered to me; yes, we are the Living Body of Christ.

With the recent introduction of bowing, individual acts of piety now disrupt the experience and the visibility of communion, our union with one another in Christ. There is a great deal of uncertainty now as people approach to receive the sacrament. "Should I nod or bow and even genuflect, or continue doing what I did before?" A careful observation of eyes as folks stand there to receive the sacrament often reveals simple distraction or absolute confusion. The simple act of faith is obliterated!

A second example of new rubrics valued by the sanctuary pastor is the positioning of the hands for the Lord's Prayer. The rubric now directs people to join in this prayer with their hands extended in the same manner as the priest at the altar. This rubric is unsettling and disruptive for those who have been accustomed to join hands for the Lord's Prayer. I have listened to many complaints from folks who recognize that the simple gesture of holding hands during this prayer gives a visible, symbolic and sacramental expression to the mystery we are, the Living Body of Christ. Ironically the new posture of extending the arms unintentionally reinforces the very thing good liturgy can counteract, the excessive individualism so rampant in our culture. This "we = a community," not "me = a single individual" join in this prayer. "We = a community," not "me = a single individual" prepare to eat and drink the Sacrament that deepens the Christ life within us. "We = a community," not "me = a single individual" are the Living Body of Christ.

Vestibule pastors recognize there is nothing wrong with the laity! The laity simply have a different perspective of church than the ordained who are sanctuary pastors. They know that our *"Amen"* when receiving the Sacrament is an affirmation of the Risen One present in the sacrament and in us, the Living Body of Christ.

Since at least the thirteenth century until the Second Vatican Council, there was a broadening gap between those ordained (clergy) and those not ordained (laity). As this gap widened the stage was set for another development. The church gradually forgot that Eucharist is the source renewing our life as the Living Body of Christ. The attention of scholars and the hierarchy drifted to the academic exercise of trying to explain the real presence of Christ in the bread and wine. The community no longer understood Eucharist as Augustine had.

The medieval period fostered extensive theological controversy and debate. The faithful became obsessed with external rituals as their misunderstanding of the Eucharist separated them further from the Mass. The great theological disputes raging around them only added to the confusion. In 1215 Pope Innocent III called the Fourth Lateran Council. That Council issued a definitive pronouncement about the Eucharist. With the concept of transubstantiation that Council defined the Eucharist in most literal terms.

Jesus Christ himself is both priest and sacrifice; and his body and blood are really contained in the sacrament of the altar under the species of bread and wine, the bread being transubstantiated into the body and the wine into the blood by the power of God.[12]

That Council inadvertently promoted the practice of worshipping the consecrated host that became common practice among the faithful.

That sort of host magic was backed up by a literalizing doctrine of the Eucharist. Such practice became even more widespread during the thirteenth and fourteenth centuries. The Eucharist became an object to be venerated or adored.

Mystery cannot be explained. Yet the concept of transubstantiation was the church's effort to provide a philosophical explanation of Eucharist, even though Eucharist is mystery! Mystery gradually was replaced by practices and customs that easily conveyed the impression of magic. These controversies did not rekindle a desire in the faithful to receive Communion. Perhaps if anything the controversies and the emphasis on transubstantiation even intensified the common sense of unworthiness that burdens most people.

In place of receiving the body and blood of Christ, the faithful in the medieval period became eager to see the Eucharist. The custom developed of exposing the seldom-received Sacrament for people to see and adore. By the fourteenth century the customs of genuflecting to the sacrament, of lengthy elevations of the host and the cup, and eventually blessing the people with the sacrament had become normal. Such customs replaced the reception of Communion as the normative practice of the faithful. Only the priest ate and drank the Eucharist. By the seventeenth century tabernacles became common and more important than the altar-table on which they rested.

There are two ways in which the appearances of magic gradually developed around the Mass and the Blessed Sacrament. One was around the pious custom known as Benediction with the Blessed Sacrament. The other was the manner in which various rubrics of the Mass were acted out.

The bread and wine of Eucharist are commonly referred to in our Catholic household of faith as the Blessed Sacrament. Among our very ancient Catholic traditions is that of providing communion to those among us who were absent from the liturgy because of illness, and for those who are dying. The Latin word *viaticum* was adopted meaning food for their journey to God. This custom requires us to keep the Blessed Sacrament in a secure place that has come to be known as a tabernacle.

Centuries ago, when people seldom received Holy Communion during Mass, and then only after going to confession, it became popular to spend quiet time in prayer before the tabernacle, or as most of us commonly expressed it, before the Blessed Sacrament. That was and remains a good form of prayer. However there is always the possibility that such a pious practice begins to consider Eucharist or the Blessed Sacrament as an object to be venerated or worshipped. Clearly Jesus did not invite us to gather at the Table of Eucharist to venerate or worship him in the Blessed Sacrament. Eucharist is not an object. Eucharist is an action, a prayer in which the entire community is engaged and in which the Living Body of Christ is nourished.

The practice of prayer before the Blessed Sacrament eventually led to the custom we now call Benediction with the Sacrament. It is a custom that clearly perceives and treats the Eucharist as an object. In my own history, soon after being ordained a transitional deacon, the opportunity was offered for me to be the minister for Benediction with the Blessed Sacrament. For this service the Sacrament was removed from the Tabernacle and placed in a special gold vessel called a monstrance. This was placed on the high altar for all to see and venerate. When the prayers and incensing were finished, the minister took the monstrance in hand, turned to the community, elevated the sacrament and blest the community with it in the form of the cross. When the concluding prayers were said, the Sacrament was returned to the Tabernacle and the service ended.

The devotion was so ingrained into our spirituality that no one ever questioned it. From my youth and for many years thereafter it was a significant element of my own Catholic life. Our common language spoke of Jesus as God. Jesus equaled God, present in the sacrament. Therefore the conclusion seemed obvious. We ought to kneel before the sacrament in adoration.

To be the minister for Benediction meant wearing special vestments. It meant reaching into the Tabernacle and removing the Sacrament. Apprehension welled up in my soul the first time it was my privilege to do this. As all Catholic people at that time, we who were preparing for ordination also were besieged with concern about being worthy or unworthy to touch the Sacrament. Wild, crazy, scrupulous thoughts and feelings awakened and rushed through my spirit on that occasion. In retrospect, those thoughts and feelings seem humorous because they were bizarre.

Various customs and/or practices easily and unintentionally created the appearance of the magical. This is what has happened historically when the Blessed Sacrament was seen and/or treated as an object.

Today this form of piety is out of sync with the pre-Reformation Eucharistic theology that has been reclaimed by John's Council. There

101

was no deliberate effort to end the custom of Benediction. The apparent demise of Benediction was not deliberately caused. It simply was a consequence of the liturgical renewal called for by the Council. That renewal enabled people to appreciate Mass in a more personal manner and to actively participate in the liturgy. As we witnessed a rapid increase of the numbers receiving Holy Communion, the piety expressed in Benediction simply disappeared.

In a recent issue of *New Theology Review*, Mary Christine Athans, B.V.M., offers a new horizon for understanding the presence of Christ in the Eucharist. She discusses the Jewish roots of our Catholic liturgy. She argues we find a new perspective and understanding of Eucharist when we learn from recent studies in Hebrew language, in the Hebrew scripture and in the synagogue prayers. Remember, Jesus was a Jewish man! She argues that in the tradition in which he was raised, the words body and blood have a far more holistic meaning than our recent Catholic tradition has given them. For Jesus and his Jewish peers,

The word 'body' represented the whole person; 'blood' represented life! Now I hear Jesus saying in the words of the priest: 'This is my whole person for you!' and 'This is my whole life for you!'[13]

Perhaps when we lost this more holistic understanding of those words, various habits developed because of which those outside our Catholic culture viewed our liturgical and pious customs as magical rites. We were absorbed in our prayer and our salvation. We did what we thought was needed doing to save our soul. If faith and religion are disconnected from the gospel, ritual practice easily becomes magic.

In an article titled *Can We Get Beyond Religion*, Anthony Gittins makes this observation:

Jesus was plagued with religious questions by people caught within a legalistic (magical) mindset. What must I do to inherit eternal life?' 'Who is my neighbor?' 'How many times must I forgive?' 'Who is the greatest? All of these are religious questions, seeking unambiguous answers – and Jesus answers none of them. Inevitably, in every single case, Jesus calls people to be imaginative rather than purely rational, loving rather than narrowly legalistic, and open rather than firmly closed.[14]

Religion always seeks clear answers. Faith walks in hope and trust. Religion restricts and limits. Faith is openness to the unexpected. Religion becomes complacent. Faith hungers for justice and seeks to know God. Religion requires the performance of deeds and the acceptance of dogmas. Faith is response to mystery perceived but unknown. Religion seeks control, turning mystery into magic. Faith is relationship. Our relationship to God, even in and through Christ, is and must always be mystery. To live in relation to the Holy One we name God is to dwell in mystery.

Father Thomas Merton was a Trappist monk whose life of contemplative prayer led him to appreciate the profound connection between Eucharist and the social, political and economic issues transforming and shaping our world. He became a vocal critic of so much in our world and church that contradicted the life and teaching of Jesus. His superiors disapproved of his activity and of the content of his writing. Some of his work was critical of United States foreign policy and activity. He was forbidden to continue writing and publishing his ideas. His experience is an illustration of what is meant when we say that in the decades preceding Vatican Council II, the church as the people of God, the Living Body of Christ, was asleep.

Prior to the CivilWar, our household of faith was soft and gentle about racism. With good intention church leaders misused scripture to justify slavery. Following that war, in the period of reconstruction, racism became a virulent cancer spreading throughout the social fabric of our nation. Racism was simply ignored. The leaders of the church remained passively uninvolved at the best. Some even engaged in racist practices. In the post World War II period many Catholic people remained indifferent to the racism and domestic poverty in our country. That same indifference infiltrated the period of the war in Vietnam and continues today.

Gradually the civil rights movement brought these moral evils into our church buildings and called for our attention. As we awakened to the racism among us, we also began to recognize the evil of Vietnam, especially as the carnage of that war affected members of our own immediate families or local communities.

I was already an ordained priest during the days of the civil rights campaigns and the anti-Vietnam war protests. I am ashamed to admit how many years passed before it dawned on me that as an ordained minister of the gospel I was responsible to address such moral evil. For many years I stood daily at the altar to celebrate Eucharist, oblivious to the profound connection between Eucharist and the social, political and economic issues transforming and shaping our world.

Many of us within the Catholic culture were like the majority of our fellow citizens in the United States. We were so conditioned and propagandized by the turmoil in the twentieth century that we were unable to see a connection between the dominant culture in which we were living, our Catholic faith and what we did at Mass. In World War II our nation participated in the carpet-bombing of cities in Europe and Japan. Millions of innocent people were killed. The Church said nothing. A nuclear bomb was exploded over the city of Hiroshima. Then another a second was exploded over the Catholic Cathedral of Nagasaki. Hundreds of thousands of innocent people were killed or injured. The Church said nothing. War in Korea, then war in Vietnam and war, war, war became a normal part of American life. The Church said nothing.

At least some of this perception of Catholic life as filled with magic can be attributed to the individualistic piety in which most of us were immersed from our childhood. The Mass was about Jesus and me. Devotions to Mary in a wide variety of forms like the rosary, novenas and May Day observances were about Mary and me. Individualistic piety was the norm. The motivation behind our prayer and devotions was to save my soul, or to get to heaven. The overemphasis on self was neither healthy nor respectful of the teaching of Jesus. Yet that was our life. In spite of the individualism it generated, the practices within our Catholic culture resulted in much that was positive and good. Our culture provided us a great respect for the Mass. It led many of us to a well-established discipline of prayer.

There was another simple crack through which some light broke into the individualistic piety of my life. That was the doctrine of purgatory. Our common belief during my early life was that when we die, most of us would spend time in a spiritual place of purification called purgatory. Depending on what we had done in our lives, after a suitable time of purification, we eventually would be joined with God in heaven. The practice of earning indulgences for those who had died was born of that doctrine of purgatory. We were convinced that by reciting certain prayers and fulfilling a variety of other conditions, we earned indulgences. An indulgence gained early release for the poor souls in purgatory. The value in this doctrine was that it turned our attention to others and their needs.

The doctrine of purgatory occasioned my first serious theological problem with a bishop. I was the pastor of the parish ministering to the University of Montana. We sponsored an evening of inquiry into Catholic life. The pastors from the four other parishes in town came to

Christ the King and we formed a panel for open discussion with a large group of people who gathered. Unbeknown to any of us, a reporter from our local newspaper was present. He did an excellent job of reporting the event.

I was then and still am careful in responding to questions about faith and Catholic life. We who are ordained are obliged to state clearly what the church teaches and why. Then, if the doctrine or practice seems unclear or unsatisfactory for me personally, it seems that honesty requires me to speak about my own struggle and how I resolve it. Through my years as an ordained Catholic priest, I always have been careful to follow this approach.

Unfortunately for me, the reporter from *The Missoulian* quoted only comments about my own struggle with the doctrine of purgatory and what I believe. At that time our local bishop carefully read the newspapers from around the diocese. He never allowed us to forget that as our bishop he was the custodian of orthodoxy. He read the report of our evening of inquiry and immediately wrote to me. It was not a note of appreciation for what we had done! He was upset and demanded that *The Missoulian* was to issue a clarification in which my unequivocal belief in the doctrine of purgatory as taught by the church was to be stated.

Last year, forty-six years after serving in one of our diocesan parishes as my first assignment, I returned to preach a Lenten mission in that parish. The various priests who served that parish in pastoral ministry since then were good men. I have no doubt they brought the vision of the II Vatican Council to that community. Many opportunities for theological, spiritual and liturgical growth were provided that community over a long span of many years. Even so it was evident in many ways that magic retains its power in some of the faithful there.

Here is one simple, clear example of what I mean. Part of that parish mission included celebrating a weekday Mass. I invited those present for the Mass to remain so we could discuss the Eucharistic liturgy. Some insightful comments were made and various folks expressed concern that it seems various reversals of the Council's vision are being introduced. During the liturgy one woman had remained alone, off on the side, apart from all those gathered near the altar. During the discussion she offered this biting criticism. "It is the law! No priest can change anything in the Mass." Then she stood up and without waiting for any discussion, she walked out. Perhaps her comment gave expression to the magic mentality that remains so deeply rooted among us and seems to be returning today. Now in senior status with the opportunity to preside and preach in various parishes spread across North America, I am discovering how deep rooted, extensive and persistent that mentality is. I have felt it lash out at me on more than one occasion.

Pope John XXIII called us to *aggiornamento*, a spiritual renewal. In doing so he was calling our Catholic household of faith to move away from magic and return to mystery. Mystery draws us deeper into and awakens an enthusiasm for the Christ life within us. It enables us to see things as they are in relationship to God as Jesus made that Gracious Mystery known to us. Some today still feel uncomfortable when immersed in mystery. Mystery seems nebulous, too uncertain. Magic helps us feel that we are in control. Our drift back into magic is disappointing to say the least. It is the consequence of trying to put everything back into the box.

Prior to the II Vatican Council, law and obedience to law were central to Catholic life. In summoning the bishops of the world to an ecumenical council, Pope John XXIII said it is time "for the church to bring herself up-to-date where required."[15] The Council endorsed his call to *aggiornamento*, and awakened us to the freedom we share as children of God, brothers and sisters of Christ. The Council reminded us that in Christ our lives are based in love of God and neighbor. Laws and rules are very important to the stability of our community, but always only in so far as they foster love.

Here is a final illustration of the insidious way in which magic repeatedly intrudes into mystery. The name of the priest has been changed and the parish/diocese are not identified. At the time I concelebrated with him, Father Andrew had been ordained for one year. His devotion to the Mass reminds all of us how privileged we are to celebrate liturgy. It seems that he, and other recently ordained men, have been trained in that Jesus and I piety that was so common prior to the Council. He does not show indications of scrupulosity, but the potential is there. He has resumed the very stance and mannerism of that scrupulous professor of so many years ago. While celebrating Mass, Father Andrew ignores the community gathered, leans down over the Table with his mouth nearly touching the host, and breathing slowly onto the host, his eyes skipping back and forth from the missal to the host, slowly, carefully and distinctly says "this is my body." In a similar fashion he holds the cup of wine, leans down over the Table with his mouth nearly touching the

106

cup, and breathing slowly into the cup, with his mouth nearly touching the chalice, eyes skipping back and forth from missal to chalice, <u>slowly, carefully</u> and <u>distinctly</u> saying, "this is the cup of my blood..."

Here we are again! To anyone watching, it would seem he was engaged in some sort of magic ritual, rather than in a communal act of remembering and celebrating Christ present in this community. If we are returning to that mentality of say the words and the result is achieved, then surely magic is again replacing mystery. Eucharist is not magic! It is a mystery of faith. It is about we who gather becoming the Living Body of Christ. This chapter may suggest ideas you will want to discuss with your pastor or the priests in your parish.

CHAPTER 9

"SONG OF JESUS CHRIST" BY JOHN SHEEHAN
"Deep within us, shared among us,
may we ever keep the mind and heart of Christ."

IT'S ABOUT THE HEART

Hiking is another of the major passions in my life. It is physically demanding and forces me to learn about myself and to cope with my own limitations. Walking in the wilderness requires us to respond to situations or circumstances beyond our ability to control. A day of hiking in the mountains of western Montana, regardless of destination, is strenuous, stimulating and refreshing. Walking carefree among craggy mountain peaks, mountain flowers, rocks, tree roots on the trail, alpine lakes, an occasional sparkling stream, the sweet air and the brilliant sky absorb all of one's attention. Occasionally a fork in the trail requires the hiker to be more alert. Several times in my excursions, my companions and I wandered away from a clear trail seeking a shortcut. Unexpectedly we found ourselves confused. We convinced ourselves to say with confidence that, "We are not lost. We know where we are. We just don't know where the truck is." It was somewhat like our situation in the Catholic Church today.

I have never used and do not know how to use a global positioning system. A G.P.S. as they are commonly known, is an electronic devise that provides the user with his or her exact location on this planet at any given moment. I think of the G.P.S. as a metaphor for Christian faith. In the lengthening span of my life, faith has been a sure and constant guidance system enabling me to know where I am going at any given moment. Faith also has guided me as I have tried to honor and live out the vision of the Second Vatican Council. My education and formation within the Catholic Church provided me a strong conviction about the meaning and the ultimate direction of my life. It was drilled into my mind, heart and soul. Our purpose is to know, love and serve God in this world, and to be happy with God in the next. That may sound almost simplistic but I really believe it. I have lived my life out of that conviction. It has served me well. I am indebted and grateful to those responsible for providing me such a constant.

My years of collegiate and theological studies provided knowledge and information while opening doors and windows to new dimensions of life and a vast array of possibilities. As my life experience expanded, I became even more aware of my personal need for constant assurance about the meaning of life and my ultimate direction. Faith kept me on course.

I was twenty-five years of age when I completed the third year of theological studies and spiritual formation at St. Thomas Seminary. On behalf of Bishop Gilmore, the rector and faculty of the seminary called me to be ordained a Sub-deacon. That call marked a moment of significant change in the course of my future years. Late on the evening before the ordination, after a day of doubt, anguish and confusion, I visited my confessor. He then sent me to the rector of the seminary. Over their objections I persisted in my decision. I informed them that on the next morning I would not be ordained with my classmates. The consequence of that decision could not be foreseen.

Many young men followed the long course of studies and were ordained Catholic priests. Most of them served our local diocesan church. Others went off to religious orders whose charism was in the field of education or to foreign mission lands. Many young women from my hometown entered the convent. As vowed women religious they served the Catholic Church in many places both near and far distant from our home.

Reflecting on our youth it is obvious there were many reasons why vocations were so abundant. A major factor was the influence of our families and the faith that permeated our homes. Another may have been economic. The prospect of carrying a lunch bucket and spending our lives working on the Anaconda smelter was not appealing.

The Anaconda smelter provided many local students temporary summer employment beginning the year we graduated from high school. We were fortunate to have such employment available for us. At the age of eighteen, I joined the *Mill and Smelter-Workers Union*, bought my work clothes, steel-toed boots, canvas gloves and a lunch bucket. I worked at the smelter for eight summers. From my first shift I received a real education. In many ways it was more real and of equal importance to all the education provided for me in college and the seminary.

The very nature of a copper smelter requires that it operate twenty-four hours a day, seven days a week. The furnaces are shut down only when needing serious repair. That process is both laborious and costly.

My first job began on night shift (11:00 p.m. to 7:00 a.m.) in a section of the smelter known as the Ferro Manganese. The night foreman took me to my workstation. It was a large concrete slab, probably five feet wide by eight feet long. It was one of four such slabs set side by side near an exterior wall. The building was long, noisy, poorly lit and the high temperature filling the space carried the aroma of gas furnaces and molten metals. The foreman pointed to my tools. They included a green rubber water hose, a twelve-pound sledgehammer with a stout handle, and two large iron sled-like buckets, each approximately the size of an automobile.

Then the foreman outlined my task. Ferro Manganese comes out of a furnace in molten form. In my eight hour shift the overhead crane would come and drop a block of hot Ferro Manganese on the concrete slab. The metal was encased in six to eight inches of slag on the top and six to eight inches or more on the bottom. My job was to use the sledgehammer to break that block of hot Ferro Manganese into whatever pieces I could lift and load into the metal buckets. In one bucket I was to load the chunks of slag. The slag was relatively porous, almost sponge-like. While that meant those chunks were somewhat easier to lift, the slag reduced the effectiveness of the twelve-pound sledgehammer. It bounced off the slag, increasing the number of swings required in breaking the mass apart. The other bucket was to be loaded with the chunks of Ferro Manganese. The chunks of Ferro Manganese were, dense, heavy and therefore very difficult to break. The weight of the metal required me to break them into smaller pieces that I could lift.

That was only part of the bad news. These blocks were hot, very hot, and the foreman told me that as they broke into manageable pieces, it was important to cool them down by directing cold water on them. This would lessen the intense heat radiated by the blocks. In theory that made swinging a twelve-pound sledgehammer easier. Finally the foreman told me where I could get additional canvas gloves when I needed them to replace the ones I brought with me. He said my leather gloves would deteriorate from the roughness of the blocks and the heat.

111

Then he announced the really bad news. When that first block was finished, the crane would return and drop a second one. The good news was that when the second block was finished I was free to go to the locker room and rest for the remainder of the shift. I finished the task, but just barely, before the shift ended. When the smelter whistle signaled the end of the shift at seven in the morning, this very tired young man departed for home, more determined than ever to go to college.

During our student years, we were fortunate to be hired and grateful for whatever work assignment was given to us. At the beginning of each summer we were often moved from one department of the smelter to another. Some buildings like the huge Converter building or the building holding the Calcine furnaces were hotter, dirtier and more dangerous than others. The jobs in these areas involved rotation through three swing shifts. Other jobs were outdoors and straight dayshift.

Our co-workers were generally good men, some alcoholic, often single. Most had only very basic education that was reflected in the coarseness of their language. Their lack of education was reflected in but did not limit the creativity of their vocabulary. That helped me set aside any doubts about going to college. The work was dangerous, dirty, physically demanding and provided motivation for me to pursue a higher education.

Probably one of the more significant factors influencing decisions to enter the convent or the seminary was the quality of the wonderful Catholic Women Religious who taught us, and the priests who served in our parishes. Today my response as I read and hear about clergy pedophilia is the quick rejoinder that was not my experience!

This is not the place to list their names and unique qualities of each. The "Sisters" were good, some even great teachers. I treasure the influence Sister Marie Jerome, O.P. (now Sister June Wilkerson, O.P.) had on my life. She provided a foundation for Catholic social teaching that still directs my life. The priests were good men, apparently happy and always available to us in a variety of ways. I honor with gratitude the Catholic sisters and priests who in my youth served us and influenced our lives so deeply. Their goodness and the sincerity of their lives were always apparent.

In my student years, basketball was a passion. As a senior in high school, St. Thomas College in Minnesota was tempting with the possibility of receiving a basketball scholarship. That is when Father Bernard Topel entered my life. In his role as diocesan vocation director, he visited our high school to interview all the senior boys.

The memory of that interview remains vividly clear. He was a thin, ascetical man wearing rimless glasses and was sitting behind a desk. He began by asking, "Have you ever felt you have a vocation to the priesthood?" Most Catholic boys in Anaconda would answer, "Yes, I had felt that at one time or another." But basketball was more important to me at the moment and I explained my hopes.

He looked sternly at me and said, "If you have a vocation to the priesthood and do not accept it, it will be very difficult for you to save your soul!" That would get the attention of any high school student, even today. He said I should consider attending Carroll College!

So I enrolled at Carroll without any clear direction for my life except for my desire to play basketball. The coach of the Carroll basketball team at that time was another diocesan priest by the name of Raymond Hunthausen. He was our coach for two years. When he was appointed President of the college, he was replaced by his brother, Jack Hunthausen, also a priest of the diocese. Both of them were kind men and men of faith. Anyone who participates in intercollegiate sports under the direction of such coaches is very fortunate. Their influence reached far beyond the basketball court. Under their guidance we learned far more than basketball. They inspired us to be men of virtue, taught us the meaning of teamwork and became role models we wanted to imitate.

Carroll College was like a large extended family. Daily Mass was a routine for those of us living on campus. Our professors were good. Our basketball teams were successful. The spirit among us in the student dormitories generally was exuberant. The four years passed swiftly. By the time of graduation, philosophy was my major field of study with a second major in history and a secondary teaching certificate.

At some point along the way I made the decision to become a candidate for the diocesan priesthood. Bishop Gilmore assigned me to St. Edwards Seminary, later to become St. Thomas, in Seattle. The seminary grounds were situated in a vast, isolated and lovely park-like setting at the north end of Lake Washington.

The years in the seminary were a mixture of spiritual struggle and rigid discipline modeled on monastic life. The course of studies was not over-demanding. Our major texts, examinations and our communal prayer were in Latin. The house rules were designed to form and prepare us for a life of prayer and service. They were far more rigorous than realistic. The required participation in handball, field sports or walking helped us keep some balance in our daily living. Minor infractions of the rules resulted in immediate dismissal from the school.

In retrospect, through the lenses of forty-eight years of ministry in Catholic parishes, there was little in those four years of formation that prepared us for parish ministry. The spiritual formation I received at Carroll College, especially under those who coached our basketball teams, carried me through those years and continues today.

The four years of theology were interrupted by summer breaks during which we returned home. Our bishop assigned us for several weeks each summer to simple forms of youth ministry in rural parishes of our diocese. Then for me, the remainder of the summer meant work on the smelter and enjoying family and the wonder of nature that surrounded our hometown. There were mountains to climb, fish to be caught in clear mountain streams, and lakes in which to swim or water-ski.

As noted earlier, at the end of the third year of theological studies and spiritual formation, my classmates, who still remained, and I received official calls to ordination as Sub-deacons. At that time, this was a major, irrevocable step. Diocesan priests do not make vows of any sort. We are expected/required to promise obedience to our diocesan bishop and the laws of the church. In the weeks before ordination the implications of that promise, especially the requirement of celibacy, were impressed upon us.

I listened, prayed and doubted. My unresolved fears were burdensome. During those years as a theological student my youthful ideals were tested by summer assignments in rural parishes. From the perspective of an idealistic young student, the priests in those rural parishes seemed to be lonely men. It seemed their life of prayer was limited to saying Mass and the daily recitation of the Divine Office. They seemed lonely and their life-style unhealthy.

One of the pastors with whom I spent several weeks was considered a scholarly aesthetic. His lifestyle confirmed the rumors. His up-side-down night and day patterns confused me. He seemed to survive on coffee, cigarettes, Coca-Cola and peanuts. He lived alone and seemed far removed from other people. I did not want to live that sort of life.

As I mentioned earlier, all of that came to a climax at the age of twenty-five when I allowed fear of loneliness and anxiety about lifestyle to control my spirit. I declined ordination. On the night before ordination my confessor tried to convince me to change my mind. So too did the rector. Finally, both accepted my decision. My parents, brother and

114

grandmother had driven to Seattle for this big occasion. In the morning they respected my decision. They were supportive and we sat together during the ordination ceremony. Then it was time to return to Montana. The summer offered several opportunities to visit with Father Raymond Hunthausen. He listened carefully to the unresolved fears behind my decision. He was wise and offered two simple bits of advice.

First and above all he encouraged me to avoid being pusillanimous. That means don't be small-hearted. More importantly he tried to help me understand that the most certain way to a life of inner harmony and purpose was in making the choice to be magnanimous. That means being large-hearted. In retrospect it is my conviction this is the very heart of faith. He explained that the choice to be large-hearted resides in one's willingness to trust in God. That meant following what I heard myself called to be. It is our common task.

I am writing these lines so many years later in that season when the darkness of winter is upon us. It is the liturgical season of Advent. These winter nights are long. They speak to me, call me, remind me of the wisdom of the songwriter Paul Simon.

Hello darkness, my old friend. I've come to talk with you again.
Because a vision softly creeping, left its seeds while I was sleeping,
and the vision that was planted in my brain still remains, within
the sounds of silence.[1]

Men and women who struggle to live in faith do so within the same darkness. When we listen with our inner ear, we hear a gentle voice whispering, speaking to us. It is a voice heard only dimly, speaking love, inviting trust. It is the voice of the One who made our world and us for a purpose, the One who cares for our world and us. Faith is the willingness to listen and live with a magnanimous spirit.

It was apparent to me that Father Ray Hunthausen lived his own life out of such trust. If he could be the sort of man and priest he was, his counsel made sense. It was a challenge. It required a major act of faith to trust my life totally into the hands of God. Once made, the decision seemed easy!

His second piece of advice was equally important. Today, I suspect he did not, could not have realized the future implications of his advice. Again his words were simple. Basically he asked me to understand that if I was ordained priest, my lifestyle did not have to be like that of other priests. He pointed out that it was for me and me alone to decide how I would live as a Catholic priest.

Through his counsel I began to appreciate several things. If relationships are important to me, and they are, then it is my responsibility to reach out to include people in my life. There is no need to be lonely unless that is what I choose to be. The same applied to a life of prayer. Prayer is an important element in my life, if I choose it to be. That decision was for me to make.

Those summer months were consumed with my inner struggle. As the weeks past, the need for me to live with a magnanimous spirit and to assume responsibility for my own life became the bedrock of my life. In his *Song of Jesus Christ*, John Sheehan gives expression to what I was discovering at that time in my life, "deep within us, shared among us, may we ever keep the mind and heart of Christ."[2]

As the end of summer approached, my path seemed clear and so I returned to the seminary and accepted the call to ordination. Eventually at the age of twenty-six I was ordained priest with my classmates on May 27, 1961. Thus began this journey as a Catholic priest of the most common variety, a diocesan or secular priest.

For some years I was privileged to teach a course at the University of Montana about the Ethics of Non-violence. The course allowed ample opportunity to engage students in conversation about the ethical values at the heart of the gospel. The life and teaching of Mohandas Gandhi and Dr. Martin Luther King, Jr. were key elements of that course and teaching about their struggles made me aware that my own journey has engaged me in personal struggle similar to theirs.

We who are secular or diocesan priests are called to ordination by a diocesan bishop. The ministry of diocesan priests is an extension of the local bishop. He sends us to serve the various communities of this local church. Our primary responsibility is preaching the gospel, forming faith-community, and celebrating the Christ-life with our people in liturgy and sacrament. We are called secular priests because we live in the world with and among the people we serve. It is a wonderful life.

In the early nineteen-sixties, ordination to Catholic priesthood was a major cultural affair in our hometown and diocese. Many of my family and friends traveled to the cathedral in Helena for the ordination and two days later gathered again for my First Mass in my home parish. The church was full and later in the day there was a flood of people into the social hall of our local Catholic high school. The enthusiasm, joy and pride of the community were tangible. It was an extremely humbling experience! People, lots of people, who knew me since I was a little boy came and knelt before me asking for a blessing from this newly ordained priest. The significance of being a Catholic priest was like all things Catholic at the time. It was magnified and multiplied many times over!

Decisions about my own prayer life were simple. I felt then and continue to feel a deep inner need or calling to seek intimacy with God. The choice to make prayer an important element of my daily life was made early in my student days. That choice was reinforced a few years after ordination at a national conference. Father Henri Nouwen admonished us to mark an appointment time on our daily calendar for prayer, and then to treat that time as we would any other appointment. His advice made sense and remains a guiding principle for scheduling my daily life.

In returning to my theological studies, it was with an inner conviction there was no need for me to be lonely if I chose not to be. The great fears about a life of loneliness that distressed my soul as a theological student proved to be empty.

Early in parish ministry it became obvious that reaching out to people enabled them to respond with real friendship. My second pastoral assignment moved me to a large city in the western part of our diocese. In that deanery there were no other priests my age. Those with whom I skied and shared life were now several hours away by car. It was time to find new friends, or hike, ski or go to plays or concerts alone.

Every person I know is ultimately alone, even those in deeply committed marriages. That is our common existential reality. Being alone is different than being lonely. Reaching out in friendship to people set a pattern in my life. Eventually when it became possible for me to live in less institutional situations, I invited people to my residence for meals or socializing. In my first assignment as a pastor, I told the community I would like to be invited to their homes to share meals with their family. I also promised they would hear me on the phone inviting myself to their homes for a meal. Perhaps there is no better way to become an integral part of a community. For me it proved to be very effective.

Fifteen years ago and during my final assignment as a pastor, my doctor informed me I had prostrate cancer. He recommended various treatments but placed radical surgery at the top of the list. He was emphatic that recovering from such surgery required rest and exercise. I consulted other doctors for a second opinion. It was clear the cancer was slow moving. There was no hurry to act so a date for surgery was set in the spring after Holy Week and Easter. By then most of my nonnegotiable obligations and responsibilities would be behind me.

On the first Sunday of Advent I informed the parish of my situation and promised to keep them informed, asking for their prayers for guidance and healing. The mood in the sacred space was definitely serious. So two weeks later I returned and shared the second opinion and my decision to have surgery in the spring. Again the mood was rather serious, so in order to lighten it up I closed my announcement in a very serious manner. I told them there was only one major concern in my heart. I asked them to pray for me. I told them my one major concern was, "That about two or three weeks following the surgery, the current pope (John Paul II) would die, and the newly elected pope would change all the rules. For me it would be too late!" This was a Catholic community. Needless to say, the place exploded with laughter.

I share that story simply to illustrate the significance of trying to live in a spirit of magnanimity. Remember that my biggest reason for declining ordination those many years ago was my fear of loneliness. My fears of being lonely were so ungrounded.

As the date for that surgery approached, the concern expressed by so many suggested there would be a flow of visitors to my hospital room. Ironically my long ago anxiety about being lonesome was now replaced by a real concern that there would be too many people in my life, no quiet time to recuperate. It seemed wise to post a list of names with the hospital staff asking that the number of visitors to my room be limited. It proved to be a good decision.

The doctor advised me to arrange eight weeks for recuperation. I found a Jesuit priest willing to assume some of my pastoral responsibility for that period. Then I asked the parish members to care for me, especially by assuring a nutritious meal was delivered to my home each night for the eight weeks. Members of the parish brought me dinner every night. Most asked to stay and share the meal with me. Those early fears of loneliness were clearly an illusion.

Accepting the call to ordination was only the beginning and in some ways the easiest part of my decision. The real challenge was assuming responsibility for my own life. As my life progressed, the various parish and teaching assignments from our bishops provided me a variety of opportunities to discover gifts and talents of which I was unaware. It was a blessing to be placed in parochial circumstances that made it possible for me to follow the advice given to me in that summer of 1960.

Father Hunthausen had assured me that if ordained priest, my lifestyle did not have to be like that of other priests. That was good in theory. There is a great deal of social pressure inside a clerical culture. It is no small challenge to be true to one's inner calling. In addition, ordinary people put priests on a pedestal. Their expectations of a priest's lifestyle were well established among the laity. I remember my own reaction to those priests in our diocese who were the first among us to abandon clerical dress.

The inner turmoil and struggle that led me to decline ordination clarified many things for me. So much of our training was modeled upon monastic life. In some instances that is still the lifestyle some parish priests try to live. We who are diocesan priests are called to a lifestyle that differs drastically from that of the monk in the monastery. We do not live in monasteries but among the people who are church. Trying to develop and embrace a non-monastic lifestyle is not something that every bishop is willing to bless. It was inevitable that many of my choices and decisions were not in sync with typical clerical life.

To be a secular priest is to be in the world with and among the people. We share the lives of people in as many ways as possible. It eventually became clear to me that wearing a black suit and Roman collar was often a source of privilege. Clerical clothing also establishes an invisible barrier separating us from people.

Few if any realize how pampered we priests were in the 1960's. Being a Catholic priest then was like all things Catholic at the time, magnified and multiplied many times over! In my first two parish assignments I lived in a rectory with two or three other priests. It was a presumed fact that a live-in housekeeper was part of rectory life. I would rise early in the morning for meditation and then celebrate one of the six o'clock Masses. When I returned to the rectory, breakfast was waiting and my bed was already made. Much has changed in fifty years!!

In the nineteen-sixties, clerical dress was an unchallenged norm and expectation. After ordination we dressed in proper clerical attire, a black suit, white shirt with cuff links, a Roman collar, the required hat and long black stockings. Around the parish and when teaching in the grade or high schools it seemed normal to wear a cassock. The elementary school children loved to count the buttons on my cassock while I was trying to simplify some profound theological idea for them.

My parents once traveled with me to San Francisco. One evening we were going out to dinner and dressed appropriately. I was in black suit and Roman collar. It was a dark night and raining heavily. I dropped my parents at the door of the restaurant and went to park the car. The waiting area was crowded with people. When I entered the restaurant, my dad informed me "the maitre'd said we have to wait about an hour and a half." As we discussed the situation, the maitre'd came up to me and said, "Father, how many in your party?" I told him. Immediately he said, "please follow me Father" and moved us ahead of all those people waiting in front of us. That gracious but embarrassing moment initiated the questions that eventually led me to set aside clerical dress.

For me it became more and more obvious that while people love and respect me as a Catholic priest, their love and respect is most authentic when they love me because of who I am, not because of what I am. That sort of love and respect is all any of us need and does not exclude respect for me as a Catholic priest.

Prior to all of the anger and sadness caused by clerical pedophilia, people of all faiths respected Catholic priests. Many privileges were extended to us simply because of our clothing or uniform. Such respect is suitable when earned through personal engagement in the lives of people. It certainly is inappropriate if extended simply because of dress or status.

The advice given to me during that summer of indecision is the sort of basic wisdom we all need to hear. First, be magnanimous, bighearted," be willing to trust God and seek to live in harmony with the call placed in your heart! Second, take responsibility for your own life! This spiritual wisdom simply deepened and strengthened faith as the guidance system for my life and ministry.

A close examination of the life of Jesus, and especially of his ministry of healing, makes it abundantly clear he was calling us to be people of faith. He never engaged in the use of magic words. Repeatedly he told people, "Your faith has healed you."[3] His reference to faith is not simply about believing in the existence of God or even the power of God. Faith is an essential tool we all need in our struggle to become fully human. For him, faith was "a particular kind of consciousness, the consciousness of God as loving and caring toward us."[4] When he affirms that someone has been healed because of their faith, he simply recognized their willingness "to trust that God will do what is best, which may not be what you or I want."[5]

In his ministry,

And above all in the events leading up to his death on the cross,
we are presented with a dramatic image/story of one who appears

to have trusted God absolutely, and in consequence was enabled to interact with his fellow human beings with love and care and to forgive even the enemies who were bringing about his death.[6]

In this chapter I have tried to present the greatest challenge placed before all who are willing to follow in the way of the Risen Christ. It certainly is the greatest challenge for us as Catholic people today. It is the challenge of being magnanimous, trusting in God. For all of us who want to know and live in harmony with the creating will and purpose of God, doing so means listening and responding to what we hear ourselves called to be and to do in the world.

Our ancient Catholic tradition is clear. The ultimate teaching authority of the Church is not the bishop of Rome. That ultimate authority is expressed in a universal council of the Church gathered in union with the Bishop of Rome. We believe that the Holy Spirit guides and directs our efforts to live in the way of the Risen Christ through such a conciliar body. It was within this tradition that Pope John XXIII summoned the bishops of the world to gather in Council with him.

There still are Catholic people, even adults with advanced university degrees asking, "how can you change a tradition that goes back to Jesus himself?" There is no question about the sincerity of those who ask such questions. Their questions make it apparent that our efforts to help people understand the rich theological and scriptural foundation for the vision of the Second Vatican Council and all that happened since that Council were inadequate and ineffective.

Since the very day the Council was announced by Pope John XXIII, even on the day the Council concluded and increasingly more since, it has been quite obvious that the minds and hearts of some Cardinals, bishops, pastors and people were closed to John's invitation. They did not appreciate, endorse or appropriate the vision, the teaching or the new paradigms set before us by the Council.

For all of us, the Council tests our faith, our willingness to trust that the Holy Spirit of God is leading us. It is no easy task to be magnanimous, large-hearted. It was a challenge at the time of the Council and today remains a challenge for us still. We will become fully human only as we learn to trust in God. Such trust measures the authenticity of our faith as Catholic people in this century.

I know, but am still learning, that life at every stage of our development is about the same issue. Either I choose to believe in the existence of a loving God, or I choose not to believe. If I choose to believe, then it makes sense to trust that God guides us. If we are willing to trust, willing to speak our yes, "all shall be well, and all manner of things shall be well."[7] As the theologian Karl Rahner suggests, to be a person of faith is to engage in "a journey of discovery into the virtually uncharted territory of our own lives."[8] Above all else this means that our choice to be people of faith is a "journey that ends up being a journey of mind and heart into God."[9]

Jesus spoke of the will of the Father. In my youth I thought the will of God meant God has a specific plan for each and everyone of us. I made choices based on my belief that it was my responsibility to discover and respond to that plan. My decision to return to theological studies and to accept the call to ordination was rooted in my intention to trust God's will for me. I reflect back upon my life with deep gratitude for that decision. However my understanding of what it means to speak of God's will today is far different than it was when lying on the floor of the St. Helena cathedral. My conviction that faith is "trusting that God will do what is best"[10] has not diminished. But I no longer believe there is an abstract will of God out there somewhere setting an absolute course for each person. I no longer believe God has established a slot for each of us and our task is to discover that slot so that in the discovery and response we will become who we were created to be. That was never how our Catholic tradition expressed the will of God. But there were times in my own life when that was descriptive of my understanding.

In the course of forty-eight years of pastoral work I have learned a few things. I learned that people who are magnanimous, people who trust the Holy Mystery we name God become very human. They live out of the conviction that God surrounds us with unconditional love. Almost inevitably they are the ones who seek the common good of all people. "The common good is whatever is best for the whole human family or the whole community of living beings or the whole universe in its grand unfolding."[11] Surely this is what Jesus is about. He came announcing the kingdom of God, an entirely new way of being and living that fills us with concern for the common good of all.

It has been far more than fascinating to reach my present age. As I became a priest in senior status, I had to deal with the sadness of letting go of a long life of parish ministry. That life has been both challenging and deeply rewarding. As I moved into senior status I was surprised that once again the old fears rose up in my soul. The fear of loneliness is something we all experience apparently at every stage of life. I thought it had left me many years ago. I had to confront the fear that life may have no meaning, no purpose without the demands and expectations of others.

At the end of my third year of theology I learned and am continuing to learn there is only one way to resolve that fear. There is only one way to embrace a wholesome life. It is to live with anticipation and confidence in the faithful presence of God. This Gracious Mystery has guided me to this point and continues to guide me into the uncharted territory of my life.

It is easy to pray without hesitation, "thy will be done on Earth as it is in heaven." Praying and living can be two different things. I know those words are an authentic expression of my faith when they express my willingness to imitate the radical trust so evident in the life of Jesus. Faith is the guidance system that has given meaning and direction to my life. It has kept me on course, even today when fear and anxiety crawl out of the corners of my soul as they did so many years ago when I was a student and declined the call to ordination. On the two occasions when my companions and I have felt disoriented or lost while hiking in Montana, we could easily have panicked. We didn't and allowed our natural environment to guide us. Perhaps you sometimes feel lost today as you pursue your determination to live within this Catholic household of faith. I invite you to trust as I do that the Spirit of God is leading us and no matter how persistent in their efforts, those who are trying to do so will not be able to put everything back into the box.

CHAPTER 10

"THE LONG PATH." BY PEYTON PALMERTON:
The long path I walk has dead ends.
  It has fallen trees and broken bridges
    and there are times when there is no path at all.
But that does not stop me.
  I find light in darkness.
  I find treasure in tears.
  I find happiness in the most disastrous situations.
I keep going on; the long path.

THE WONDROUS GIFT

As noted earlier I live in a fertile valley in western Montana. Rivers flow through our city draining the snowfields that mantle the peaks of the Bitterroot and Rattlesnake Wilderness Areas. Often the high mountain snows remain until mid or late summer. Missoula is a paradise for those of us who enjoy the challenge and reward of hiking in the mountains.

People were incredulous when they heard of my intended journey. My only reply to their quizzical looks and critical comments, like "you are seventy-one years of age!" was, "I have nothing to prove!" After serving in the diocese of Helena as a Catholic parish priest for forty-five years and my twenty-two years as pastor of Christ the King parish were coming to a end, I was about to become a priest in senior status. To walk the ancient pilgrimage route to the basilica of my namesake, James the Apostle, seemed an excellent transition experience. Three of us planned to walk five hundred miles of the Camino de Santiago de Compostela. We would begin at St. Jean Pied de Port in southern France, cross over the Pyrenees and then walk across northern Spain.

Transitions can be easy or difficult. Margaret is a dear friend of mine. I have known and loved her husband since he was in the fifth grade at St. Anthony grade school I witnessed her marriage to Mike thirty plus years ago. One day, she and Mike were golfing. They reached the thirteenth green. She laid her golf bag down and said "Mike, I am going home." He said, "You forgot your golf clubs. Are you taking them home?" She looked at him, smiled and said, "No, I will not need them any more," and went home. Some transitions are easy. Some are difficult.

Thousands of pilgrims have walked or attempted to walk the Camino de Santiago de Compostela. Legend has it that the body of St.

James is buried in the cathedral of Santiago in Galatia, Spain. It may be so, or it may be pure legend. In any case my companions and I do a lot of hiking in the mountains of Glacier Park and western Montana. We were confident we could do what thousands of pilgrims have done before us and walk the five hundred miles in thirty days.

St. Jean Pied de Port is a lovely village tucked into the base of the Pyrenees in southwest France. Night's darkness still hung over the village as we stepped out of our hotel. The first light of day embraced the small village with a magical morning. Trees lined our way as we began our ascent over the Pyrenees Mountains. Flocks of birds, as if monks chanting in their monastery greeted us and raised their voices in morning praise. I wanted to sing with them.

On this first day we walked the old Roman road. I was conscious we were following the footsteps of Caesar, Charlemagne, Napoleon and many others. Green slopes and tall mountain peaks surrounded us. Slowly and silently vultures circled in the sky above. As the hours passed the trail seemed like the headwaters of a mighty river. In the early morning there were three of us, a tiny stream. Then as the day progressed the number of pilgrims steadily increased. It was never apparent to me from whence they came. The river of people on this pilgrimage walk grew larger. I was delighted when I caught, greeted and passed a happy Italian whose donkey carried his baggage up the steep slope. His wife carried their small dog.

Our intended destination on that first day lay far beyond the mists that shrouded the mountains. The Camino stretched out uphill in front of us. Five hundred miles seemed daunting but our daily goal helped it seem more reasonable. We knew we could walk a daily average of fifteen to twenty miles. On that first day we set out with confidence that we would easily reach our destination, the monastery at Roncesvalles in Spain.

For many years I was privileged to lead groups of pilgrims to the Holy Land. It is a serious responsibility that gradually taught me that for those making a pilgrimage, the journey is more important than the destination. So in preparation for this pilgrimage to Santiago I tried to carefully identify my purpose and the daily objectives that would stimulate my determination.

The physical challenge of walking five hundred miles was clear. The real issue was how I would allow the Spirit energy of God's freedom to mold my own spirit as I walked each day. For this to be a pilgrimage it had to be about far more than walking. It was my hope that each step would lead me to something deep within myself. The outward journey was the vehicle for an inward journey.

The backpack I carried was both practical and symbolic. A twenty-pound load seemed reasonable. To respect that limit meant leaving so much behind. Doing so was symbolic of leaving behind all that my life as a pastor had been, especially the twenty-two years at Christ the King.

I set out with enthusiasm more than anxiety. My objective each day was to walk with steady movement but consciously aware I was walking in the eternal present. With every step a new world would open to me. I wanted to watch for it in the environment and the people to be encountered. I wanted to embrace it with my heart.

A transition implies a change of rhythm. It implies crossing a threshold, entering a new space or a new time. Transitions always are *kairos* moments, filled with grace. In the weeks of preparation before my departure someone suggested a great idea. I accepted his suggestion and decided to carry a limited number of poems with me. Then while walking, some part of each day could be engaged with reciting and memorizing poetry. The words and sentiments could melt into my soul. It was easy to accumulate the sort of poems that seemed full of potential. I sent an appeal out on the Internet to those who receive my weekly homilies. The response was like Christmas and some of those poems were included in my backpack.

The airplane trip across the Atlantic interrupted the physical rhythm of my body and my life. It was easy as we set out on the Camino to feel we had entered God's time (*kairos*). We expected that first day to be extremely difficult. We were not naive and realized a nineteen-plus mile walk that involved a vertical ascent of nearly five thousand feet and a similar descent on the other side would be physically demanding. We also knew we could do it. Mountains are an integral part of my life and literally thousands had done it before us.

Soon after leaving the village of St. Jean Pied de Port and our initial footsteps on the Camino were behind us, a powerful headwind awoke and began to slow our pace. It seemed to be pushing us backward. At times that wind actually knocked me off-balance as if resisting my purpose, saying do not go any further!! My companions estimated the wind at forty plus miles per hour. It continued on throughout most of the morning and subsided only after reaching the summit. We estimated that wind added the effort of an additional two miles to our walk. It took seven and a-half hours of steady effort to reach the monastery at Roncesvalles in Spain.

It was a welcome diversion to have a poem in hand, allowing it to enter my soul as the journey took me higher into the beautiful scenery of the Pyrenees. I do not remember the author or source of the poem I tried to absorb that day, but the words remain vivid.

Awakening, dawn's chorus welcoming the day new,
untouched, waiting to be filled, and will we paint a rainbow,
with all its promise, or dull the canvas sadly seen?
Each day brings its own colors to be chosen,
mixed pigments of joy, happy moments, smiles and laughter,
and which will you choose? For life is choice.
We all are painters in our own way. All needing to create
something of worth, of lasting beauty, making our journey.
I clean my brushes, choose my palette of vibrant, living colors,
and begin to fill today's blank canvas.

The words, images and feeling were so right for that day and those to follow! They continue speaking to me with vibrant meaning. On that early morning I wondered if the misty, shrouded mountains were symbols of life closed to my participation or perhaps hints of forthcoming mystical experiences. The poet's words assured me there was a canvas to be filled and it is the canvas of my life.

As we pushed upward into the mist, the sun emerged, coating the green foothills and mountains with morning's unique glow. Late in the day as I descended into an old birch forest, a filigree of light and shadow played through the gently swaying trees.

After the steep descent to the monastery, we sought welcome refreshment and rest. I was tired and hungry. The *albergue* (pilgrim hostel) was a newly renovated facility housing one hundred beds in a single, long room. There was also a small hotel near the monastery. The intensity of that first day moved us to opt for the hotel rather than the *albergue*. The simple pilgrim meal of green salad, trout, potatoes and red wine rekindled my spirits as much as my body. It is amazing how such a day like that can reduce the complications of life to the simple resolve of perseverance.

We awoke early the next morning and almost literally fell or climbed out of bed. In spite of a good night's sleep, our bodies felt the burden of the previous day's climb over the Pyrenees. With first light, we set out again. Our legs were stiff and sore but we remained confident in our ability to walk the seventeen plus miles to Larrasoana. That morning was a fresh awakening and reminder that only days before my body had reached the age of seventy-one. It did not surprise me, that like the rising sun, my steps were slow but determined. The sun was bright. The walk was pleasant.

Among the poems received before my departure was one that I selected for my walking meditation on the third day. The parents of a twelve-year-old boy encouraged him to send his poem to me. His parents had been students at the University of Montana and active in Catholic Campus Ministry. I still treasure them. Their son's name is Peyton Palmerton. The creative spirit and talent in our young people is extraordinary in many ways. To know such young people is to be filled with hope that God is leading us to a bright and good future. Initially his poem spoke to my situation while attempting to walk the Camino de Santiago de Compostela. Now it has become for me a description of our current situation within the Catholic household of faith. Peyton titled his poem *The Long Path*. I used it to introduce this chapter.

Many who have dedicated much of life energy to the renewal called for by John's Council at times feel we are confronting dead ends. I have among my notes this undated reflection by the editor of the journal *Celebration*. He wrote,

> Many of the remarkable scholars and educators dedicated to implementing the vision of the Second Vatican Council have died. After long careers of service they struggled with official misinterpretations of Council reform and the discounting and dismantling of work they had completed.[1]

The reality in which we live is that we experience obstacles blocking our path, and at times the confusion makes us feel there "is no path at all."

We were tired after our third day of walking, but less so than the previous day. That poem led me into a deep awareness that this time of transition in my life was nothing new. The cycles of my life all involved change, sometimes grief, and always growth. That young boy's poem is a summation of life and at that moment was calling me to embrace the new opportunities before me. To embrace life is to acknowledge the power of God working with us.

I expected the first days of this journey would be physically difficult and challenging. They were that. I also expected to gradually adjust and grow stronger, and I did. As we set out on the fourth day, my body was beginning to feel the rhythm of the journey. My stride was steady and strong and the profusion of wild flowers that surrounded us on the seven hour, thirteen mile plus mile walk to Cizur Menor bolstered my spirit.

Friends of mine who live along the Camino picked us up and drove us back to their village. They invited us to join them for a stroll and a wonderful meal in the city of Pamplona, the city of the running bulls. As I set out early on the morning of the fifth day, my confidence was reinforced. Walking five hundred miles to Santiago was beginning to seem possible. On this day, I walked nearly seventeen miles in six and one-half hours. For most of those hours the Camino was a long, gradual walk through rich green fields of grain that stretched as far as I could see. Off in the distance mountain peaks rose up inviting us to continue.

Sometime during the afternoon my metatarsal arch began to bother me. I first had that problem about twenty-five years ago. At that time I played a lot of tennis. I went to a podiatrist seeking relief. He fitted me with a pair of orthotics. They corrected the problem. When pain leaves us it is easy to forget about it. Over the years those orthotics disappeared into a box somewhere. I forgot about them. As I trekked along the Camino, I was wishing I had them.

At the end of that day, the same friends who had taken us to Pamplona the previous evening picked us up again to stay one more night with them. That evening, even with my metatarsal arch cramping, I felt relaxed and strong enough to spend another evening socializing in Pamplona. I was wearing sandals. As we made our way through the narrow, crowded streets I kept walking on my toes. That seemed to lessen my foot pain. We had a great evening sharing tapas, beer, the music of the Basque people, and Celtic music from the region of Galatia.

The next morning our friends drove us back to the village we had reached the day before. As I set out on the Camino in the first light of the morning, I felt a deep serenity and peace. Unknown to myself, it was to be a day of transition. As the day progressed I was amazed how prophetic the poems were. I was enjoying a wonderful morning and walking briskly. Sometime around mid-morning I felt a twinge of anxiety. It had been some time since I saw the familiar yellow arrow indicating the direction of the path. I trusted my instincts and continued. A farmer informed me I had missed a turn but his directions were clear and eventually I reconnected with the Camino.

I was approaching a small village and my body clock was reminding me it was nearly noon, time for a lunch break. Then the Achilles tendon on my right foot began to pain me. I found it increasingly difficult to walk. So I limped into the village of Estella and found a nice place to eat my simple lunch of bread, cheese and an apple.

Walking the streets of Pamplona on my toes was not a good decision. Doing so had alleviated the pain in my metatarsal arch. Apparently it also had stressed my Achilles tendon.

After a refreshing nap, my tendon felt better so I headed out of the village and up the hill. Within a few kilometers the pain returned and my inner dialogue became more interesting. After descending the hill the Camino crossed a highway. It only took a moment for me to decide my walking for this day was finished. I stuck out my thumb and within five minutes was in a car speeding along to the next *"albergue"* at Villamayor.

Once I had claimed a bed, stowed my backpack and showered, I had time to sort out my situation. The Achilles tendon on my right foot was very painful. "What can I do? What should I do? What will I do?" Already the answer had been given to me in a poem that had been my companion several days previous. Again I do not know the author or source, but the words are still so familiar:

How silently, how silently the wondrous gift is given.
I would be silent now, Lord, and expectant,
that I may receive the gift I need,
so others may become the gift others need.

Yes, I was about to discover the deep implications of these words. As others limped or walked briskly on to Santiago, I began to realize the gift I had received was the gift of being lame. My attitude remained positive but it was clear I needed to disrupt my walk, rest a few days, perhaps not walk all the way, but do only what my tendon would allow.

My dinner companions that evening encouraged me to press forward. Our conversation was lively and helped me recognize that for me, the goal of this pilgrimage was the same as all those years of pastoral ministry had been. The poem I had carried in my heart several days earlier now returned. That poem spoke about "how silently the wondrous gift is given," so "others may become the gift others need." Lame or not, there was purpose for this pilgrimage and it would become apparent as I followed the long path.

In the morning after breakfast the manager of the *albergue* was kind and offered me a ride to a nearby village where intercity buses were available. The next major city was Burgos so I accepted his offer. I knew there was a Benedictine monastery a few kilometers south of Burgos. The monks were internationally known because they recorded the Gregorian chant of their divine office and sell the compact discs. That seemed a good place to seek refuge and allow my tendon to heal.

At the bus station in Burgos I met John from New York, a man my age. He was ending his walk and not going beyond Burgos. His plan was to rest for a few days and then return home. He is a retired judge from New York City. As we spent time together I learned that he, like others on the Camino, is a poorly informed Catholic, an agnostic, and unforgiving of Muslims. When he learned I was going to the Monastery of Santo Domingo de Silos, he asked if he could accompany me and if I would help him get a bed in the monastery.

It became apparent on our one-hour bus trip that John is a talker but a poor listener. Perhaps this is because his hearing is somewhat impaired. We arrived at the monastery too late to get a bed. So we went our separate ways looking for a hotel room, having agreed to meet the next day for Morning Prayer in the monastery.

The monks welcomed us graciously. The guest master led us to our simple cells, each with a single bed, a desk and a chair. They invited us to share their meals and me to concelebrate the Eucharistic liturgy which I did each day. The decision to seek refuge in the monastery was excellent. It provided a place to rest and heal, while continuing the inner pilgrimage of transition in my life.

Peyton's poem from the first days on the Camino provided me the precise wisdom needed for my circumstance. His title, *The Long Path,* was suitable and fitting not only for the journey on which I had embarked but for the realities encountered along the way.

I repeat his poem again because his images apply not only to those on the Camino or walking the high mountain ridges near my home. They apply to life for all of us. These lines describe our common journey.

The long path I walk has dead ends.
It has fallen trees and broken bridges
and there are times when there is no path at all.
But that does not stop me.
I find light in darkness.
I find treasure in tears.
I find happiness in the most disastrous situations.
I keep going on; the long path.

Sitting in my monastic cell provided a great setting for the wisdom of that twelve-year-old boy to seep into my soul. I applied it then to my experience on the Camino. Clearly it applies to all of life and our current experience within the Catholic Church. There always are obstacles and opportunities in life. We really have no idea or need to know what is next. If we simply adjust to every new and unexpected circumstance and move on with confidence and hope, it seems inevitable that I will "receive the gift I need, so others may become the gift others need."

My new companion from New York wanted to talk about everything: parenting, faith, relationship with his wife, retirement. I was, and was not surprised to learn that he never discusses such things with his wife or family. It is amazing how many people never speak with their loved ones about their spirituality, their yearning for God and their struggle to find meaning inside their daily struggle. As I listened to John, I wondered if perhaps this is why so many undertake this pilgrimage. Walking the Camino opens new avenues of sharing with people you will never see again.

On our second day in the monastery a second John came into my life. I named him John of Barcelona. He told us he is the retired conductor of the Sydney symphony in Australia. He is a pious Spaniard and returns often to the monastery for long periods. He seemed anxious to speak English and shared all of our meals with us. It quickly became apparent that John of New York and John of Barcelona were kindred spirits. Both were Catholic, retired and in full agreement that it is not realistic to work for peace or to expect peace.

In the few brief days at Santo Domingo de Silos, a third John came into my life. His name was John Marie. The monks all left for an overnight excursion and gave the key to the monastery to me. John Marie invited us to join him on a drive to several nearby villages. Here was another interesting man. He also is Catholic. He likes the Catholic life. He visits the monastery often. He does not belong to a parish and does not participate in Sunday liturgy. This John was a gracious driver and guide. He is the married father of three, a bank teller and a scholar of the Apocalypse.

John Marie came to the monastery to study. Apparently in the monastery's library there is an ancient manuscript of the Apocalypse and a commentary on that book. While sharing a delicious lunch in a rustic village cafe, he explained his reason for such study. He considers the Apocalypse a book of hope. According to him, after Islam was

133

expelled from Spain, the Spanish people found hope in this book. Today he fears Islam will soon re-conquer Spain by the simple process of immigration.

The three Johns were a case study in Catholic life today. I welcomed them with full recognition they would challenge me to enter into real dialogue, truly listening with empathy, but also trying to invite them to consider the gospel and the Mystery of Christ. In their negative mental energy I could hear some of my own brokenness. In their prejudices and narrow-mindedness I recognized various ways in which I neglect, ignore or reject the possibility of living in harmony with others and thus with God.

The three are good men and sincere about their convictions. They readily condemn the violence of others while claiming divine approval of their own violence. In the case of the two Spaniards, they return to the monastery frequently, for rest, not for Christ. They deeply appreciate the monastic singing. It is beautiful, but external. It is ritual done well but maintains Christ as a mysterious, remote presence. While at the monastery they received Communion but apparently remain untouched by the gospel, perhaps even oblivious to the reality of Christ.

I was still limping as John of New York and I walked with John of Barcelona to the bus stop. He wanted to bid us farewell. I wished him peace and urged him to work for peace. He became very agitated and upset with my suggestion. He spends weeks in the monastery. Without hesitation, the last words he spoke to me strongly affirmed that Caesar is his god.

Of the three Johns, two are Spanish and probably typical of most Spanish males. They name themselves Catholic. They like things Catholic. But where is the fire? Where is the awareness of Christ? Where is the yearning for justice and peace? If the faith they claimed is only a cultural form and if Eucharist is simply a mode of expressing that culture and no more, then Spain may well become something other than Catholic. In many respects it seems it already has. Surely the fire of love, a yearning for peace and an awareness of Christ must roam in the hallways of their heart. It simply was not apparent to me. Perhaps John Marie intuitively is correct in anticipating that Islam will again conquer Spain. If it does, it is more likely it will happen, not by immigration alone but by converting the Spaniards to Islam.

As the bus took us away from the monastery, I knew my decision was clear. A transition had occurred. I remained one additional night in

Burgos, hoping that perhaps I could resume walking the next day. It was not to be so. My days of walking the Camino were finished and I was going home early. The bus ride to Santiago marked another transition. I was no longer a pilgrim on the Camino. So I sat back in my seat and enjoyed the beauty of the countryside as I left the challenge of the Camino behind me.

After settling into a hotel in Santiago, in spite of my painful limp, I followed a procession through the narrow streets until we reached the ancient Cathedral. Then I limped through and explored the interior of the building as well as I could. This cruciform building is ancient and it is enormous. It was late in the day so I sat in the stillness, listening to the silent echoes of all those people who for centuries have come to this place as pilgrims or searchers or as both.

The distinction between pilgrims and searchers is ambiguous. Searchers are looking, seeking and do not have the foundation of faith that pilgrims have. Early the next morning I again limped through the narrow streets, joining the newly arrived pilgrims for Sunday liturgy. Fortunately I arrived early and front seats were still available. The pews filled quickly. Most gathered for the liturgy seemed to be pilgrims. Pilgrims celebrate God and Christ and life as gift received. I think pilgrims are happy, laugh and sing. The appearance of those gathered around me was somber and reserved.

A bell rang and we could hear music, of an orchestra, behind the altar. Altar boys led a procession into the church. The orchestra followed them, and then the Cathedral Canons and several vested con-celebrants. They stopped when they reached the cross aisle. You could appreciate this only if you saw it.

Eight men stepped into the middle of the church. They lowered an enormous silver thurible from the ceiling. It may have been three feet in diameter. They fired up the charcoal, poured incense onto the burning coals and raised it up above our heads. Then by manipulating the ropes, the eight men began swinging the smoking thurible back and forth, nearly touching the ceiling on both sides. Now the gathered assembly looked like pilgrims. All had great shining grins on their face. They swung the thurible in this fashion for a while, and then raised it back up to the ceiling. The procession continued into the church.

There was constant distraction high up behind the altar. Legend claims the body of St. James the Apostle is buried behind the altar and so an enormous statue of St. James peers across the nave. Pilgrims climb up a series of steps and hug the statue from behind. That goes on all through the liturgy.

Folks seemed to actively participate in the liturgy and seemed engaged, some even deeply affected by the experience. Even so, for me much of it seemed religious in the negative sense of the word that edges on magical. I prayed but had no sense of celebration. There was no interaction among us that would suggest we were aware of Christ present. I suspect that few in that assembly even thought of us as the Living Body of Christ. Eucharist was celebrated. Every Eucharist is meant to be a transition. I left wondering what it means to celebrate as we did?

Mt. Sentinel is the mountain that rises up immediately behind the campus of the University of Montana. A large, whitewashed "M" is situated six hundred twenty feet above the valley floor. It overlooks the campus and our valley. That "M" is one hundred twenty five feet wide and one hundred feet long. For many years and still now in these years of senior status I continue my habit of climbing to the "M" at least six days each week.

While pastor of Christ the King, I always spent a few minutes at the end of the Sunday liturgy with little children circled around me. I tried to open the Sunday gospel for them with a small story or a question that could lead them into the gospel. I will always remember the moment when I asked them, "How many mountains surround our city?" Without hesitation a five-year-old boy responded, "twenty-five!" WOW!

The next day I climbed Mount Sentinel. I sat up there and tried to count the peaks that surround us. I counted and recounted several times. I have lived in Missoula for nearly four decades and never realized twenty-five mountain peaks surround us. I wondered how that little boy knew. Perhaps because like all children he was aware life is gift.

My effort to walk the Camino was marking a time of transition in my life. I am grateful for all of my experiences on the Camino. Those weeks reminded me again that life is gift. Everything about the journey reminded me not only, "how silently the wondrous gift is given," but also and more importantly the journey reminded me that even when it seems there is no path at all, our presence and continued effort is important that we "may become the gift others need." I try to retain those words in my heart as I am touched by the efforts of those seeking to put everything back in the box. They too are pilgrims with me on the Camino of life.

CHAPTER 11

ACTS OF THE APOSTLES 2:46
*"'They devoted themselves to the apostle's teaching and
fellowship, to the breaking of the bread and the prayers."*

RETURN TO WHAT?

Dorothy, in *The Wizard of Oz,* was filled with a yearning to go home. To some degree our personal identity is rooted in our childhood home and we are programmed with a nostalgic yearning to go home. Perhaps that explains the yearning among some among us to return to yesterday. The inherent question in that yearning is, "Going back to what?" I was surprised and continue to be dismayed that Pope Benedict XVI recently extended permission for priests to set aside the liturgical reforms of Pope John's Council and resume using the Tridentine Mass.

The liturgical reform mandated by the II Vatican Council is about far more than externals. That reform called us back to the understanding and appreciation of Eucharist that formed and fired the earliest Christian communities. In his letter to the Church of Corinth, St. Paul reminded them,

As often as you eat this bread and drink this cup, you proclaim the death of the Lord until he comes. ..... For those who eat and drink without discerning the body, eat and drink judgment on themselves.

Paul was not taking about discerning the body of Jesus in the bread; his reference is to the Body of Christ into which those participating in the Lord's Supper have been transformed. "People who meet as Church are essentially different from people who gather to watch a football game."[1]

Through our history of two thousand years, various aspects of the liturgy were emphasized over others. Those in the earliest periods gathered to celebrate the presence of Christ in and among them were aware of their own identity as the Living Body of Christ. In later periods, all awareness of Christ present in the community was diminished or disregarded. This shift hindered the transformation of the world.

I am disappointed with the pope's announcement allowing the Tridentine Mass. His desire to mollify some Catholics who never accepted John's Council is noble. Unfortunately for many others his announcement diminishes, disregards, or eliminates the possibility of them awakening to their own identity as the Living Body of Christ.

We who were ordained priest prior to the Second Vatican Council were trained in abstract theological concepts and laws. There was little fresh or stimulating in our courses of study. For fear of Vatican reprisal, biblical, liturgical and catechetical research and study was done behind closed doors and we were never given the keys.

Orthodox Jewish religious thinking is rooted in the conviction that God acts in human history. The earliest Hebrews did not speak of resurrection life. However there is in their tradition a discernible movement toward the idea of resurrection life. In their earliest teaching the Hebrew people had no developed concept of life beyond death. They simply accepted that the dead go to an undifferentiated, shadowy place below the Earth called Sheol. It is sort of a storage house of the dead.

We see early in their sacred texts, the gradual development of what the Hebrew people later believed about death and life after death. The earliest indications of such a development appeared eight centuries before Christ in the prophet Hosea. Hosea expressed hope for life after death when he invited his peers,

Come, let us return to Yahweh. He has torn us to pieces, but he will heal us; he has struck us down, but he will bring us back to life; after two days he will revive us; on the third day he will raise us up and we shall live in his presence.[2]

Today we hear Hosea's metaphorical language through the lenses of the Risen Christ. We adopt his description of the hoped for restoration of the Hebrew people as a description of resurrection life.

In the sixth century BCE, the apocalyptic author Daniel was more explicit than his predecessors. He was convinced that,

When that time comes your own people will be spared, all those whose names are found written in the Book. Of those who lie sleeping in the dust of the earth, many will awake, some to everlasting life, some to shame and everlasting disgrace.[3]

Centuries later the unjust suffering of good people of faith led to a further shift in Jewish theology. It was in the second century BCE that the family known as the Macabees refused to abandon their heritage and religious convictions and were cruelly tortured and subjected to violent deaths. They expressed the then emerging Jewish belief that resurrection was something that would happen to all God's people at the end time.

At the time of Jesus, some Jews rejected the notion of life beyond death. Others in the Jewish community were beginning to believe in the possibility of resurrection.

The fundamental, bedrock conviction, because of which we are Church is that Jesus of Nazareth was crucified, died and was raised up to new life. Some of his companions claimed they encountered him after his death. We do not know what they saw. We do not know what experience they had. They testify that they had some glimpse of human life far beyond any previous experience.

All they could say was they understood something new about human life and they had derived this understanding from their experience of it being lived by Jesus after his death. "They were not stressing they had seen Jesus' body as something merely physical, but their testimony is they had met Jesus himself."[4] They were convinced. He is alive! It is because of this conviction that we live in the manner we do.

I think these reflections on resurrection life are fundamental to the question expressed as the title of this chapter. The resurrection of Christ and our hope in resurrection are so significant and essential to the meaning of liturgy that we cannot ignore that mystery in our discussion.

We who were ordained before the Second Vatican Council were trained to say Mass according to the ritual of the Tridentine Liturgy. It was called Tridentine because it was a reform of the liturgy instigated by the Council of Trent and issued by Pope Pius V in 1570. The Tridentine Mass was characterized by two major concepts. First, it mirrored the Jewish Temple practices of offering the blood of animals sacrificed on the altar in atonement for sin. Second, it transformed Eucharist into an object of veneration by stressing the real, permanent presence of Christ in the bread and wine. The rubrics of the Tridentine Mass contained minute details to be observed by the priest. These rubrics were designed to assure that the un-bloody sacrifice of the cross is offered properly and that the bread and wine are consecrated properly.

These two characteristics explain why the Mass was essentially the work of the priest. He was trained, and stood apart and above the people, separated from them by the communion rail. The altar was situated facing the wall, more like a shelf than a meal table. The priest faced the wall and recited the prayers in a low tone of voice in Latin, a language unknown by most.

The primary role of the congregation was passive. They were to kneel in adoration looking at the host and/or chalice when elevated above the priest's head. That was considered the central moment of the Mass. The bells rang signaling the moment of transubstantiation. That was the moment when The Son of God was present in the bread and wine. Genuflections were introduced in imitation of what one did before kings or princes. We genuflected to Jesus, the King of kings. It seemed obvious to me that ringing the bells also served the practical purpose of telling people to wake up and pay attention.

The few who received communion came forward and knelt at the rail. The priest was the only one whose hands could touch the consecrated host. He stood before each person, spoke a rapid formula in Latin, and placed the sacrament on the tongue. Communion under the form of wine was reserved exclusively to the ordained. After returning to their pew, the faithful knelt and covered their face with their hands, supposedly to commune privately with Jesus.

All of this together created the myth that priests are holier than the baptized and of course bishops holier than priests. This also mirrored the Jewish Temple practice of identifying those who were pure and those who were impure. It was exclusionary rather than welcoming.

The non-ordained submitted to this theology. They never disputed it but apparently never really believed it in any way that related to real life. I began to realize this almost immediately after my ordination. Most pastors and parishioners were unconcerned with the rubrics. Good men were considered good pastors if they were efficient in saying Mass. It was not uncommon for priests to say Mass in twenty minutes or less. Students today label that a microwave Mass. In those first years after ordination I was more than surprised when some folks were upset with me because of the "manner in which you say Mass!" "You are too slow!" We were expected to pray, in Latin, swiftly! It is a fact that no one could say all of the Latin words correctly and make all of the gestures and motions called for by the rubrics in less than thirty minutes. The rubrics of the Tridentine Mass required the washing of hands, a variety of blessings, multiple signs of the cross, hands extended over bread and wine, elevations of the sacrament, genuflections, index finger and thumb held together, hands properly extended during prayer and many other gestures. Put everything back into the box? Return to what?

Following the Council, among the theological experts who came to our diocese was Father Godfrey Diekmann, O.S.B. His insights about liturgy as celebration of the Paschal Mystery jolted me away from the theology of the cross that characterized the Tridentine Mass. He was emphatic that liturgy celebrates the death-resurrection of Christ. This highly respected scholar of patristic studies and liturgy made it abundantly clear that our oldest traditions affirm that the Church is the Living Body of Christ! He laboriously explained that,

Every baptized Christian is an active, co-responsible member of the body having a distinctive contribution to make. Vatican II became the Magna Carta of the laity, the basis of active participation in the liturgy and in the great social movements of the time.[5]

He was insistent that liturgy is truly Catholic liturgy when, and only when the assembled community recognize, realize and respond as the Living Body of Christ. Then the liturgy changes us, transforms us into the Living Body of Christ.

An associate professor of theology at the Washington Theological Union said it this way:

According to the "Constitution on the Sacred Liturgy" (1963), the entire celebration of the Eucharist, rather than only the words of institution, is an expression of the Eucharistic faith of the Church. And so, we can say that the deep pattern of the celebration of the Eucharist, the Liturgy of the Word, Eucharistic Prayer and participation in Bread and Cup is a text in action that is both a model of what we believe and a model for what we believe and its ethical implications.[6]

Put everything back in the box? Go back to what? From my perspective and experience, the church is far healthier today because we realize the entire community acts as celebrant of the liturgy. Even priests are healthier when they realize that "they exercise their distinctive role as a member of the community, rather than as a person who stands between the community and God."[7]

Under the mantle of the Tridentine Mass, the catechism of my youth and my theological training were negative and individualistic. Both emphasized sin and the suffering and the death of Jesus on the cross. The theology of the cross was central. The spirituality derived from that

141

theology was about sacrifice offered to atone for our sins. We forgot that the Risen Christ and the new life we share in him are the heart and core of our faith.

Yes, Jesus of Nazareth suffered and died a violent death. Many people have! But God raised Jesus from the dead and that makes all the difference! The resurrection is not simply one doctrine among others in the creed. The resurrection is the core and central message of Christianity from which all flows and upon which all depends. We believe that God raised Jesus from the dead and that makes all the difference! Without the resurrection his crucifixion would have been forgotten, as were the crucifixions of so many others killed by the Romans.

There are many nominal Catholics, nominal Christians in our world. They speak the words of the creed without comprehension. They sit with arms crossed as the scriptures are read. They kneel around the Table with a passive face. Their bodily posture and gestures are non-verbal indicators they are determined to remain untouched by the Risen Christ among us.

As I previously mentioned, backpacking in the high mountains is an exhilarating experience, at least when all goes well. Those who have enjoyed backpacking know the importance of finding dry wood, especially when the ground is wet or it is raining or cold. A small gas stove is adequate for the preparation of food and clean water. When it is cold, only a wood fire can provide the needed warmth to cold hands and feet. Dry wood ignites quickly and burns well. It is almost impossible to call fire out of wood that is wet. Wet wood is an image of the human heart saturated with concerns, worries, ambitions or distractions. The fire of God's Spirit cannot ignite fire in such a heart as it does in the hearts of those who actively engage in Eucharist. We who gather around the Table of Eucharist are offered a fire whose blaze could spread from us outward. It could leap from the Table awakening hearts to love, justice, and peace.

To be Catholic means to live out the implications of our baptism. When we experience the Risen One as a real presence, we learn to recognize him in one another. Such experience liberates us from our false self and awakens something within us we did not know was there. It enables us to live by a higher law, the law of love. When Christ lives in us, we find ourselves able to love, even those we perceive as enemy.

The bishops in the II Vatican Council allowed the Risen One to guide them. The evidence of this is in the vision they set before us. They remind us that liturgy "is the summit toward which the activity of the Church is directed; and the fountain from which all her power flows."[8]

Church is an extensive worldwide community. We need rubrics to help us maintain our union with one another and to enable us to know we are home whenever and wherever we gather around the Table. The rubrics provide a pathway or markers to guide us so that wherever celebrated, our liturgical experience reawakens us, unites us and confirms our conviction that we are the living body of Christ.

We need rubrics so we never forget St. Paul's reminder to the community in Corinth,

The blessing-cup, which we bless, is it not a sharing in the blood of Christ; and the loaf of bread which we break, is it not a sharing in the body of Christ? And as there is one loaf, so we, although there are many of us, are one single body, for we all share in the one loaf.[9]

In those words St. Paul sets before us the primordial rubric. All other rubrics exist for the sole purpose of enabling us to realize this first rubric. All who gather at the Table of Eucharist, priest and people, gather to share the Lord's Supper. The rubrics exist to assure we do that with intention.

It may have been apparent to many of you in my generation there were serious leaks in the ceiling and the plumbing of our old mansion that were being ignored. I have been trying to describe our situation in the preceding paragraphs by asking the question, return to what?

Perhaps Benedict XVI and the bishops are not rushing us forward into the past. Perhaps we are simply experiencing the backlash created because many basic elements of renewal called for by the Council were ignored and are still being ignored today. All of us realize our young people are absent from our Sunday Assemblies. So too are many others. It does little good to lament their absence. Their absence tells us something about how we are church. It is important that we seek to understand their absence. There is still time for us to make necessary repairs. While the bishops are trying to do so, it seems to me they would do better by challenging us to implement the vision of the Council instead of abandoning that vision.

On the road to Emmaus, two of his disciples encountered the Risen Christ. "Their eyes were kept from recognizing him." The two invited this fascinating stranger

To stay with us. ... So he went in to stay with them. When he was

*at table with them, he took bread, blessed and broke it, and gave
it to them. Their eyes were opened and they recognized him.*
They returned to Jerusalem and reported their experience to the eleven
and their companions, saying "how he had been made known to them in
the breaking of the bread."[10]

Ever since, we have recognized Christ in the breaking of the bread
and in the cup shared. Eucharist is so simple. Bread is placed on the
Table. A cup of wine is placed on the Table. The community gathered
invokes the Holy Spirit to transform these into the sacrament presence
of the Risen Christ. The one Bread is broken and shared. The one Cup
is poured and shared. In this way the sacrament clearly expresses our
common life in Christ who is present in us, among us, with us. Then we,
the Living Body of Christ, are sent into the world to continue his work.

Within easy walking distance of my current residence there are four
small bakeries and two supermarkets. All of them offer an enormous
variety of freshly baked, tasty, nutritious breads. One of the smaller
bakeries offers a slice of fresh bread free to everyone who walks in the
door. It is not unusual to find dozens of high school students stopping
there for a slice of hot bread at lunchtime or after school adjourns each
day. They would never associate this good bread with Eucharist. Recently
I heard a very pastoral bishop say the aroma of freshly baked bread
reminded him of Eucharist. I wish it could be so. Perhaps he is using an
unauthorized recipe! Such good wholesome bread is available today. We
ought to use the best available. Most of our communities don't.

One day a priest friend said to me in all sincerity, "I have no trouble
believing in the real presence. I do have trouble believing this is real
bread!" He was referring to the hosts commonly placed on the Table of
Eucharist in most parishes. At least he intuitively recognized those hosts
are simply inadequate signs or symbols of Eucharist.

Recently a married couple and several older university students
shared a meal around the table in my residence. Both husband and wife
are members of the university faculty. She is Unitarian and her husband
is a long-time member of the Catholic Alumni Association. (That is
code language for non-practicing.) They told us their adopted daughter
was invited to a gathering with friends who are part of an established
alternative form of Catholic community. Her parents presume Mass was
celebrated during that gathering. When their young daughter returned
home they encouraged her to share the experience with them. She
reported that among the activities she had been given a sip of wine and

a cracker! Apparently they use some form of hosts. When real bread is broken and shared, it is never misjudged to be a cracker.

Several years ago I was privileged to celebrate Mass with a large community of Haitian people in a parish in New Jersey. The church was large and the community warm and welcoming. The scripture inspired songs engaged all of us. The amplifying system was excellent and those proclaiming the scriptures did so with conviction. It was truly a celebration of faith. After the sign of peace, the deacon poured from the one cup into smaller cups as I was breaking the one very large host. As I did so I heard snap, snap, snap audible above the voices singing Lamb of God. It was distracting at least to me.

Some parish communities have been persistent in trying to use real bread for the sacrament. The currently mandated recipes for baking bread to be placed on the Eucharist Table overshadow the efforts of those communities. The product of those mandated recipes generally are rubbery, pasty and tasteless. It simply fails to provide an authentic sign or symbol of Eucharist.

When I was ordained in 1961, on behalf of our family, my parents, younger brother and grandmother presented me a gracefully designed chalice. It is a piece of art crafted by Brom Silversmiths in Utrecht, Holland. It is large enough to provide the sacrament for a sizeable community. I treasure it even more now since those family members have died. When celebrating liturgy, that chalice is a visible connection with my parents, brother and grandmother.

Although that chalice has such importance for me, I seldom use it. At the time of my ordination, our Eucharistic theology was expressed in an exaggerated emphasis on the divinity of Christ. No one questioned the mandates requiring that all the vessels used in the Mass were to be made of silver and/or gold. The Eucharistic theology recovered by the Council restored our understanding of the Mass as a meal in which we, the Living Body of Christ, are nourished in his life. As communion under the form of both bread and wine became our accepted custom, we also turned to the use of more practical vessels like pottery or glass. Such vessels also are works of art and suitable for the purpose of holding the sacrament.

Apparently there is a directive somewhere either suggesting or requiring once again that the vessels used in the liturgy be made of gold or silver. There is another directive that the wine be poured into the small communion cups prior to the words of institution. This practice of pouring the wine in advance seems to be spreading. The result is a multiplication of cups and plates on the Eucharist Table rather than the strong symbolism of one cup and one loaf. Of course this immediately diminishes the effectiveness of the outward sign of the sacrament. It also eliminates the purpose for the prayer known as the Lamb of God that is sung while the sacrament is broken and the cup poured in preparation for communion.

As I said above, the celebration of Eucharist is so simple. Bread is placed on the Table. A cup of wine is placed on the Table. The community gathered invokes the Holy Spirit to transform these into the sacrament presence of the Risen Christ. The one Bread is broken and shared. The one Cup is poured and shared. In this way the sacrament clearly expresses our common life in Christ who is present in us, among us, with us.

Symbols communicate without words. A clear message is given when one loaf of bread is broken and shared. A clear message is given when one cup of wine is poured and shared. A clear message is given when everyone present eats of that one loaf and drinks from the one cup.

There are highly skilled potters whose artistic skill enables them to create large cups capable of being poured into smaller cups for sharing the sacrament. When parish communities use one large cup, the unity of all gathered is expressed as the Sacrament in one cup is poured into smaller cups to be shared by all.

These elements of this sacrament are able to communicate a powerful positive message about our common life shared as the Living Body of Christ. They can so easily become a negative message. When you invite people for dinner and conversation, you spend time preparing a wonderful meal. Guests arrive and together you enjoy telling stories. Eventually you set the wonderful foods on the table. You would not think of serving leftovers from the refrigerator. It amazes me that today, in spite of direct and repeated directions from the Vatican, there is one rubric generally ignored more than any other. That rubric is clear. The Sacrament shared in communion during the liturgy is to be from the bread broken and the wine poured in that celebration. Today in almost all parish liturgies the practice persists of bringing the Blessed Sacrament reserved in the tabernacle to the Table for distribution. Without intending any irreverence, that is a subtle message that negates the meaning of one cup and one loaf, the one life of Christ shared with us.

146

Food and drink are essential to our physical life. Adequate nourishment keeps us healthy. Food and drink that is not nourishing or that is improperly cared for will make us ill. The food and drink we consume become part of our physical body. We are what we eat and drink. This is why we are careful about what we consume. In spite of the abundance and variety of food available to us, we are part of a fast food generation accustomed to cafeteria-style meals. Many students come to the University with little or no established habits of sharing family meals. University dining services provide well-prepared and nutritious food but most students eat and run and many even eat alone. That is a growing concern about family life.

During my first weeks as pastor of Christ the King I recognized and realized that one of the simplest ways to contact university students and establish relationships with them was to invite them to my residence for meals. This provided them an experience of sharing meals with others, and of establishing friendships with other students and with me. Most young people have never been invited to the home of a Catholic priest for anything, especially not for a meal. Some students were hesitant to accept the invitation. Those who did found the dinner table a safe place to ask questions and share challenges with their peers, faculty or members of the parish community.

"Eating is one of the most basic functions of every living being."[11] Eating common meals is one of the most characteristic expressions of what it is to be human. As we grow in our ability to share food and drink with family and friends, we also begin to grasp the potential of eating as a theological metaphor. This sort of experience prepares us to gather at the Table of Eucharist.

Having students in my home for meals reminds me of life in my childhood home. I remember time spent together in our kitchen preparing food. The preparation was as important as sharing the meal around the table. I habitually asked students to join me in the kitchen and to assist in preparing the food. This helped create an atmosphere of home. With eight to twelve of us seated around the table, we laughed a lot and someone inevitably led us into serious conversations about faith, Catholic traditions or personal concerns and needs. Everything that happened in these meals had Eucharistic implications.

We understand Eucharist only by sharing food with others. We learn to participate in liturgy by sharing around the dining room table. It saddened me that some students never came to Sunday Mass because they felt like strangers and feared being alone in the one place safe community is available to them. Often, after sharing a meal in my home, some began to gather with us for Sunday Eucharist.

These meals were a core and essential ministry of my twenty-two years as the pastor of Christ the King and director of Catholic Campus Ministry. Food and drink shared becomes part of our bodies while connecting and bonding those of us who share meals. Such sharing leads us to appreciate Eucharist as a meal in which the Holy Spirit transforms us into the Living Body of Christ. The manner in which we gather and interact, the environment, the music and especially the bread and wine placed on the table contribute to that transformation.

"Take and eat. This is my body." Christ is present in the form of bread. "Take and drink. This is the cup of my blood." Christ is present in the form of wine. The symbol is strong. All of us eating of the one bread and drinking of the one cup are the Living Body of Christ. The oldest testimony to this fundamental conviction of our faith is the comment of St. Augustine about those who gather in our Sunday Assemblies.

We who eat and drink the sacrament of Christ's life become that which we eat and drink. We eat and drink the body and blood of Christ. That is what we become.[12]

By the simple word "amen" we affirm with absolute certainly that yes, this is the body of Christ; yes, this is the blood of Christ; and yes, we who eat and drink at the Table of Eucharist are the Living Body of Christ!

When the one loaf is broken and the one cup is poured, it more readily communicates to us that it is the Risen One who welcomes all to eat and drink the sacrament of his life. When we finally begin to celebrate the Eucharistic meal as the Council has summoned us to do, there will be no need for anyone to put everything back in the box, and no one will be asking, "return to what?"

CHAPTER 12

GENESIS 1: 1-2
"In the beginning when God created the heavens and the earth,
the earth was formless and void
and darkness covered the face of the deep."

CREATION EVER NEW

I treasure opportunities to sit with friends around a campfire under a sky filled with brilliant stars, or in a local pub sharing a glass of local brew. By telling our stories to one another we reveal who we are. Earlier in these pages I told a story that reveals a lot about me. I described an incident in a local Ace hardware story. The clerk was being helpful and accommodating. He opened a box thinking it might be the sort of gift for which I was searching. It was not. He then attempted to put the item and its packaging back into the box. In chapter four I offered that incident as a metaphor of what is happening in the Catholic Church today.

Our ancestors in faith tell us that "in the beginning darkness covered the deep."[1] There is so much about this cosmos we do not know. My Celtic ancestors believed there is a thin veil separating us from reality beyond our reality and moments when that veil parts allowing a glimpse of that Gracious Mystery we name God. The Greek word *kairo*s names such moments. Blessing or curse, we live in such a moment.

The II Vatican Council was a *kairos* moment. By instigating the process of spiritual renewal, the Second Vatican Council opened a box containing the Christ mystery and the gospel values and ideals that are the essence of living the Christ life. These are the treasured item in the box. Opening the box meant removing all the contents, all the traditions that formed the sub-culture through which we established, maintained and expressed our identity as Catholic people. That Catholic sub-culture

149

may be likened to the various protective packing materials surrounding the treasured item in the box.

That which we have known as the Catholic sub-culture served us well, but Pope John recognized it was dying. The death of a sub-culture does not imply the death of the mystery embodied in it. The core of our faith is the Christ mystery. That core will not die for it is the mystery of God's engagement with all of us in the human family.

Look and listen to the voices around us. When I did so in recent years, I found myself embarrassed by the name Christian. The name has been corrupted. It originally applied to people who embraced the way of the Risen Christ. Christians were those who made his value system their own. In doing so they found themselves out of sync with the value system of the dominant culture in which they lived.

In recent years some loudly claiming the name Christian were aligned with the dominant ideology of our culture. There is a letter on my desk from a highly educated professor asserting that because of fundamentalist Christians, he will no longer refer to himself as a Christian. He is disturbed that Matthew's Sermon on the Mount has been replaced by "a pro-rich, pro-war and pro-American ideology." It is his conviction that such ideology underlies much of the discord and increasing divisions within our Catholic household of faith. Too often the name Christian came to signify a value system that contradicts and is opposed to the life, the teaching and the way of Christ. In our nation at least, the word Christian became supercharged with overtones of fundamentalism, nationalism and militarism. This has been obvious for many years in other countries where political parties claim the name Christian and engage in all sorts of activity that contradict the gospel. Today in the United States, it is common to hear that name invoked by folks who justify war and capital punishment or policies that favor the wealthy and disregard or even victimize the poor and the marginalized. When I feel embarrassed by how the name Christian is used, it is because the meaning of the word has changed, not me.

Aggiornamento is not a call to compromise the gospel. It is a call to live the gospel and to design and develop new packing materials in which to express the values of the gospel. Our faith cannot be expressed or shared with others unless we develop a new cultural expression that is relevant to the times in which we live.

Every day, every one of us responds to the various pressures and influences that impact our living. We do that unconsciously but always to the best of our ability. That is exactly what Pope John was asking of we who are the church.

As I indicated earlier there were some during the Council determined to keep everything in the box. Today others persist in that determination. These are good folk who treasure our faith heritage as we do. They want to retain the old sub-culture we named Catholic and pass it on to new generations. Not every Catholic watches Mother Angelica and WETN-TV. Those who do watch that channel receive encouragement to maintain the sub-culture that has become irrelevant to the lived experience of so many.

Now that we are a distance from the Council, there are many who never heard of, have forgotten, or simply choose to ignore the wisdom of John XXIII. He reassured us that our faith tradition is ancient and the core of our faith does not change. At the same time he was emphatic that we must infuse our faith with new vitality and find new ways of presenting it. The metaphor of the box helps me to understand the tremendous pressures and conflicts within our household of faith today.

Our transition from one sub-culture to a new one is a *kairos* moment. Our privilege is to create new ways to incarnate the gospel and church in this emerging age of high technology. While enormous and challenging, the task is both opportunity and privilege.

During the past forty years, we have been developing new ways to speak about Christ and to proclaim the gospel in ways the dominant culture can understand. The process has been random and lacking in clear direction. As old customs and practices became less meaningful and relevant to the world in which we are living, many of us simply adjusted those customs and practices to create meaning and relevance for today.

Transitions always involve risk. That became very clear to me throughout the years since my ordination. Prior to the Council our faith tradition was like a vacuum-sealed package. The Creed contained all one needed to know to be a good Catholic, or so we claimed. Doubts were to be treated as bad temptations. Questions were discouraged. I understand why it was so. The Catholic sub-culture into which my generation was born and lived was rooted in the authentic personal faith of our parents and pastors.

However the images we received from our ancestors in faith have been shattered or at least are challenged by the new cosmology, quantum physics, psychology, biology and scripture studies. As one scholar notes,

> *We are living through a major period of change in science, a paradigm shift from the idea of nature as inanimate and mechanical to a new understanding of nature as organic and alive.*[2]

Our ability and willingness to engage in the process of transition requires that we be responsive to this paradigm shift.

Like our parents and pastors before us, we need well-defined and clear images of who Jesus is. This requires that we develop and be able to articulate clearly just what we mean when we affirm that Jesus is the Son of God. His life, death and resurrection are important only to the degree that each of us acquires a clear understanding and conviction of why they are important.

After his selection, the newly elected Superior General of the Society of Jesus addressed his Jesuit brothers saying, "I have a feeling, still imprecise and difficult to define, that there is something important in our religious life that needs attention and is not getting it."[3] His words reveal his sensitivity to the uneasiness that is so pervasive in our society and church. His words invite us to recognize "an important factor in the perception of people that should drive us to some deeper reflection"[4] about the gospel and what it means for us to be church today. In his address to his Jesuit brothers, Father Adolfo Nicolas, S.J., did not speak directly about a new Catholic sub-culture. Yet it seems to me that is exactly what he is describing when he refers to that "important factor in the perception of the people that needs and is not getting attention."[5] The old is dead or dying. We are in transition to the new.

After ordination I, like the other young priests in our diocese, was assigned to teach religion classes in our Catholic high schools. Over a period of eight years I taught in four of our Catholic high schools. That was in the nineteen-sixties. Students had questions and were not satisfied with canned answers. Soon their questions were my own. It swiftly became clear that I had to find satisfactory answers for myself, if I was to help students discover answers that satisfied them.

It was probably in the third year after ordination that I had my first personal experience of continuing education. A priest friend and I attended a workshop at Gonzaga University in Spokane. Father Bernard Haring was a moral theologian, an expert at the Council, and clearly a holy man. His reflections and comments on Paul's *Letter to the Ephesians* were fresh and relevant. As we sat listening to him and entering into conversation with him, the texts of our sacred scriptures began to make sense to me for the first time in my life.

That marked the beginning of my own transition and effort to understand and appropriate our faith tradition into my own lived experience. That meant asking questions. It was unsettling to do so then. It remains unsettling today. Questions are inevitable as new information and knowledge raise new doubts and open new doors of possibility. Responding to questions and doubts always feels risky because once allowed to begin, the process is like a whirlpool that draws us ever more deeply into itself. There is always the lurking fear that all the familiar and secure will evaporate.

It is easy to understand why people who choose to remain at whatever level of faith development they reached in their childhood or adolescent years resist the Council's vision and call to renewal. After passing through their adolescence, many people do not want to question and think. Conformity is valued over conscience. Once the transition process began for me, it gradually became clear that some of our local diocesan bishops had little or no patience for innovation of any sort. One sought my compliance assuring me that if I cooperated I would someday be named a bishop. He seemed quite shocked when I told him I was totally satisfied with being a parish priest and had no ambition or desire to be anything else, least of all a bishop. Then that bishop attempted to gain my compliance through threats of various sorts. For a time I really thought he would remove my faculties to minister in our diocese. His threats became so troublesome that eventually I scheduled an appointment with a local psychiatrist asking him to evaluate my mental health. His reassurance strengthened me to maintain my personal integrity.

Because there are risks involved in any transition, it is quite natural for people to resist change. So often folks respond in a negative manner because they feel the clear identity markers that provide security are being disturbed or challenged. Any and all efforts to bring forth a new Catholic/Christian culture involve such risks and the task is challenging. Talking about those risks may help to alleviate and significantly reduce the perceived threat.

The experience of hiking in the wilderness of western Montana is exhilarating. There is little that compares with the silence broken by the chatter of birds, and the peaks rising up higher than the trees, and cold mountain lakes emptying into sparkling streams. A few times in my life my companions and I experienced nature's beauty turn threatening. When that happens it is not comfortable. I suspect it is even more unsettling for those who climb rock cliffs when they are forced to let go of familiar handholds as they seek to climb higher. We who are Church are in a somewhat similar situation today. As we struggle to design and develop new packing materials in which to express the values of the gospel, our images of God and of Jesus will mature. Our faith, our trust in God, directs us to let go of and set aside our uncertainties, our discomfort and our fears.

Twin wars in Afghanistan and Iraq, and the swiftly mushrooming economic mess bequeathed to us by President George Bush's administration have drained our emotional and spiritual lives. These obscure the massive transformations taking place within the human family. Most of us go about our day-to-day business oblivious to the magnitude of the change. We are caught in the vortex of a major evolutionary transition within the human family and being drawn into something entirely new. If at times it feels challenging, even threatening, remember that is because this transition is filled with new possibility. Pope John XXIII seemed to anticipate this awakening of a new human consciousness. He foresaw the need for a new spirituality and a new level of faith.

The II Vatican Council is still in its early stage of development. The agenda of that Council planted seeds in our hearts and imaginations. These seeds have lain dormant within us for several decades. I hope that you and I are among those who will persist in the challenge of nurturing those seeds until they blossom. Among the most significant of those seeds is our developing awareness of the mystery we name God. Today the image of God embraced by most folks is amorphous and poorly defined.

The island of Molokai is the least developed of the Hawaiian Islands. It is the island where the Belgium priest Father Damien gave his life ministering to people suffering from Hansen's disease. Prior to the twentieth century no cure for that disease was known. Victims were banished to Kalaupapa Peninsula on the island of Molokai, abandoned and left isolated to care for themselves. The black lava peninsula sits at the base of magnificent green cliffs rising up three thousand feet from the blue waters of the Pacific. It offered no possibility of escape.

Since reading about Father Damien as a child, there has been a lingering desire in my heart to visit that site. When the opportunity finally arose I chose to walk the three-mile trail down the face of the cliffs. The steep trail is rocky, rough and zigzags through tropical greenery until reaching the black sand beach of Kalaupapa. There a rickety old bus waited for about twenty-plus folks who rode down the trail on mules or walked as several of us did. The visit to the sites where Father Damien and others lived and cared for the residents reminded me of what being church is about.

The two-hour plus climb back up the cliffs on a hot, muggy afternoon provided opportunity for me to know a couple from Portland, Oregon. Debra and Steve were enjoyable companions. Later that evening we shared a burger, fries and a beer in a local restaurant. They knew I am a Catholic priest and of course the inevitable happened. Shortly after joining me at the table, they initiated a conversation about institutional religion, spirituality and God. I never had to ask do you believe in God? Debra very clearly does, although her husband's conviction was less apparent. Our conversation never led us to discuss our images or concepts of God. That was unnecessary. The bottom line and the only real issue when discussing the mystery of God is the degree to which one's belief in God makes a difference in the way we live, how we build our social life and how we express our relationship to the created world in which we live. It was clear to me, that the image Debra was expressing when she spoke the word "God" had a strong positive influence upon my newly discovered friend.

"Theos" (Greek), "Deus" (Latin), "Allah" (Arabic) and "God" (English) are simply words. They refer to the divine, the ultimate ground of our being, the ultimate reality beyond and behind this material world in which we live.

The faith of our brothers and sisters in the Orthodox tradition and of Eastern rite Catholics is grounded in what is called apophatic theology. They affirm, as we Roman Catholics do, that the Gracious Mystery we name God has made God's-self known to us. They also affirm we are capable of receiving the gift of God's Spirit. At the same time they emphasize that God "is so radically unknowable that ordinary language and concepts fail utterly to get at"[6] God's reality. Their method helped me clarify my own image of God by clarifying what God is not. God is not an object, not an abstraction, not some sort of supernatural being, in addition to reality, as we know it. My image of God is no longer the image of one who rewards or punishes us.

The Anglican Bishop and scripture scholar Thomas Wright put a slightly different spin on the same idea. He put it this way. "Speaking of God in anything like the Christian sense is like staring into the sun. It's dazzling." Our personal faith can be real and meaningful only when we clarify what our image of what God is like. It is inadequate simply to repeat what we received from others. We want and need our images of God and of Jesus to be authentic for ourselves and congruent with the worldview out of which we live every day. Otherwise those images sort of drift out there apart from our thinking, judging and acting.

The word God awakens ideas and emotions and these produce my image of "God." Many years ago, in a source I no longer remember, the theologian Langdon Gilkey expressed the classical image of God in these words:

The word or symbol 'God' referred to one, supreme, or holy being, the unity of ultimate reality and ultimate goodness. So conceived, God is believed to have created the entire universe, to rule over it, and to intend to bring it to its fulfillment or realization, to save.[7]

This image of God as separate and apart from us is "supernatural theism." It is an image that still resonates with many of us today. We image God as a human-like male; a Supreme Being presiding far above the clouds; or the heavenly judge who will reward or punish us. This image is both misleading and inadequate.

The science fiction author Arthur Clarke captivates me in ways both entertaining and stimulating. About fifteen years ago I was reading the final book in a series he titled *Rama*. I finished it near midnight and found myself filled with inner turmoil. His description of this vast cosmos we inhabit was so overwhelming that my image of God seemed shattered. As I crawled into bed I feared I could not continue in active ministry as a Catholic priest. A refreshing night's sleep cleared my confusion. My old images of God were shattered, but his ideas opened me to a far more realistic appreciation of this mystery we simply cannot know. Clearly "no human words, no human formulas, and no human religious systems will ever capture that reality."[8]

A similar paradigm shift is occurring for many as we move on into this twenty-first century. For many folks the well-defined and clear images of God commonly accepted by my generation have been shattered or challenged by modern science. Some find that disturbing. This paradigm shift in our understanding of the cosmos in which we live calls us to a radically different imaging of the ultimate mystery we name

God. Study. Discuss. Contemplate. Pray. In the process we discover God in new and unexpected ways.

God and Jesus are separate and distinct, yet often are blended into one. There is historical and theological reason for this. Our Catholic tradition affirms Jesus of Nazareth is both fully human and fully divine. Our tradition is unable to explain or clarify what that statement means. So people speak of Jesus as God.

In his classic study of God, Rudolph Otto spoke of the divine or the presence at the core of all experience as The Holy, or in his more poetic words, as "a mystery at once awesome and attractive."[9] The Jesuit theologian Karl Rahner simply refers to the Gracious Mystery we name God. That speaks to me. Mystery implies inability to know or to comprehend the source and presence "in whom we live and move and have our being."[10] God is around and within us and yet far beyond our ability to comprehend or express. God "is so radically different from the world, so wholly other, that human beings can never form an adequate idea nor arrive at total possession."[11] This is why we must repeatedly and continuously seek to clarify our God image. In the journey of faith there always is the danger of falling into overtones of magic. Magic captivates us, promises to open locked doors, to provide explanations, and some sense of control and assurance. Unfortunately magic has sometimes infiltrated our Catholic culture. Once that happens folks refuse to let go of the magical to the detriment of their own faith.

In any liturgical gathering in any church on any Sunday there are a wide variety of images with which people conceive of God. Certainly a poll among us would produce interesting and surprising results. Our images overlap and intermingle with the images put forth by the institutional church. As you read this try to clarify your own God image. These few abbreviated ideas may be helpful as you do so.

I mentioned above the very common God image is that of "supernatural theism." Another common image is "pantheism." Pantheism is identifies God with the world, and the world with God. The identification of God and world eliminates the otherness of God. It is my understanding that the theory of pantheism is characteristic of the Hindu tradition and other traditions derived from Hinduism. It also was an image "popular in the ancient Greek and Roman worlds of the first century"[12] Pantheism perceives a spark of the divine in all of us and in everything that exists. This includes trees, mosquitoes, horse flies, spiders, rocks, tsunamis, and so on. If God and the material world are the same, and everything is God, then God is the source of evil and evil is part of God. It is difficult to believe that the yellowjacket that just stung me is divine.

"Deism" is another common way of imaging God. Deists see us occupying this small rock named Earth, spinning in the vast darkness and immensity of the cosmos. They conclude that,

God is a far-off, detached being, perhaps responsible in some sense or other for the creation of the world, but he – or perhaps one should say 'it' – is basically remote, inaccessible, certainly not involved with the day-to-day life, let alone the day-to-day pain, of the world as it now is.[13]

Our Catholic tradition differs distinctly from supernatural theism, pantheism and deism. Some are comfortable describing our tradition as "panentheism." Scholars may disagree but it seems to me this is the image of God contained in the beautiful poetry of Gerard Manley Hopkins. "The world is charged with the grandeur of God."[14] It is our belief there is only one God who is present to and actively engaged with creation but separate from creation. God is the creative energy expressed in the evolving cosmos. The cosmos is sustained by, yet always distinct and separate from God. We Catholic people view creation with sacrament-conditioned eyes. We see God in nature, but nature is not God. We see God in other human beings, but human beings are not God. Both the yellowjacket that stings, and we who are stung, exist in and are sustained by God. Neither we, nor the yellowjacket are God.

Jesus of Nazareth employed the word Father in speaking of the divine. My biological father always stood out as a model and inspiration in my life. There was never a moment's doubt that he loved me and cared about me. His presence throughout my life was consistent. Because of that strong relationship with my father, it has always been natural, comfortable and meaningful for me to name God Father. That is not true for all people. Many today are unable to know or speak of God as Father and find other words to express the mystery. It is important for them to do so and for us to understand and respect their sincerity and faith. Because Jesus spoke of God as Father, our tradition eventually used the word person to give expression to our image of God. The word person is anthropomorphic and inadequate to express the reality of God. Yet the word conveys so much of what is important to me. In spite of it's limitations, I continue using the word because it is an implicit statement that the divine is not some sort of static being. God is self-giving love that creates and sustains; a presence within the depths of all that is; the life force and the energy within and beyond the cosmos; the love in all, with all and through us all. Father Karl Rahner helped me by referring to God as Gracious Mystery. Gracious means living, dynamic, generous, loving, absolute fullness of life and all the wonderful and good qualities and attributes summarized in the word person.

My experience and personal understanding of God today is vastly different from my experience of God as an adolescent or even while still an active pastor. As my life experience has changed and continues to change, it is quite logical that my descriptions of God also change and continue to change. Our faith journey is rooted in the historical person we name the Christ. It is in and through Christ that we know God as Gracious Mystery. Understanding God in this way frees me from any feeling that it is necessary to put everything back in the box.

CHAPTER 13

MARK 10:17
"Good Teacher, what must I do to inherit eternal life?"

GURU or SON OF MAN

In Mark's gospel a rich young man came to Jesus searching for a guru in the spiritual life. He was looking for an expert who would tell him infallibly what he must do to gain eternal life. Remember, this young man is rich but unsatisfied. His inner longing for meaning and for happiness leaves him restless. He is a first century Jew, which means he is not asking about life after death. For him, eternal life means a full life, a successful life here in this world. He is in search of a reliable guide, an expert in goodness who is able and willing to tell or show him how to silence his inner longing for happiness and satisfaction.

The gospel writer tells us that Jesus looked at the rich young man and loved him. He also saw behind or beyond his question and refuses to be a guru. He says there is only one who is good. He is referring to God whom we do not see. Only God is good! No other ought to be elevated to the level of expert in goodness.

The request of that young man represents a fundamental longing in most of us. On the surface we want to know exactly what we must do to be happy and satisfied. That is normal, especially in a time of social uncertainty as is typical in any period of transition. Employment separates families and requires frequent movement. This splinters and fragments our communities and creates a general social turbulence. It is common in the culture of North America for people to look for an expert, a guru who will resolve the stress produced by that social mobility. A recent poll indicates that fifty percent or more of our population in this country go church shopping. That is not surprising in a culture built on consumerism.

In their search for a church most folks are looking for a guru but

161

not a church that will challenge them to imitate Christ or inspire them to place their life into God's hands. Most are looking for authentic community. In the fragmented society in which we live, folks need a home in which they are welcome. This basically is what Twelve-step programs offer to those struggling to recover from addictions. All of us hunger for community in which we are known, loved and supported.

Four documents provide our primary source of information about Jesus of Nazareth. They are the written gospels of Matthew, Mark, Luke and John. Each tell the story of Jesus but no one of them claims to be an historical account of his life in the manner we understand history today. They are expressions of the oral tradition passed among the early Christian communities. That tradition developed because their experience assured them that Christ was raised up by God and continues to be alive!

In those years before the gospels were written, the core of that oral tradition was recorded in the letters, attributed to St. Paul, to various Christian communities. He repeatedly speaks of the Mystery of Christ. For Paul the reality of the Risen Christ is so much greater than the historical Jesus. Paul's primary message was the fact of Christ's resurrection. In his first letter he seeks to assure the church in Corinth that his teaching is reliable. "The tradition I handed on to you in the first place, a tradition which I had myself received. . . "[1] He continues,

That Christ died for our sins in accordance with the scriptures, and that he was buried and that he was raised on the third day in accordance with the scriptures, and that he appeared to Cephas, then to the twelve. Then he appeared to more than five hundred brothers and sisters at one time, most of whom are still alive, though some have died. Then he appeared to James, then to all the apostles.[2]

Paul also wanted those early communities to understand and appreciate the implications of Christ's resurrection for them and their own personal history. To the church in Ephesus he wrote, "God has put all things under Christ's feet, and made him, as he is above all things, the head of the Church."[3] He is telling them the Risen One is the head and they are the Living Body. He wrote to the community in Colossae about Christ as,

The image of the unseen God. ... In him were created all things in heaven and on earth, everything visible and everything invisible, thrones, ruling forces, sovereignties, powers – all things were

created through him and for him. He exists before all things and in him all things hold together. He is the beginning, the first born from the dead, so that he should be supreme in every way; because God wanted all fullness to be found in him and through him to reconcile all things to him, everything in heaven and everything on earth, by making peace through his death on the cross.[4]

Paul's soul was filled with a passionate yearning to help those early communities appreciate the Mystery of Christ. In chapter fifteen of his first letter to the Church in Corinth, he makes this connection. "Christ has been raised from the dead ... so all will be made alive in Christ."[5] In chapter eight of his letter to the Church in Rome, he writes,

... you live not by your natural inclinations, but by the Spirit, since the Spirit of God has made a home in you ... When Christ is in you, ...the spirit is alive ...; and if the Spirit of God who raised Jesus from the dead has made his home in you, then he who raised Christ Jesus from the dead will give life to your own mortal bodies through his Spirit living in you.[6]

In the *Letter to The Philippians,* the author inserted a great Christological song. He introduces that song to his readers with the simple challenge, "Make your own the mind of Christ Jesus."[7] With this simple admonition, "make your own the mind of Christ Jesus," he is stating that the significance of Jesus is determined by the degree and manner of his influence on their development as human beings.

For several decades after the resurrection, the initial companions of Jesus of Nazareth struggled to appropriate some positive meaning for his humiliation on the cross. As those initial companions told others that God had raised from him the dead, more and more people were attracted to Jesus and to his teaching. Those who eventually joined the movement grew in their conviction that he is the Christ, the center of all things. They spoke of him as the vine, the light, the energy, and the life that flows through us. They became more and more convinced that he is the one through whom all of us have access to God. They then and we now affirm that in him we are given a limited glimpse of what God is like.

Eventually, over several decades, the oral traditions were collected in four distinct written gospels. They share a significant amount of common material. However each gospel was written for a specific community. Each presents an account in a manner suited for the needs of their community. While they are rooted in actual events and the teaching of Jesus as remembered in those communities, they,

Were put into their present forms by second (or even third) generation authors. ..... The gospels are the church's memories of the historical Jesus transformed by the community's experience and reflection in the decades after Easter.[8]

Study the four gospels carefully and you quickly realize that Jesus of Nazareth neither said nor did anything indicating he expects to be the center of our attention. He neither sought nor expected our admiration or worship. He consistently pointed away from himself to that Gracious Mystery we name God. He never in any way was about getting us to praise him. He never spoke about saving our souls. He was about bringing God's new creation into being. "He did not want to die on the Cross and he never thought to declare inhumanity and torture to be signs of a true trust in God."[9] This Jesus is the one we affirm is both fully human and fully divine.

When questioned about paying taxes, Jesus said to the crowd, "give to Caesar what is Caesar's, but give to God what is God's."[10] The four evangelists set the Risen Christ before us as one who directs our allegiance to God before and above all others. Giving allegiance to someone means allowing them full and complete access to my heart and life. Full and complete means such allegiance cannot be divided. The current Caesar, whoever it may be, always embodies power and violence. The God made known to us in Jesus is love and nonviolence. Yes, we ought to pay taxes. Yes, we ought to vote. In doing so we always remember that our primary allegiance cannot be given both to God and to Caesar. Only one can be primary. The implications are serious and significant.

Throughout the several centuries in which the early church was emerging, our ancestors in the faith engaged in serious debates about the nature and status of Jesus. Some insisted he was divine and only seemed to be human. Others insisted he was human and not divine. Eventually, the letter to the Philippians gave directions to the early fathers of the church as they struggled to settle those debates and clarify the nature and status of Jesus. The conclusion, now embedded in our Creeds, was that Jesus of Nazareth is both fully human and fully divine. This creedal statement puzzles many of us and confuses others. In spite of that confusion this statement is part of our inherited tradition. So we struggle with the meaning of that text as we seek to identify a well-defined and clear image of who and what Jesus is for us.

The Jesus image that folks embrace is important. Most assume their image of Jesus accurately reflects the historical person who lived in first-century Palestine. At the very best, our image of Jesus will always be tentatively accurate. We simply do not have access to detailed information about the historical Jesus. The degree and/or manner in which our image of Jesus influences or does not influence my personal life is the real issue.

If our image of Jesus is to have any validity it is important that it be rooted in and reflect the tradition contained in the written gospels. I readily affirm and continue to live my own life out of the conviction that in Jesus from Nazareth in Galilee, God has chosen to reveal God's self to us. The tradition of our Catholic household of faith is clear. I affirm our creedal statement that he is both fully human and fully divine. This creedal statement is in harmony with the authors of the New Testament. Having said that, I caution you. Beware that debating, discussing, and even preaching about the nature and status of Jesus as divine does not distract you from the task of imitating him. It is so easy to reduce our faith to an intellectual enterprise while our hearts and lives remain unaffected. So rather than attempting to analyze, categorize and understand what it means to affirm that Jesus is both fully human and fully divine, it seems far more important that we concern ourselves about the injunction in the *Letter to the Philippians* and imitate Christ by thinking, judging and acting in ways that are congruent with the gospel.

So in your effort to clarify your own image of Jesus, be mindful of how your image affects you and the manner in which you live. I think this obviously means focusing entirely and exclusively on the humanity of Jesus. His humanity was not simply a mask put on by God for a brief moment in the unfolding of the cosmos. Jesus, a Jew from Nazareth, was fully human as we are. Keeping the humanity of Jesus as your focus does not deny the creedal statement that he is fully divine. It simply does not engage it.

As in our struggle to clarify our image of God, identifying an authentic image of Jesus also requires serious discipline in study, discussion and prayer. During my years of ministry to students at the University of Montana, I often recommended books for them to read. They and we all need guidance and direction in our effort to clarify our image of Christ. Among books that seemed extremely helpful to students is a small volume by the Dominican priest, Albert Nolan. The title, *Jesus Before Christianity,* suggests the importance of trying to discern the historical person around whom our doctrines and dogmas formed. My reason for recommending this book is summarized in the author's observation:

When one allows Jesus to speak for himself and when one tries to understand him without any preconceived ideas and within the context of his own times, what begins to emerge is a man of extraordinary independence, immense courage and unparalleled authenticity, a man whose insight defies explanation. To deprive this man of his humanity is to deprive him of his greatness.[11]

I appreciate an illustration used by N. T. Wright in discussing the various images of Jesus. I referred to it in Chapter Twelve:

Speaking of Jesus is like staring into the sun. It's dazzling. It's easier, actually, to look away from the sun itself and to enjoy the fact that, once it's well and truly risen, you can see everything else clearly.[12]

I borrow his idea here and twist it a slight bit and offer it to you in identifying your own image of Jesus. Try to do this in harmony with both the New Testament and our creedal affirmation that Jesus was fully human and fully divine. Instead of staring into those creedal statements, turn away from them and consider the struggle in which all of us engage as we try to understand Jesus of Nazareth.

In my youth we were taught, and I believed, that by rising from the dead Jesus proved he is God. That is what I tried to teach during the early years of my life as a parish priest. I would never speak that way today. A careful reading of New Testament texts makes it clear that Jesus did not raise himself from the dead. Jesus, fully human, was fully dead. His companions had no doubt about this. His lifeless body was in a tomb as were the bodies of all who die. The scripture texts tell us that Gracious Mystery we name God raised Jesus of Nazareth from death. I find it helpful in forming my own image of Jesus to ask a simple question. It is this. Why did God raise Jesus of Nazareth from death? In developing my answer the following ideas have been helpful to me.

In the book of Genesis we are told that God created us in goodness with freedom of choice. We are free to love or to be cruel to one another and we do both. The book of Genesis suggests some guidance in our effort to develop our understanding of why we do evil things by describing a conversation between a talking snake and a human. The snake makes a promise. If you ignore the divine prohibition and warning, "you will be like gods, knowing good and evil."[13] The humans eat the forbidden fruit, and the serpent's promise is fulfilled. They sense their nakedness, feel shame and realize death will claim them. This suggests we humans are responsible for the cruelty and violence in our world.

If that is so, and I think it is, I find it helpful to consider the implications of evolution. Perhaps the evil we do is simply the result of our genetic instincts. Survival and reproduction are strong animal and human instincts. Some scholars suggest the Genesis story is a primitive way of describing the emergence of human consciousness. Since the beginning, prior to our awakening or becoming human, humans died. Prior to our conscious awakening, we didn't know that we die! Once our knowledge awakened, our instincts for survival and reproduction became stronger than ever before and pushed our humanness aside. As a consequence we do whatever is required to protect our own life, family or friend.

Our primitive instincts entice and move us to seek success, status or power. We can name the evil that results. Names like Antietam, Shiloh, Pearl Harbor, Dresden, Auschwitz, Hiroshima, Vietnam and Baghdad are familiar to us. We know the inhumanity, the cruelty and the evil represented by those names. For me it seems reasonable to conclude that all the evil we see in our culture, as well as the violence that murdered Jesus, can be linked with primitive instincts for survival and reproduction. The church's obsession with sexual morality may be an intuitive recognition of this.

Matthew, Mark and Luke tell us that Jesus went into the desert and fasted. He was alone, hungry and weakened. He experienced a testing of his humanity and of his fidelity to God. He is confronted with a choice. Those deeply rooted primitive instincts were as strong in him as they are in us. He could submit to them choosing success, status and power or he could sublimate them into service for those who are alone, hungry and weak. He made his choice and apparently that choice set the direction for his public life, his ministry among the people, and his final confrontation with evil at Calvary. In making this choice he was the first of us to set those instincts aside without reservation and the first of us to be fully human.

Jesus turned away from and sublimated those primitive instincts and thereby became the prototype of what it means to be fully human. As St. Paul seems to have understood, Jesus is the model for us to imitate. We are to become Christ. For the remainder of his life we see in him an absolute trust in God. In story after story we see a man who is so fully human and fully alive that he respects the dignity of every human person.

167

Even in the most serious confrontations between himself and the various religious leaders his response is always nonviolent and loving. When they engage him in discussions designed to discredit and embarrass him, his response is nonviolent. When they threaten to stone the woman accused of adultery, his response is nonviolent. When he confronts and discharges the moneychangers and merchants in the Temple, he does so in a nonviolent manner.

Finally we see the fullness of his humanity in the passion narratives of the four gospels. From the moment of his arrest in the Garden of Gethsemane he is subjected to violence and his response is nonviolent.

One of the followers of Jesus grasped his sword and drew it; he struck the high priests' servant and cut off his ear. Jesus then said, 'Put your sword back, for all who draw the sword will die by the sword.[14]

When his adversaries verbally abuse him, degrade him and speak falsely about him, his response is nonviolent. Matthew tells us simply that, "Jesus was silent."[15] They physically abuse him, nail him to the cross and expose his broken body to public view. Luke tells us his response is nonviolent. "Father, forgive them; they do not know what they are doing."[16] Caesar could not provoke him to violence even by subjecting him to cruel torture and a murderous death.

I am suggesting our primitive instincts of survival and reproduction are at the base of all human violence. They are the residue of our origin and our condition prior to that evolutionary moment in which God breathed the human spirit into us. At that moment we became something much more than those other living beings that still are guided and controlled by their primitive instincts. We humans became a new species capable of embracing a life of nonviolence and unconditional love. These strong base instincts remain within us but need not control us, or how we think, speak or act.

Read Matthew's account of what is commonly referred to as the Sermon on the Mount. That text is Matthew's agenda for imitating Christ. It is a roadmap guiding and directing us in our vocation to become fully human beings. An encyclopedia could be compiled defining and explaining what that means. Most of us intuitively recognize that it means being free of all that hinders our ability to love others. It is being able to live without barriers of any sort in harmony and union with people, the natural world and with God.

Imitating Christ, following the way of Jesus is the major challenge.

It has been my experience that in every conversation about imitating Christ, at least one person will interrupt the discussion with the same observation. "Jesus was God. We are just human. We cannot be expected to forgive our enemy or to love those who harm us!" It is so easy to excuse oneself from thinking and acting as Jesus did, and/or as he taught us to do. Simply recall that he is fully divine. Then logic compels the conclusion that it is impossible to think and act as he did or taught us to do. He is God and we are not. That really confuses the reality of Jesus and the meaning of the gospel.

I return to the question, "why did God raise Jesus of Nazareth from death?" The answer that makes sense to me is this. In Jesus we see what it is to be fully human. The written gospels tell us Jesus referred to himself as the Son of Man. By borrowing that phrase from the prophets Daniel and Ezekiel and applying it to himself as his own self-identification, Jesus claims that he is "The Human Being," the prototype, and the model of what it means to be a human being. Jesus is the first human being to become fully human, to live fully in harmony with God's creative will and purpose. God raised Jesus from death as an affirmation of all that Jesus embodied in himself.

In the various communities with whom I gather, I encourage people to consider the gospel as God's invitation for us to become fully human. As I mentioned earlier, people raise objections to that idea. Apparently some are conditioned to think there is something negative about being fully human simply because we still carry some basic primitive instincts within us. Survival and reproduction are fundamental and essential instincts in all of us. Neither is intrinsically bad or evil. Neither is the emotion of anger. We contain within us the genetic patterns of those from whom we evolved. The goal of becoming fully human engages us in the task of submitting our basic animal instincts to our higher capability of love. Study of the gospels from that perspective has convinced me, that the call to be more fully human is the core of both the life and teaching of Jesus of Nazareth.

I wrote this chapter hoping to encourage you to examine and clarify your own image of Jesus. I offer a final word about the Mystery of Christ within the context of our contemporary cosmology. Our small blue planet Earth is like a speck of dust in the galaxy we name the Milky Way. This galaxy is but one galaxy of millions. We still are probing to discover the extent of this cosmos which has been evolving for fifteen billion years. Modern science is helping us understand that everything that exists is inter-related, inter-connected and inter-dependent. This is the mystery hidden from ages past, now being discovered by modern science. I think the mystery made known to us in Christ is the very same as that shown to us by modern science.

The human DNA genetic code is unique and differentiates us from all other beings in creation. Consider what is happening as more and more of us become what Christ is, and embrace his way of unconditional, nonviolent love. God's new creation about which Jesus consistently spoke is being realized in and among us. As more and more of us are taken into the Christ Mystery we think, judge and act as he did. In the process we become more fully human and this mystery we name salvation or redemption becomes conspicuous in our world. In Christ we have been given a new DNA. We are a new creation. Yes, We Are! The Living Body of Christ.

CHAPTER 14

THE LETTER TO THE ROMANS 8:16
"The Spirit himself joins with our spirit
to bear witness that we are children of God."

CHILDREN OF GOD

We believe the final three days in the life of Jesus of Nazareth had cosmic significance. In our Catholic household of faith we celebrate those three days liturgically on Thursday, Friday and Saturday nights of Holy Week. It was my resolve to suspend writing and devote these days to prayer and reflection. Work on this manuscript would wait until post-Easter. Two events overcame my resolve because both left me frustrated.

I concelebrated the Roman Catholic liturgy of Holy Thursday. On Good Friday I joined our local ecumenical Good Friday service. The two experiences dampened my yearning to enter into the mystery celebrated liturgically. In both the Catholic liturgy and the ecumenical service, the words spoken irritated my soul. The content and vocabulary of both were negative.

Late on Good Friday morning, fresh snow fell upon us. It was cold when we began our simple, silent walk along the river. We were small in number from various Christian communities in town. We took turns carrying a large wooden cross. Our walk was interspersed with scripture readings, prayer and silence. We concluded in the downtown Methodist Church. The television evangelists are certainly not the sole distributors of a theology of sin and sinfulness. Preachers repeatedly tell us that Jesus came to save us from sin. Protestant and Catholic stand shoulder-to-shoulder repeating the same message. Last night, the Catholic liturgy and again today the ecumenical service both were punctuated with reminders that we are sinners whom Jesus came to save.

Pre-conciliar manuals of theology contained lengthy, complex treatises about sin. This was considered essential in preparing students

171

for ordination and the responsibility of forgiving sin in the sacrament we then called penance or confession. Catholic tradition teaches that original sin is inherited, not committed. In our theology manuals, the nature of original sin was distinguished and described as a category separate from the concept of personal sin.

I found two quotations among my notes with no indication of source or author. I share them here because I think each speaks significant truths that need to be considered in our continuous struggle to understand evil. The first describes a conversation between an old Cherokee and his grandson about the battle that goes on inside people. The old Cherokee said,

> *My son, the battle is between two 'wolves' inside us all. One is evil. It is anger, envy, jealousy, sorrow, regret, greed, arrogance, self-pity, guilt, resentment, inferiority, lies, false pride, superiority, and ego. The other is good. It is joy, peace, love, hope, serenity, humility, kindness, benevolence, empathy, generosity, truth, compassion and faith." The grandson thought about it for a minute and then asked his grandfather: "Which wolf wins?" The old Cherokee simply replied, "The one you feed.[1]*

We all engage in that battle on a daily basis: evil or good, death or life.

The other quotation does not attempt to explain evil but simply expresses the reality and problem of evil.

> *The Central American country of Guatemala endured a thirty year civil war which left more than two hundred thousand people killed or disappeared. The years of terror and the hundreds of massacres, perpetrated in great part by the military and their death squads, left a blanket of deafening silence over the people. Rarely did anyone speak the truth of what had really happened, for to speak the truth was to nominate oneself to appear on the next death list. It was a strangulating silence, which, with a few heroic exceptions, only began to be broken after the signing of the Peace Accords in 1996.[2]*

Most of us would agree that moral evil is the result of choices made by individuals or social conglomerates. That is the story of the book of Genesis. In the fifth century, St. Augustine, as many before him and we today, struggled to understand evil. He developed the concept of original sin. That doctrine is his response to that long shadow originating somehow in our ancient genes.

In our personal living one choice leads to another choice and to another and so on. It is impossible to foresee the consequences inherent in that initial choice. Had they been foreseen at the start, the original choice or decision may have been deferred or never made. Human choices seem to accumulate a sort of primal force greater than the original choice could conceive. Individual choices set events in motion. Eventually the magnitude of the events requires some sort of bureaucratic institutions to manage them. Then as money, power and energy multiply and accumulate, those institutions assume an independent life with their own momentum and unanticipated consequences. They shape and mold us with a power of their own.

The theologian Walter Wink, in his stimulating work on *The Powers,* coined or popularized the phrase "the dominant culture" to identify the institutional milieu in which we live. For me that phrase has become a meaningful identifier for my experience of institutions that exercise influence and control over us. The phrase seems to fit nicely when speaking about our nation as well as about the institution we call the Catholic Church.

The dominant culture has its own agenda and its own idea of what is real and what is of value. Its influence is obvious and apparent in our decisions of how we ought to behave in various social environments. The dominant culture influences how we dress, the sort of car we drive or house we live in and the lists go on.

Jesus of Nazareth lived within the dominant culture of his time but called his peers and us to a new reality beyond the dominant culture. He named that new reality the Kingdom or Reign of God. That new reality is not the church. The church exists to promote that new reality.

Originally we create institutions to promote the common good. Institutions require management. As they grow and age they tend to become highly impersonal. Perhaps they forget the original decision or purpose for which they were created. When that occurs it is easy for some form of systemic evil to develop. The terror and massacre that drained the life-blood of two hundred thousand Guatemalan peasants is an example of such systemic evil. The examples are many.

In their dissertations about sin, our pre-Counciliar manuals of theology contained lengthy, complex definitions, descriptions and examples trying to clarify the nature of sin. Those manuals never presented a simple, precise definition of sin. They devoted pages making distinctions between mortal sin, venial sin, internal sin, and external sin. In many ways such distinctions are helpful in developing a conscience capable of making informed moral decisions. Yet the basic word sin continued to be ambiguous.

In the Hebrew Bible sin was anything that was considered unclean and therefore offensive to God. Early Hebrew tradition equated sin and ritual impurity. Ritual impurity was anything that excluded a person from the Temple. Christian theological concepts were influenced by the Hebrew tradition. The significance if not the practice of many Hebrew temple practices and regulations were woven into the Christian Bible obscuring and distorting the significance of the life, death and resurrection of Jesus.

Peter J. Gomes was the pastor of The Memorial Church at Harvard when he wrote *The Good Book*. In a few pages of that book he provides some great ideas that helped me sort out and disengage the tightly woven connection between the gospel and sin. He wrote the following:

There is good news, and that is why they call it the gospel. The news is not that we are worse than we think, it is that we are better than we think, and better than we deserve to be. Why? Because at the very bottom of the whole enterprise is the indisputable fact that we are created, made, formed, invented, patented in the image of goodness itself. That is what it means, that is how one translates being created in the image of God: It means to be created in the image of goodness itself. We are cast from a perfect die and the imprint is on us, and it cannot be evaded or avoided. God made us, male and female, in the image of goodness, and goodness itself is who and what we are, and God pronounced it good, and hence it is good, because as the kid in the ghetto said, 'God don't make no junk.' What God makes is good.[3]

A few pages later he adds,

To be created in the image of God means that we are in some sense a picture of God. There is that of God in us, there is that of God in the poor and destitute of the world; in them there is something of God. Sin is when that something, that image is distorted or denied or deprived or twisted.[4]

In our churches today, the words sin and/or sinners are used so often and in so many contexts that are vague. I suspect most folks cannot define the word in any clear manner. Certainly sin is more than culturally unacceptable sexual behavior, abortion, bad language or missing Mass. These are symptoms of sin.

174

In the written gospels, the word sin seems to apply to those attitudes and behaviors that lessen one's own humanity or that of others. In whatever way the Gracious Creator brought us human beings into existence, we exist as and are called to become fully human. At the most basic level sin means missing the mark. Jesus is the only one among us who is fully and completely human. He renounced all and everything that diminishes our humanness. Read Matthew's Sermon on the Mount. It is clear that Jesus calls us to embrace our humanness without reservation. It seems to me the Ten Commandments do the same on a less sophisticated level. Reading the gospels through this sort of lens led me to insert the word violence whenever the biblical text uses the word sin. Try it and you may be amazed how well that fits. It certainly is in harmony with the overall context of Christ's teaching and his response to people.

Violent behavior of any sort toward self or another misses the mark. For most of us, hopefully for all of us within the Catholic household of faith, it is obvious that anyone who engages in or is responsible for the torture or killing of others, or other similar behavior, is missing the mark. They are being less than human. The Creator's gift of goodness still resides in such individuals but their personal choices thwart that goodness, diminishing their own humanity.

In our day-to-day living most of us seldom achieve the ideal and day after day we settle for the possible. Even so we are and remain children, sons and daughters of God. That is the good news we are commissioned to bring into our world.

On Good Friday, sitting in the Methodist church, listening to a local pastor whom I respect and admire in many ways, as he repeated the word sin over and over, the large stained glass window behind the sanctuary diverted my attention. The window reminded me of the significance of the Middle Ages, a period whose theology reflected the lived experience of the church at that time. Medieval art was extraordinary and the magnificent cathedrals with stained glass and sculpture provided visual lessons in the biblical story and doctrine. Through such strong visual imagery the theology of the middle ages imprisoned our minds and restricted our imaginations.

It was in that period that St. Anselm developed his theory of atonement theology. He proposed that sin damaged God's honor. The death of Jesus was the necessary recompense for that injury. Anselm ignored the resurrection and emphasized the suffering and death of Jesus as the active cause of salvation. His theory continues to capture the imagination of Christians today. It shapes and molds our images of Jesus, and our understanding of the life and teaching of Jesus, far more than the written gospels.

Anselm's theory of atonement affirms that we are sinners in need of redemption. Today such vocabulary saturates most preaching and prayer. Yet the images and language of atonement theology seem to have little or no influence upon our actions or behavior.

This week in both the Catholic liturgy of Holy Thursday and the ecumenical Good Friday service the words sin and sinners were repeated many times. We washed the feet of others, knelt and kissed the cross, perhaps feeling that we are responsible for the death of Jesus on the cross. Then we walk back into our city and nothing changes. As I write this, the few reliable non-government sources available to us continue to report the massive violence of our two wars in Afghanistan and Iraq. We have created and continue to create enormously dehumanizing situations. Our national debt balloons and basic human needs are ignored and neglected.

If sin means to miss the mark, then surely we are doing that when we dehumanize others in any way and treat them as less than images of God. Perhaps it is time for us to break free of the medieval mind-sets that keep us from proclaiming good news. Church exists to proclaim the good news that we are better than we think; to awaken us to what it means to be fully human and to inspire and support us in our struggle to be like Christ, fully human and free to help others be human.

The gospel is good news. Consider just the eighth chapter of the *Letter to the Romans*. In this text St. Paul reminded the church in Rome,

All who are led by the Spirit of God are children of God. For you did not receive a spirit of slavery to fall back into fear, but you have received a spirit of adoption. When we cry, "Abba! Father!" it is that very Spirit bearing witness within our spirit that we are children of God, and if children then heirs, heirs of God and joint heirs with Christ. In fact, we suffer with him so that we may also be glorified with him.[5]

We ignore this text in our Catholic rites for baptism. The Roman Sacramentary has a sin mentality. Paul is emphatic. Yet we simply ignore his reminder that, "All who are led by the Spirit of God are children of God." His words point to our deepest truth. He admonishes us to be mindful that we are children of God.

Among the great theologians of the Second Vatican Council, Father Karl Rahner was one of the most significant. He provided us new insights and convictions that are in harmony with the Christian Bible and our own lived experience. He wrote, "it is not established historically beyond dispute whether the pre-resurrection Jesus ... interpreted his death as an expiatory sacrifice,"[6] and Rahner's theology offers us the direction to move away from the atonement theory of Anselm. As I understand Rahner's theological perspective, he is more in harmony with St. Thomas Aquinas arguing for our deepest truth as sons/daughters of God, made in the image of goodness itself.

The indications are subtle and may seem few, but the Council's call to renewal continues. Eventually the spiritual renewal of the church will blossom as we reclaim the gospel as good news. I found a major reminder of this several years ago when I visited Our Lady of the Angels Cathedral in Los Angeles. That cathedral is a proclamation of good news. It is an affirmation that we are the people of God, sons and daughters of God, the Living Body of Christ.

Many, including myself, were disturbed by the expense involved in the construction of that cathedral. It was a mega-million dollar project. Several years ago my cousin invited me to celebrate his wedding in southern California. Of course I accepted because of the privilege involved. Another of my cousins has struggled for many years with addictions. He has lived on the streets of Los Angeles and occasionally has been incarcerated. The occasion of this wedding provided me an opportunity to spend time with this wonderful young man. We took a ride touring the city and beaches of Los Angeles. Along the way I surprised myself when I suggested we go out of our way to see the new Cathedral. It had never been my desire to do so. Fortunately my young cousin agreed.

As we approached this massive building my expectations were low. Even as we climbed the stairs to the large plaza my expectations remained low. Then my astonishment grew as each step awakened a great appreciation of this complex. On the broad plaza many people were seated enjoying their lunch. Huge doors on each side of the plaza open into long corridors stretching along the sides of the cathedral. The light in the corridors is dim. Small chapels are set along the interior side of each corridor. These offer tasteful space for individual piety. One chapel remembers and honors the victims of AIDS!

At the end of the corridor, a right angle turns into the central nave.

My attention was drawn immediately to the holy pool of baptism. On the wall behind the pool hangs the first of the magnificent tapestries that accentuate the space. It is a face-view of John the Baptist pouring water over a kneeling Jesus whose back is to us. We took the waters of this pool and signed ourselves to remind us of our own baptism. The location of the pool is a strong reminder that we, sons and daughters of God, are the Living Body of Christ.

This cathedral is a modern building that truly is sacred space. There are no stained glass windows. Natural light filters through windows of white alabaster creating a warm ambiance. Turning from the holy pool we immediately felt drawn to the ambo and altar. The floor sloops gently forward. Gradually I realized I had joined a large company of others, all looking at ambo and altar. Massive tapestries drape the walls; each with a single human figure, all turned slightly facing forward. These are the holy people of God: Hebrew saints, Mary Magdalene, apostles, John XXIII, Dorothy Day, a migrant farm worker, and a variety of figures representing all of God's holy people, all of us. There is nothing about sin or sinners or sinfulness in this space. Here we are affirmed as children of God, the living Body of Christ gathering to celebrate and affirm our life and destiny.

We lingered and eventually joined several hundred people for a mid-day celebration of Eucharist. The interior space is immense. Yet even in this small assembly it was possible to realize the presence of the Risen One in and among us. I received communion and my "amen" was strong and intentional for I had experienced and was reaffirming that yes, we are the Living Body of Christ. I remain grateful that my young cousin was willing to stay and participate. He also was grateful for our shared experience and as we continued on our tour I think he was at least a slight bit more aware that in spite of his addictions he is made in the image of goodness itself.

CHAPTER 15

BOOK OF PROVERBS 29:18
"Without a vision the people perish."

PRAY FOR RAIN IN A TIME OF DROUGHT

Summer in western Montana can be a festival of sensual delight. The fireweed was brilliant as we began our climb to Mount Enias. It was a good summer for wild flowers. White daisies with their gold button and red paintbrushes draped the hillsides with wild glee. An abundance of huckleberries tempted us to stop, to conclude our hike right there and spend the morning picking and eating their small purple fruit. On another day high up on Lolo Pass, the camas flowers blanketed the mountain meadows and appeared from a distance, to be shimmering, blue mountain lakes. Earlier in July a group of us climbed Shining Mountain in western Montana. It is a beautiful symmetrical peak that points to the cloudless sky over the Nine Mile area west of Frenchtown. As we moved higher up the mountain, single file, up through the towering ponderosa, the beargrass stalks stood tall, their white delicate bulbs draped as if nodding in sleep. Each stands separate and alone, yet it is quickly apparent that they never grow independently. In the years in which they bloom, it is always in relationship with other stalks and the higher we climb, the more abundant they become.

When the winter snows are scarce and the summer rains inadequate, the hills and mountainsides of western Montana turn brown and our hearts fill with anxiety. It is justified. While far less intense in smoke in the summers since, memories of the fires in the summer of 2000 will hide in my heart for many years to come.

Ordinarily summer in western Montana means long days and short nights. July and August bless us with soft twilight and long gentle evenings. The days of summer 2000 were hot. The forests were dry and the rivers low. Smoke poured into our valley and our skies were darkened for weeks with smoke. On some days the streetlights came on at 5:00 p.m. The mountains were closed; no hiking, no backpacking. No fishing either for the water in our rivers was too low and too warm. Folks chose to stay indoors. The air was not fit for breathing.

As I write this, our drought continues, oppressively. With only a skiff of snow in town, more in the mountains, the ski areas suffer and the land grows in thirst. Our rivers have become more like creeks. Yet, like all that is beautiful, it is the variety that attracts. Montana remains this place of pristine wonder, like a prophet reminding us that God exists and Earth is precious.

Perhaps in summers like these recent ones, we are seeing the effects of global warming. Fires and drought remind me that the cosmos and this planet Earth are far more than lifeless resources for us to manipulate. Rocks, trees and water are not simply inanimate objects for us to consume or manipulate for our own personal needs. Perhaps we are beginning to realize we cannot simply extract oil and coal, cut down trees, pollute air and water, and go on our merry way shopping for items we don't need. The cosmos and this planet Earth are mystery and sacred for they reveal that Gracious Mystery we name God. When we see them as sacred we more readily see people as sacred, uniquely created, each loved by God and to be loved by us.

Perhaps you remember and value the wisdom in the Hebrew book of *Proverbs*, "without a vision the people perish."[1] A "vision is a picture of the future that produces passion."[2] The Bible recounts the stories of our ancestors. Those stories set a dream, a vision before us, especially the vision lived and spoken by Christ. It is a vision of what we are to be and how we are to live. In his studies about the dominant culture in which we live, Walter Wink observed,

> God uses visions to excite leaders because excited leaders get the most out of those who follow. The positive power of vision lies in its capacity to force us to face threats of unimaginable proportions.[3]

Visions galvanize efforts at self and social transcendence.

The institutions, systems and structures of the dominant culture that organize our society tend to block the Christ-vision and tempt us to remain less than human. We see this today in the complexity of our life experience. Enormous societal transformation, significant demographic changes and the influence of technology are reshaping Earth and Earth's inhabitants. No single person or group is capable of understanding the transformation occurring in our world. Those in political or ecclesial office are no better equipped to understand and respond to our situation than most of us. So it is of no benefit to blame anyone for our situation.

Unlike the dominant culture, we in the Catholic household of faith persist in our conviction that Christ planted a new vision in our brains and hearts. It still remains softly creeping into reality. The Christ mystery is universal, unconditional, nonviolent love. Christ refused to act like the wild beasts, or wild humans who launch missiles rather than love. The vision he spoke and lived is God's peaceable kingdom, first spoken among us by the Hebrew prophet Isaiah. God is intimately with us! God is in our every thought, desire and gesture! Nothing can stop us from becoming holy! It is possible for us to turn swords and missiles into plowshare and to plant crops of peace!

Those of us who welcome the Christ-vision are convinced that Jesus of Nazareth, and he alone, is the one human being who offers us life in ways no other has or is able to do. No other is as human as he. No other challenges us so clearly to struggle for justice and peace. No other in all of history, makes that Gracious Mystery we name God known to us as he does. Where there is no prophetic vision or revelation from God the people are cast adrift. Without a vision to inspire and direct us, folks inadvertently set aside all restraint and sooner or later no longer remain faithful to God's Word. Without a vision we too easily find ourselves wandering and confused.

In Chapter Thirteen I wrote about faith as the equivalent of the now popular, high tech Global Positioning Systems. As I said in that chapter, the life and teaching of Jesus of Nazareth has provided direction to my life. According to Mark's gospel, during the week preceding his arrest and murder, Jesus was asked "which is the first of all the commandments?" He replied,

> *Love the Lord your God with all your heart, with all your soul, with all your strength, and with all your mind. And the second is like it. Love your neighbor as yourself.*[4]

The written gospels all agree with Mark's. Many of us try to live out of the conviction that the Risen Christ is alive in all of us, and is continually revealed to us, generation after generation. His message for us today remains the same. Love God. Love neighbors. Love self. Love those perceived as enemy. His words, the vision he sets before us, are as vital and urgent today as they were when he stood among the people of Galilee. Love is the way to become fully human.

That vision of the transforming power of love is a precious gift. We are seekers and wanderers but with faith are able to find our way even in dense fog. More importantly we live with hope in a world where so many seem to wander with no direction. We are able to accomplish anything when we have a vision, a dream and a hope for which people yearn. "Without vision, the people perish." With vision, people discover the vitality that makes them creative and daring.

Our bishops know that something is wrong in the church and across our land as well. They recognize this but their response in recent years confirms the implied suggestion of a recent article in *Commonweal* magazine. The author is a strong advocate for the election of our bishops. He acknowledged that many of our current bishops seem aware of the challenges and negatives that confront us. Then he presented his reasons for asserting that few of them seem able to offer viable solutions to inspire us. In his opinion they seem unable to inspire us with a vision for our future because they are preoccupied with the task of rushing us forward into the past as swiftly as possible!

We have seen the return of legalism replacing compassionate pastoral ministry. We have seen the return of authoritarian decision-making replacing the positive spirit of collaboration that reflected the vision of Pope John XXIII. To ignore his vision as developed and set forth by the II Vatican Council only contributes to the problem. A relapse into dogmatism and a judgmental spirit that is exclusionary rather than welcoming only stifles both young and old.

Our bishops are not ordained to be administrators of property, fundraisers, or regional managers for a large multi-national corporation known as the Vatican. Many see these as their responsibilities and do them well. Bishops are not ordained to protect the home office and to communicate the latest directives to the field agents, clients and customers. Because so many of them perceive this as their role, they and we increasingly are lost in a fog of confusion and frustration. We need them to be pastoral leaders who are free of ambition, possessed of wisdom and the faith or the courage to trust the church, the people of God with whom they walk.

In his book *Tales of the Alhambra,* the well known author Washington Irving, shares wonderful stories learned during the years he lived in Moorish Spain. Among those stories I found *The Legend of The Three*

Beautiful Princesses:

In old times there reigned a Moorish king in Granada whose name was Mohammed, to which his subjects added the appellation of El Hayzari or the Left-handed. Some say he was so called on account of his being really more expert with his sinister than his dexter hand; others because he was prone to take everything by the wrong end or in other words to mar wherever he meddled. Certain it is either through misfortune or mismanagement, he was continually in trouble; thrice was he driven from his throne and on one occasion barely escaped to Africa with his life in the disguise of a fisherman. Still he was as brave as he was blundering and, though left handed, wielded his scimitar to such purpose that he each time re-established himself upon his throne by dint of hard fighting. Instead, however, of learning wisdom from adversity, he hardened his neck and stiffened his left arm in willfulness. The evils of a public nature which he thus brought upon himself and his kingdom may be learned by those who delve into the Arabian annals of Granada.[5]

Our bishops have a privileged podium from which to speak. This includes a responsibility to help us understand and respond to our circumstances. If the Christ vision grows weak among us, as seems to be our situation today, it is their task to keep the vision alive.

The Pastoral Constitution of the Church in the Modern World (*Gaudium et Spes*) is one of the most significant documents written by the II Vatican Council. This document tells us that we are responsible to read the signs of the times and to interpret them in the light of the gospel. Look around and it is clear that we need the inspiration and support of pastoral leaders able to help us keep the gospel, the vision of Christ alive. We need leaders able to open the Word of God for us. We need leaders able to apply the gospel to the real circumstances of our living. If the words spoken in our assemblies are shallow, empty or filled with cliches and repetitive condemnations, then the vision weakens. If we see folks still rushing to get out of the parking lot on Sunday morning, their behavior is a blunt judgment on our Sunday Assemblies.

There is nothing to be gained by pointing fingers or creating scapegoats. Yet it is obvious to anyone listening to priests, pastors and those in the pews that many of those appointed to leadership roles in the Roman Catholic Church seem ill prepared for their task. In his book *The Holy Web*, Father Cletus Wessels O.P. expresses a discontent that is heard ever more widely. He writes,

> *Leadership is a very significant dimension of any community with a major impact on its field. Leadership creates a certain "spirit" or way of functioning within the community that can use its memory to preserve and rigidify the community and frustrate the energy of the field in a climate of fear. Or leadership can use the memory and the energy of the community to adapt in new ways to its environment and to transcend its past in a new birth. There is a crisis of leadership in the Catholic Church today that is negatively affecting the life of the community.*[6]

We who love the church recognize that we are the Living Body of Christ. It is our responsibility to speak out and call upon our pastoral leaders to be with us in ways that assure we maintain the vision of the gospel.

Many, including myself, are not in the habit of quoting recent popes about matters of the internal life of the Catholic Church. There already is far too much emphasis placed on the words of the one chosen to be the Bishop of Rome. Yet the directness of Pope Benedict XVI in an address to the bishops of Switzerland was so startling it grabbed my attention.

He observed that by allowing the church to be drawn into too many discussions about such issues as abortion, contraception, the ordination of women, etc.,

> *We give the impression that we are moralists with a few somewhat antiquated convictions, and not even a hint of the true greatness of the faith appears.*[7]

The criticism he expressed during the first Mass he celebrated as the Bishop of Rome also was striking. He spoke of the growing experience of desert in our lives, especially within contemporary, western family life. He was not speaking about our life within the Catholic household of faith today, but certainly his words are applicable to us. He said,

> *There is the desert of poverty, the desert of hunger and thirst, the desert of abandonment, of loneliness, of destroyed love. There is the desert of God's darkness, the emptiness of souls no longer aware of their dignity or the goal of human life. The external deserts in the world are growing, because the internal deserts have become so vast.*[8]

Walk into any parish church for Sunday liturgy and the probability is you will encounter an internal desert.

Why U.S. Catholics Are Heading For The Exits is the title of a recent article in the *National Catholic Reporter*. The columnist observed, "The romance of religion, the sense of awe in the presence of the Divine is seldom evident, not in the liturgy, not in the sermon, not in the music, not even in the dress." She began the article referring to a recent Pew survey on religion. That survey found that,

Ten percent of American adults describe themselves as ex-Catholics. That is a very large number, over twenty million.... Anywhere from one-third to one-half of many fundamentalist congregations once belonged to the Catholic Church.[9]

There were two articles in recent issues of *Celebration* magazine that captured my attention. Gabe Huck authored the first. He was expressing sympathy for those in positions of ordained leadership when he wrote,

The bishops and various bureaucracies have not had such a good decade or two. Lots of wrong brought into the light. Lots of folks going elsewhere. The respect of outsiders gone. Lots of blaming. In such a time those who have authority grow afraid. Rules. Control.[10]

In that same journal, I could feel that Patrick Marrin was expressing his love and concern when he observes.

The dysfunctional, self-absorbed, conflicted church thwarts its own deep identity and critical mission. When leadership focuses on protecting its own privilege and power while matters of life and death for millions of people are not being credibly engaged, the mystery of Christ, the light of the world, is being hidden under a bushel, and darkness threatens to prevail.[11]

In a time of drought, pray for rain. My intention behind the words of this chapter is to encourage all who love the Catholic Church to persist in our common effort to hold and speak the vision that brings us together. It is insufficient to complain. All the issues concerning us are important and yet none are as important as the vision that brings us together and keeps us together. Many of our sisters and brothers hunger for ordinary food and thirst for clean water. They symbolize all of us who hunger and thirst for the good news embodied in Christ, and for a world characterized by justice and peace.

Writing these pages is my way of trying to do what I encourage you to do. In a time of drought, pray for rain. Rabbi Abraham Heschel was a man of great faith and wisdom. His counsel is so appropriate for us in our household of faith today. He said, "In a controversy, the instant we feel anger, we have already ceased striving for truth and have begun striving for ourselves."[12] Allowing ourselves to become angry is no solution. Each and all of us are able and need to find ways to join our voices. It is our responsibility to call upon our leaders with love. We need them to hold the Christ-vision before us and lead us in resolving issues that diminish the vision.

CHAPTER 16

LETTER TO THE CHURCH IN ROME 7: 15,19
"I do not understand my own actions. ...
For I do not do what I want, but I do the very thing I hate. ...
I do not do the good I want, but the evil I do not want is what I do."

IDEALS and POSSIBILITIES

It seems like only yesterday that my classmates and I lay prostrate on the floor of St. Helena Cathedral. We carried ideals within us. Our many years of education and training were now complete. The future lay on that floor with us and we had no way to recognize it. We rose up from that floor with hearts full of ideals. The years since have tested our ideals as we struggled to achieve the possibilities. In the process my life has been so much fuller and richer than anything my classmates and I may have assumed on that bright sunny day in May 1961.

For nearly five decades as an ordained Catholic priest, so many people touched and blest my life. They welcomed me into their hearts and homes with enormous love. When I recall and reflect on those years as a parish priest, I am filled with astonishment and a great joy floods my soul. The good memories are far more than these pages could contain. At the same time honesty also calls forth memories that are not so sweet. There were many instances when expectations of individuals or communities were beyond my ability to meet. Of course the opportunities to make mistakes were many, and too often, seeking the ideal, I made them.

My dearest friend tells a story of her cousin's son, Peter. He is the youngest of five siblings, born and raised by parents who were Catholic to their toenails. They actively participated in daily Mass throughout more than fifty years of marriage and welcomed the Council's call to renewal with enthusiasm. A work promotion moved them to a new state. They were early into church shopping as they sought out parishes that responded to the Council's vision.

Peter was the only one of their children to move with his parents to New Jersey. There he began and finished his life as a high school student. The Catholic school in which he was enrolled provided an excellent curriculum in contemporary theology.

The unexpected happened. With good will his teachers unintentionally left him with guilt feelings. He completed high school convinced he never could do enough to correct the wrongs of the world. Eventually he was attracted to and married a young woman who was not Catholic. She introduced him to a religious tradition rooted in the literal interpretation of the Bible. The certitudes of fundamentalism were attractive to him. They freed him of his guilt and he felt in control of his own life. He, his wife and their children continue in that tradition today.

In the first chapter of his gospel, John tells us that two disciples of John the Baptist came to Jesus with questions. He lived and taught ideals that attracted them. Jesus invited them, "Come and see."[1] That is an invitation spoken to all of us. And when we do set out to follow him, we discover that he was serious when he claimed, "I am the way, and the truth, and the life."[2] First his life and most emphatically in his teaching, Jesus of Nazareth set before us the ideal or the ideals we commonly refer to as the gospel.

The gospel challenges us in many ways to be more loving, more alive and more human. At times the challenge may seem over-powering. To maintain balance we need mutual support with and from others through dialogue and discussion. We can find that most readily within small communities of faith.

It was my privilege in the early nineteen-eighties to help a parish form small, faith-based communities. These communities were very successful. Some continue still nearly thirty years later. There is no obligation to accept the current structures of the church as normative and absolute. Many folks in our Catholic household of faith form such groupings on their own. If you are not engaged in some sort of small faith community, I encourage you to form one for your own sake, to support others, and to create support for continuing the spiritual renewal called for by John's Council.

It saddens me to acknowledge there probably are some whose life story is similar to Peter's because of my good intentions and inadequate sensitivity. I know of folks who were upset about, disliked or disagreed with something I said, or they thought I said, in a homily. They walked away from the parish without dialogue or discussion. My presumption is they heard a message and like the young man Peter, for whatever reason, concluded they simply couldn't do enough to correct the evils of our world. Then, moved by feelings of guilt, they walked away from the church.

Anyone who accepts ordination and the call to preach the gospel knows this sort of dilemma. Once called to preach, our task is to keep "the ideals" alive, to hold them before the community and to encourage all to embrace and live those ideals. Not all are able to do so. Some walk away.

In retrospect it is easy to be critical of myself. I am able to be critical while also reminding myself that in the ministry of preaching, I assiduously avoided using the word must or other imperative language. For example I never said anything like you must oppose the war in Iraq. The mistake I made was in my failure to acknowledge frequently enough that not everyone is able to achieve the ideal and that we still are okay if we don't. None of us ever live our ideals to the fullest. The gospel is important to us. Christ is our ideal and we don't abandon his vision simply because we are in the fog. As people of faith we persevere in our aspiration to live the ideals, even when the challenge seems too great and we settle for achieving the possible. Maybe reading this book will help you or someone else in the struggle.

Michael is a Dominican priest whose friendship I treasure. He is an excellent homilist. On one Sunday the gospel text led him to assure folks who are divorced and remarried that the Catholic Church remains their home. It is difficult to speak this in a public forum. We treasure the ideal that marriage is a permanent, indissoluble community of faith, life and love between a man and a woman until death. That is the ideal. Not everyone is able to achieve the ideal.

Most divorced Catholics who survive a broken marriage seldom fully recover. They persevere in seeking to live the ideal. Most feel a divorce means they are no longer welcome in the Catholic Church or are second-class members. Such feelings are the result of misunderstanding. Too many previously married Catholics are abandoned in a gray zone of uncertainty. No one helped them to understand that even with the best of intention, the ideal is not possible. Some eventually establish a new relationship and regain the confidence to attempt another marriage. They want to celebrate that marriage in the Catholic Church and see no reason for delay. Most feel discouraged when confronted with the canonical process for obtaining a declaration of nullity and learn it may take one or two years for the process to be completed. The process burdens them, hinting they are somehow defective since they did not achieve the ideal upon which their heart was set. They resent the process because it means reliving all the sense of failure they have now set behind them.

In his homiletic effort my Dominican friend sought to assure folks who are divorced and remarried that the Catholic Church remains their home. He developed his homily trying to explain why they are welcome to receive Communion in spite of their canonical circumstance. Someone heard his homily and took offense. That person complained to the local bishop, and Michael endured a severe reprimand. His fault lay in being realistic and recognizing there are situations in which we need to settle for achieving the possible rather then the ideal. The reprimand he received was more than unfortunate. It was not given in brotherly love (the ideal). It was simply an authoritarian defense of law. A man of lesser character may have left the active ministry, depriving people of his unique gifts. I am thankful Michael is a man of faith. He persisted and continues to be a responsible and effective homilist, consistent in his effort to encourage and support people to achieve the ideal.

In John's gospel Jesus speaks of himself as a good shepherd. Those ordained to preside at Eucharist and speak the Word are told to be like Christ the Good Shepherd. The good and faithful people of our communities expect those of us who share these privileged responsibilities to exercise our ministry in a manner that is relevant and engaged with their lives. It is the responsibility of we who are ordained to enable people to build communities of faith, and then live among and with them as a brother who is addressed affectionately as father. These are among the ideals we carried in our hearts on that day when we rose up from the floor of the Cathedral. The years since measured those ideals against the possibilities.

Some months ago the author of an editorial in *America* magazine was reflecting on the state of pastoral ministry in the United States today. He brought the editorial to closure with a statement something like this:

A good pastor is a priest who is so in touch with his community, and willing to make adjustments to the laws of the church and the rules of the diocese, that the local Bishop considers him irresponsible.[3]

The words of this Catholic priest and long time pastor are refreshing. He recognized the distinction between the ideal and the possible.

In the seventh chapter of his letter to the church in Rome, St. Paul discusses law and sin in a manner that most of us probably find obtuse. In the middle of that text Paul acknowledges his own interior struggle to live in harmony with the ideals he taught.

I do not understand my own actions. ... For I do not do what I want, but I do the very thing I hate. ... I do not do the good I want, but the evil I do not want is what I do.[4]

As individual Christians and as communities of faith we always hold the life and teaching of Jesus before us as the ideal. Sometimes our ideals conflict with our abilities and/or the reality of our existential situation. Flexibility is a skill required of all who pursue ideals for they often elude us and are beyond the possible at any given time or circumstance.

An author friend recently told of an experience long ago in his life when he went fishing with an old moonshiner in Kentucky. The moonshiner had produced over a million gallons of whiskey that he sold in Detroit. One day my friend asked the moonshiner, "Fred, does it ever bother you that you are breaking the law?" Fred looked at my friend and with a warm smile on his face responded. "Those are men's laws and it never bothers me to break them. I never break God's law."

In any given situation, when the ideal is beyond the possible, seek to do what is possible, even though it is not the ideal. All of us aspire to honor our call to be the Living Body of Christ. We are sincere in our commitment to think and act like Christ. We intend to be nonviolent. We intend to forgive those who harm us. We yearn to love others unconditionally. My experience teaches me it is not always possible to achieve the ideal, but that is never reason to stop trying.

One of the principal characters in a delightful book about small town boy's basketball is an eccentric old grandmother. The tale is located in one of the rural communities of south-central Montana. Following a very threatening situation with an alcoholic rancher, Grandma learns some of his past history, and, "felt ashamed and foolish and angry with herself for forgetting that everyone was making his way the best he could, everyone!"[5] We all seek to achieve the ideal. Sometimes we need to settle for achieving the possible.

I inferred earlier when telling the story of my Dominican friend Michael that even Catholic bishops do not always live up to the ideal. Recently in a western diocese, two gay men, active Catholics, requested public recognition of their lifestyle. They were recognized by the bishop, but in a negative, judgmental manner. The bishop excommunicated them.

I know of another bishop who is an extraordinary individual, bright, personable and seeking to provide pastoral vision to his diocese. In one parish of that diocese there were twenty-five lay people engaged in the ministry of homiletics. All of them were serious about their ministry and some were better than many of the ordained with faculties to preach. When the pastor's term of office expired, the bishop asked him to discontinue this ministry before leaving the parish. In the bishop's judgment the ideal was not part of the possible. Most likely the day will arrive, perhaps sooner than we realize, when necessity will prompt him to recognize that the ideal is not always expressed in the code of Canon Law or mandates from the Vatican.

Both bishops are sincere in their commitment to honor their own call to think and act like Christ. They are not unlike most of us when they make decisions that to the rest of us seem judgmental or exclusionary. Recognizing that the ideal cannot always be realized may help you avoid discouragement when the decisions or the attitudes exhibited by those charged with care of the faith community fall short of the ideal.

The experience of my Dominican friend reminded me that the failure of anyone to live the ideals is never reason to doubt the existence of God or walk away from the community of faith.

Our highest responsibility is to keep before us the life and teaching of Jesus of Nazareth as passed on to us in the written gospels and the teaching church. In doing so it is necessary to trust our own maturity. The ideal is to imitate Christ until God's unconditional love is our own.

The Gracious Mystery we name God is the ultimate reality of life and of all that exists. If you believe that is true as I do, then be confidant that in the midst of the turmoil and chaos in which we find ourselves, God is leading and guiding us to a bright future

We sometimes encounter well-intended, imperious or negative statements, policies or condemnations uttered by those appointed to positions of authority. The image of God projected in such moments is out of sync with the Jesus of Nazareth we know in the gospels. The resulting inner turmoil and doubt can be a gift. In such moments we are summoned to trust our own experience of God's unconditional love. Often our own experience is more reliable than well-intended, impetuous and negative statements, policies or condemnations.

Try to live out of a deep conviction that God is the ultimate reality of life and of all that exists. Take God seriously. Be confident that in the midst of the turmoil and chaos in which we find ourselves, God is leading and guiding us to a bright future. Living with such confidence is far easier to write about than to do. It is never easy when there are issues or concerns we consider significant, or when our requests and expectations are not in harmony with church law or practice. It is never easy to have one's own bishop or pastor become angry because doing the right thing was the wrong thing to do according to Canon Law.

Being companions of Jesus of Nazareth has always meant trying to model our response to people on the example of Jesus as portrayed in the written gospels. He cared about people and their needs. He placed the needs of people above the requirements of the law even when doing so upset those in positions of authority. He never would do anything that harmed people.

The priest who wrote the previously mentioned editorial for *America* magazine understood what it means to be a responsible leader. His words provide guidance for all of us. So I repeat them with my own additions:

> *A good pastor (a good Christian) is a priest (man or woman) who is so in touch with his community, and willing to make adjustments to the laws of the church and the rules of the diocese, that the local Bishop (or pastor) considers him (or her) irresponsible.*[5]

An advisor to top management in *Fortune 500* companies produced a handbook to assist employees in dealing with the changing corporate culture. My copy has disappeared. All that remains in my notes is the following quotation without attribution. In this handbook, the author insists that corporations cannot simply conduct business as usual or stick with what worked in the past. He claims that leaders will be successful only if they are willing and able,

> *To be pioneers, willing to explore, to go forward without guarantees or a road map. Imagination is necessary. Go with some wild ideas, break out of the routine and do something different. Extend yourself and see how far you can reach.*[6]

We read about those who first followed Jesus and often fail to recognize the amazing transformation in which they were engaged. They were pioneers. They took risks, explored and moved forward into the unknown. They moved out and away from Judaism and Jerusalem. Their daring changed the church and made it possible for a sect of Judaism to become an international community. It is becoming ever more evident that we are a melting pot of culture and peoples, varied, yet unified in Christ. Today we know ourselves as the Living Body of Christ.

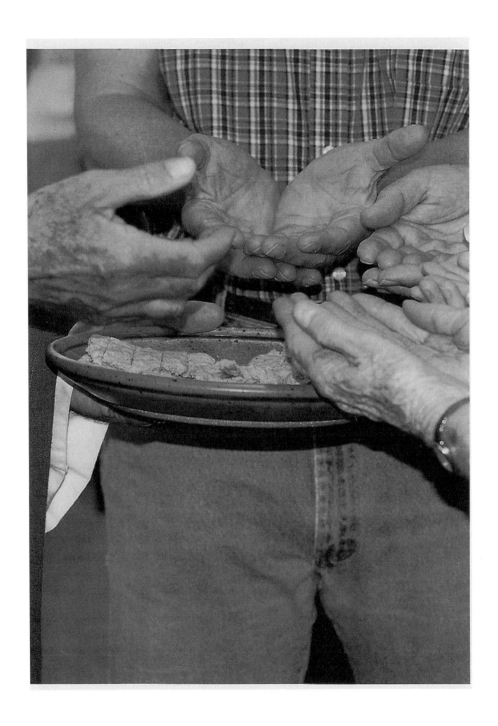

CHAPTER 17

COMPENDIUM OF
THE SOCIAL DOCTRINE OF THE CHURCH #570
"The Second Vatican Council indicated that the mission of the Church
in the contemporary world consists in helping every human being
to discover in God the ultimate meaning of his existence."

DENISE and SUSAN

I mentioned earlier that since entering senior status I enrolled in a three-week summer program of theological renewal at the American College in Louvain, Belgium. During those weeks there were many opportunities to visit other cities. Fortunately the train fare for senior citizens like myself is minimal. The weather during my stay was sunny and bright. I made weekend excursions to various cities and monasteries in Belgium. The cities I visited are truly beautiful.

One day I enjoyed touring the city of Bruges on bicycle. In the afternoon I headed out of town alone and made my way to the quaint village of Damme. While sitting at a tiny sidewalk cafe, the church bells began to chime. The tonality of those bells seemed perfect for this village. I commented to the waitress, "The bells of your local church make beautiful music." She stopped as if surprised, looked at me and with a gentle voice said, "Oh, we are so busy, we never hear them." What a sad comment, "Oh, we are so busy, we never hear them." We can become so preoccupied with concerns of life that we are unable to hear the bells, smell the flowers or see the night stars. We can be so busy about so many things that we become oblivious to the people, the circumstances or the consequences of our activity.

During my years of active ministry as a pastor I considered my primary responsibility was facilitating the growth of community. I dedicated my time and energy to this task. That means living with the people as community. As in my departure from other parishes, it was very difficult to leave Christ the King. It is a wonderful community in which people really participate in the liturgy. There is a great vitality in that parish, much of it generated by the large number of children, adolescents and young adults actively involved in the community.

Since entering senior status I have celebrated Mass in many parishes from California to Massachusetts, and north and south as well. As I visited these parishes I often found myself wondering, where all the young ones have gone. This concern is not intended to be negative, but simply an honest inquiry. For two years I was privileged to serve as an itinerant preacher begging on behalf of the poor in various parishes around the United States. The nearly universal absence of young people from our Sunday Assemblies was obvious. Their absence is a frequent topic of conversation among us.

The human body has the amazing ability to protect itself by the production of antibodies. When the system is functioning well, recuperation occurs swiftly. When the system malfunctions, or certain forms of cancer develop, our body cells have the inclination to metastasize, to spread throughout the body. Such cancers ordinarily persist against all treatments and eventually the body surrenders.

I referred earlier to a recent study conducted by the University of California, Los Angeles. That study confirms my own experience among undergraduate students over recent years. The average university student at the beginning of this decade is wired with mobile phones, Internet, text messaging, computers and I-pods. They maintain strong connections with their parents. Faculty members refer to them as helicopter parents, always hovering around their children. These students are very bright and capable, but have poor relational skills and are unwilling to make commitments or get involved. It seems an increasing number are simply far less interested in or willing to be engaged in campus life than their counterparts were just five years prior.

I was deeply involved with students at the University of Montana for twenty-two years. Each graduating class is different. In my last several years among them, it seemed that an entirely new sort of human being has or is evolving. This is not saying something negative about students. It is simply an observation that people chattering on cell phones while ignoring their immediate companions illustrate the great challenge we face in trying to pass our faith tradition to the forthcoming generation.

We are the Living Body of Christ. Perhaps the absence of our young people is symptomatic of a serious form of spiritual cancer within this body. Recently a friend invited me to lead a retreat in Hawaii. I certainly could not refuse such an offer! The retreat center is in a serene, rural, remote location overlooking the blue waters of the Pacific.

Angela is the caretaker of the residence in which I stayed. She is a warm-hearted native Hawaiian whose great smile betrays her enthusiasm for life. Shortly after my arrival, her concerns about the health of the local Catholic community began to flow out of her heart. She told me her many children and she herself have stopped participating in liturgy. She has turned to other faith traditions or practices, seeking a faith community and the spiritual nourishment for which she hungers. Her almost compulsive need to speak of this was a clear signal of the importance of her Catholic life for her.

Her local pastor has been very obedient in adopting the liturgical rubrics and norms recently published by the Bishops of the United States and commonly referred to as the G.I.R.M. (*The General Instruction for the Roman Missal)*. Given the observable consequences of this document in ordinary parish life, the acronym seems very appropriate. We know that a virus can create terrible problems in computers. In my opinion the G.I.R.M. is doing the same for the Catholic Church in the United States.

Angela's observation was sharp and critical. Neither she nor her family understand liturgy. They observe the priest-presider without much comprehension or appreciation of what he says or even less of what he does. Recent changes have made liturgy once again the priest's ritual. She, her family and her peers feel disconnected from the priest-presider. They are observers. The words and gestures do not connect with her inner life. Angela is not angry but she is sad. Her sadness was apparent as she told me the liturgy as it is now celebrated has become meaningless for herself, her family and her peers. They have abandoned the Sunday Assembly. In her heart she is Catholic and wants to remain, but cannot.

In August 2007, Dominican Sister Laurie Brink presented a very thought provoking and insightful keynote address to the Leadership Conference of Women Religious. Among her insights she was emphatic in stating,

> *Lay ecclesial ministers are feeling disenfranchised. Catholic theologians are denied academic freedom. Religious and lay*

women feel scrutinized simply because of their biology. Gays and lesbians desire to participate as fully human, fully sexual Catholics within their parishes. And young adults are drifting away from the very elements that once strengthened religious ties, set moral high ground, and created community. The hierarchy of our Church is right to feel alarmed. What is at stake is the very heart of the Church itself.[1]

During the recent ten to fifteen years, in response to events within the church and events external to us, the gaze of our bishops has turned inward. They know we face serious problems. The remedy they prescribe for our illness illustrates an absolute and narrow determination to ignore the real world and the signs of the times in which we live. It seems our bishops recognize the rapidly changing demographics within the Catholic Church and finally realize the enormous crisis we face as a liturgical community. It seems they are concerned about the absence of our young adults from our communities. Perhaps they will soon acknowledge the implications of insufficient numbers of ordained leaders and creatively respond to this developing crisis.

Thich Nhat Hahn is a Vietnamese Buddhist monk and peace activist. Consider his simple words of wisdom:

When you plant lettuce, if it does not grow well, you don't blame the lettuce. You look into the reasons it is not doing well. It may need fertilizer, or more water, or less sun. You never blame the lettuce. Yet if we have problems with our friends or our family, we blame the other person. But if we know how to take care of them, they will grow well, like lettuce. Blaming has no positive effect at all, nor does trying to persuade using reason and arguments. ... No blame, no reasoning, no argument, just understanding. If you understand, and you show that you understand, you can love, and the situation will change.[2]

Our tradition presumes that we who are ordained are given the responsibility to keep the vision of the gospel alive. This implies that we help younger generations understand the gospel, the meaning of Eucharist and all it means to be Catholic. Our Catholic tradition is a storehouse of wisdom available for us to share with them.

For some years our bishops have been busy trying to put things back into the box. Apparently they share a common opinion that John's Council and the spiritual renewal for which it called was a mistake. The declining number of vocations to ordained ministry and the absence of our young adults are read as direct results of *aggiornamento*. Apparently they think that if we put it all back in the box many young men will again be attracted to ordained ministry and our young people will return.

In the last twenty years, more and more educated Catholics recognize and resent this business of putting things back into the box. The heavy hand of church politics is resented. Once again domination and dogma are the trademarks adopted by the hierarchy beginning in the papacy of John Paul II and continuing today. It seems that a growing number of bishops and priests no longer see themselves in the role of servant ministers. They have rapidly become stalwart soldiers of the Vatican. This is evident in the near obsession our bishops have with a narrow band of moral issues, and the restoration of clerical status and culture.

The younger cells of the body we name church sense that something is askew. Dean Hoge, recently deceased, was a professor of sociology at the University of Notre Dame. In a recent report on young Catholic adults he broadly outlined differences among Pre-Vatican II Catholic spirituality, Post-Conciliar spirituality and today's young adult spirituality:

> *The highly-sentimental, ritualized and devotional spirituality of the 1940s-1950s gave way to an emerging sense of ecumenism, inculturation, a more   positive affirmation of the world at large and the Charismatic movement. Now young adult Catholics see themselves as spiritual and not necessarily tied to traditional religion. They continue to hold the Virgin Mary as a cultural icon of Catholic identity. ...[3]*

Many of our bishops are realistic about our situation and resort to the work of scholars like Dean Hoge to promote the agenda established by the Vatican. His conclusion that "the disassociation of many young adult Catholics from traditional forms of Catholic devotionalism and from the saints is having important effects" is valid. He did not indicate what those effects are. Our bishops conclude that the decline in ordinations to priesthood and the absence of our young adults from our Eucharistic Table was caused by and is a result of the Second Vatican Council.

There is no doubt that the former Catholic culture has or is swiftly disappearing. It seems a great leap of the imagination to suggest that our young adults miss what they never knew or experienced. The signs of the times in which we live are testimony that the reasons for the decline of vocations to priestly ministry and the absence of our young adults are extremely complex. It is overly simplistic to blame the renewal called for by the II Vatican Council. Consider the following.

The dominant culture in which our children are raised has a definite impact on shaping their values and ideals. Families and especially parents who are the primary educators of their children inadvertently become agents of that culture. The young of every decade are critical, skeptical observers of their parents but they learn more from the life style and behavior patterns of their parents than from the words spoken by their parents. In combination the dominant culture and families create an atmosphere in which taught values and ideals are contradicted by behavior patterns.

Many parents provide religious education for their children either in parish programs or Catholic schools. A large percentage of those same parents neglect their own spiritual development or have done nothing to nurture their own faith, even when opportunities are readily available to them. That sends a negative message to their children. Parents who have not put forth the energy to learn about and to understand the process or implications of the renewal initiated by the Council are incapable of providing the fruits of that renewal to their children. They may remember but do not understand the Catholic culture in which they were raised. They may view Mother Angelica's television channel and find it reassuring. Unable to share the vision of John's Council with their children, they only are able to pass on to them their own confused memory of that pre-Vatican II culture including some traditional forms of Catholic devotionalism. These may be attractive to young people but are out of sync with the theology of the II Vatican Council and adds to the confusion young people experience when they do go to Sunday liturgy in their parish.

Imagine the conflict in the mind and soul of a young person whose parents go to Mass on a regular basis, yet listen to and agree with public voices like Rush Limbaugh or Bill O'Reilly. The voices of such public figures contradict the voice of Jesus. If parental opinions about moral issues such as war, capital punishment or immigration are no different than the opinions of people who do not go to Mass, their children reasonably conclude that going to Mass makes no difference.

Jesus stood with the poor and the marginalized. Many Catholic families are affluent. Large trophy homes symbolize economic status. In those homes, each child has a private room, probably a computer, a television, a sound system and a mobile phone. Our young have been raised in a consumer society and are themselves consumers. Consumption requires money, so many of our young people are employed. Their job often prevents them from participating in the Sunday Assembly.

The high incidence of broken marriages impacts and influences the attitude of our young people concerning commitment. Even when reasons for divorce are valid, the repercussions for children are negative at best. This is evident in the research done by U.C.L.A. indicating our young people are hesitant to make commitments. That of course includes the commitment to be Catholic.

The dominant culture, and especially that dominant sub-culture in which our young people live, provides an environment of constant sensual stimulation and media saturation. Neither is conducive to reflection or prayer. When they are not working, they are inclined to go shopping for designer clothing or to hang out with their peers in local malls or at Wal-Mart. Such activity is more exciting, more stimulating, and thus more interesting and attractive to them than Sunday liturgy.

For some families life revolves around expensive vacations. These can be opportunities for family bonding and awaken social consciousness or simply reflect the consumer mentality of the dominant culture. It is not unusual for families to be away from their parish for major feast celebrations like Advent/Christmas or Lent/Triduum and absent as well from liturgy. Parents are seldom aware of the subtle message about priorities in life they communicate by such patterns.

Family life for many also revolves around or is controlled by academics or sports. Both are seen as avenues to economic success. Patterns of behavior make it clear by implication that soccer, skiing, golf or even fishing on Sunday are family priorities that take precedence over liturgy.

Then if our young people do join the Sunday Assembly, too often the liturgy is not experienced as prayer, or as a celebration of Christ present among us. Too often the ritual means nothing, especially when the ritual is simply ritual without soul or spirit or conviction. Too often the manner in which the prayer is spoken and/or the songs sung is routine and lacking spirit or soul. If God is not experienced as the ultimate meaning of our existence, liturgy means nothing. This easily leads to disassociation of young and old.

One year ago while hiking with a small group near Arenal volcano in Costa Rica, I was privileged to meet two young women from the Netherlands. They were attractive, bursting with vitality, well educated and Catholic. Upon learning I am a Catholic priest they became very conversant.

Denise was in a long-term relationship with a man she considered her soul mate. She heard the institutional church tell her repeatedly that relationship was sinful. She felt alienated from the church. Two years ago her companion suddenly and unexpectedly died. They were planning their wedding and she still retains her love for him as her husband. She was further alienated by the negative response of the institutional church to her personal tragedy.

Her sister Susan is younger and recently graduated with a Master's Degree in economics. Her Master's thesis developed various plans and programs to assist people in developing countries create successful businesses. Susan also feels alienated from the church because she and her boyfriend are living together. They are moving to Hong Kong and hope to work there with non-profit, non-government agencies on behalf of economically deprived people.

On the following day we found ourselves traveling on the same bus. As we arrived at our destination we decided to meet and share dinner. While hiking together on the previous day they remarked that they, like the majority of their peers in Holland, are no longer practicing Catholics. So during our dinner I asked if they could explain why. They were not hesitant but forthright in their response. The church, they said, is too dogmatic about issues of human sexuality and out of touch with the real world. Their local parish priest waggles his finger at them while preaching. In their perception the priest is boring, the Mass is boring and Eucharist has no meaning for them.

These two attractive, educated, young women intuitively sense the importance of the Mass and Catholic teaching and yearn for it to be more significant for them. They were enthusiastic as they told of Mass in their home when a Catholic priest gathers a small group consisting of their family and friends. Eucharist becomes important and means something for them in that small community. These young women believe they are both Catholic and Christian. They express this as they engage in responding to the needs of the poor. That is the direction each has chosen for her career.

A few days later, the Sunday Mass in a nearby town left me identifying with so much that Denise and Susan had shared with me. Before the Mass I introduced myself to the parish priest who was to preside. He was a warm and welcoming man and had diligently implemented the directives of the G.I.R.M. in the parish.

202

The liturgy was in Spanish, a language I neither speak nor understand. That was no problem for the Mass prayers are so familiar that it is easy for me to bridge the language difference and be united in prayer. Of course the homily also was in Spanish and as expected, was incomprehensible to me, except for the non-verbal gestures. Soon into the homily the padre's voice became strong and he kept pointing and shaking his index finger at us. On a simple, non-verbal level it appeared he was scolding us, and the tone of his voice sounded negative.

The presider kissed the altar several times, bowed and genuflected often, whispered prayers and honored the rubrics. The entire experience was remote and ambiguous. It was not because of the language difference. It was ritual lacking soul! That liturgy left me with a new appreciation for the dilemma in which Denise and Susan and so many other young adults find themselves. Neither my mind, my heart, nor my soul were touched by the experience. The Happy Birthday sung to an old man just before the dismissal was the only inspiration during that hour spent with that community of faith. Putting everything back into the box is not going to correct or remedy this situation.

CHAPTER 18

DAMME, BELGIUM
"The bells of your local church make beautiful music."
"Oh, we are so busy, we never hear them."

ONLY ONE BODY

In these pages I have attempted to engage you in a conversation that is honest but encouraging, humorous but serious. I wrote with the hope that all who read this will find a new determination to "keep on going," a new determination to study the Council documents and a commitment to be persistent in pursuing the vision.

In Chapter Ten I briefly described Mt. Sentinel, the mountain that rises up immediately behind the campus of the University of Montana, and the large, whitewashed "M" that overlooks the campus and our valley. In these years of senior status I continue my habit of climbing to the "M" at least six days each week. As I sat up on the "M" this morning, the scene before me across the Missoula valley seemed a wonderful image with which to bring these reflections to closure. It is autumn in western Montana. Autumn here in Missoula is spectacular. In the early morning as the sunrise peeks over the mountains, the valley floor explodes with the brilliance of autumn foliage. Vibrant yellows and gold, burnt umber, the red of maples and berry bushes all blend with the varying shades of greenery. They form a great chorus shouting, "Look at us! Enjoy the beauty our creator God provides for you."

I return to my residence bicycling along the banks of the Clark Fork River and through the university area. The multi-colored foliage stains the surface of the river and the tree-lined streets are paved now with fallen leaves. The spectacle embraces and overpowers my senses. In this season nature explodes with color no human made Fourth of July can match.

There is a gift in living where the seasons change with such dramatic effect. As the leaves fall and accumulate on the ground, we here in Missoula are aware winter is coming. Already snow is accumulating on the peaks that surround us. Then in a few short months spring will surprise us with new bursts of life and the cycle continues. This morning I realized anew how beautiful morning is and how each day is filled with new possibilities. Everything filled me with a renewed sense that the Holy Spirit is with us, guiding us and leading us in ways we cannot anticipate. Autumn speaks to me about letting go, and death, and putting things back into the box. Like the clerk in the Ace hardware store, it seems those in the church trying to put things back into the box are simply precipitating results contrary to their intended purpose.

You know by now that I think John XXIII had great foresight when he summoned the bishops of the world into the Second Vatican Council. My own experience of the Council was so positive. In my perception that Council created the possibility for all of us to be Catholic in more than name and to influence our nation and world in positive ways. *Aggiornamento*. The word contains great potential.

Pope John knew there is only one presence of Christ. His real presence in the bread and wine of Eucharist directs us toward the community, and his real presence in and among us. In Sermon 272, St. Augustine was instructing his local church about Eucharist when he asked, "How can bread be his body? And the cup, or what the cup contains, how can it be his blood?" He answered his own questions:

> *The reason these things, brothers and sisters, are called sacraments is that in them one thing is seen, another is understood. What can be seen has a bodily appearance, so what is to be understood provides spiritual fruit. So if you want to understand the body of Christ, listen to the apostle telling the faithful, 'You though, are the body of Christ and it's members.' ..... So if it is you that are the body of Christ and its members, it is the mystery meaning you that has been placed on the Lord's table; what you receive is the mystery that means you. It is to what you are that you reply Amen. So be a member of the body of Christ, in order to make that Amen true.*

For St. Augustine and his theological peers, the primary emphasis was not on Christ present in the bread and wine. He understood and preached that the purpose of that presence is to enhance the presence of Christ in the community.

We are still in the very early stages of the spiritual renewal to which Pope John called us. Far too often the only changes implemented at this time have been in externals. Those external changes are not accepted by all of us. The real *aggiornamento*, the renewal that Pope John set before us is a renewal of spirit. Eventually the heavy fog of confusion and frustration that diminishes our ability to see our direction forward will dissipate. Then the spiritual renewal called for by the Council will begin to spread. It will have significant influence on the dominant culture in which we live. We saw this in the years immediately following the Council. It will continue.

The process of evolution continues, even within the church. Yesterday we who are Catholic were a despised minority. Today we are a respected majority. Tomorrow we will become more fully aware of what it means to be the Living Body of Christ.

> *The 'aggiornamento' (bringing up to date) of Pope John XXIII and the documents of Vatican II were 'radical' in so far as they returned our attention to the life of the apostolic church and the earliest understandings of Christ, his mission, and our continuing role in it.*[1]

When that finally happens, we will recognize the privilege entrusted to us. It is time for more of us to make a personal commitment to follow the nonviolent Christ and direct our creative energy to calling forth God's new reality. As we do so, justice and peace will be like artisan wells flowing out from the shores of our hearts and our household of faith into the world. That is the vision of the II Vatican Council. Eventually the Council's vision will transform our hearts in spite of those who seek to put everything back into the box. Christ dwells in, with and among us here and now. Christ is the center of our lives and the source of all our living. Remember that when you speak your "amen." Speak it with conviction that, YES WE ARE! The Living Body of Christ!

NOTES

Preface
1 DeMello, Anthony. Awareness. New York: Doubleday, 1990.
2 Gaudium et Spes, Vatican City, December 7, 1965.
3 Thurston, Anne. "Honoring the Ordinary." The Furrow. Volume 58, No. 10, (October, 2007): p. 537.

Chapter One: Voice, Words, Signs
1 The Gospel of John 1: 21.
2 The Gospel of Matthew 18: 20.
3 Angelou, Maya
4 Hogan, Father Jim. A personal verse
5 Haval, Vaclav. "A Word About Words." Acceptance Speech. Frankfurt, Germany. (July 25, 1989)
6 Sirach 27:5
7 The Gospel of Matthew 12: 34-37
8 Hebblethwaite, P. John XXIII - Pope of the Council. (London, 1984), pp. 498-9.
9 Pannenberg, Wolfgang. Source unknown.
10 The Gospel of Matthew 16:3.
11 Dorr, Donal. "Reading the Signs of the Times." The Furrow. Volume 59, No. 10, Oct. 08.
12 Nothwehr, O.S.F., Dawn M. "Introduction." New Theology Review. Volume 20, No. 4.
13 Ibid.

Chapter 2: Our Task
1 John XXIII, Pope
2 Editorial. Commonweal. Volume 197, No. 4. (August 13, 2007): p. 5
3 Stanosz, Paul. "The Other Health Crisis." Commonweal. Volume CXXXIV (November 27, 2007): p.16
4 Neugeboren, Jay. "Housing The Homeless." Commonweal. Volume CXXXIV, No. 22, (Dec.21, 2007): p. 7
5 Wright, N.T. Simply Christian. Harper San Francisco, 2006.
6 Caldwell, Christopher. "The Fool's Gold of Legal Gambling." New York Times/The Week. (Jan.19, 2009): p. 14
7 Commonweal, op. cit.
8 Toolan, David. At Home In The Cosmos. Maryknoll, New York: Orbis Books, 2001. p. 128
9 Ibid.
10 O'Murchu, Diarmuid. Quantum Theology. New York, NY: Crossroad Publishing, 1997. p. 4
11 Morwood, Michael. Tomorrow's Catholic. Mystic, CT." Twenty-Third Publications, 1998. p. 25
12 Ibid. p. 23
13 Ferris, Timothy. Coming Of Age In The Milky Way. New York: Doubleday

Anchor Books, 1988. p. 384
14 New Theology Digest
15 Fiand, Barbara, S.N.D.
16 Buechner, Frederick. Secrets in the Dark. San Francisco: HarperCollins
    Publishers, 2006. p. 299
17 Dorr, Donal. "Free To Be Present." The Furrow Volume, 58, No. 9, (September
    2007): p. 471
18 Thomas, R.S. Wales: 1913-2000.
19 Julian of Norwich. 14th century mystic.

Chapter 3: Social Glue
1 Muller-Fahrenhold, Geiko. America's Battle for God. Erdmann's Pub. Co. 2007.
   p. 19
2 Bellah, Robert N. "Civil Religion in America," Daedalas 96, no. I (1967): 1-21.
3 Muller-Fahrenhold, Geiko. op. cit., p. 19
4 Kennedy, John F.
5 Martin, Diarmuid. "The Christian in the Public Square." The Furrow. Volume 58,
   No. 9 (Sept. 2007): p. 456
6 Ibid.
7 The Gospel of John 8: 12
8 The Gospel of Matthew, 5:13
9 Ron Rolheiser, OMI. Secularity and The Gospel. (New York, Crossroads) p. 70

Chapter 4: Mount St. Helens
1 Coy, Joe. "Autumn in Kilbannon." The Furrow. Volume 58, No. 12, (December
   2007): p. 672
2 Ibid.
3 Reef, Phillip. 1966. Source unknown.
4 Prabhu, R.K. (Compiler). Truth Is God: Gleanings from the Writings of Mahatma
   Gandhi bearing on God, God- realization and the Godly Way. Ahmedabad:
   Navajivan Publishing House, 1955; p. 145.
5 Ibid. p. 83
6 Wills, Garry. What Jesus Meant. New York, NY: Viking Press, 2006, p. 29

Chapter 6: John's Council
1 McBrien, Richard, gen. Ed., The HarperCollins Encyclopedia of Catholicism. New
   York, NY; Harper San Francisco; 1995. p. 456
2 Ibid. p. 370
3 Davis, S.J, Leo Donald. The Seven First Ecumenical Councils (325-787): Their
   History and Theology. Florence, Italy. January 1, 1987. Epilogue, p. 323
4 McBrien, op. cit., p. 370
5 Ibid. p. 456
6 Ibid. p. 456
7 McBrien, op. cit., p. 1300
8 Catholic Encyclopedia; Wikipedia®; 1997
9 McBrien, op. cit., p. 456
10 Ibid. p. 1301

11 Ibid. p. 1301
12 Huebsch, Bill. Vatican II In Plain English: The Council. Allen, Texas: Thomas More, 1997; p. 75
13 Ibid. p. 1299
14 Second Vatican Council. The Constitution On The Sacred Liturgy. Rome, Italy. (1963). Paragraph 14.
15 Ferrone, Rita. "A Step Backward," Commonweal (August 17, 2007): p. 15
16 Prusak, Bernard P. "Getting the History Right." Commonweal, August 17, 2007: p. 17
17 Constitution on the Liturgy; Vatican II; section 2.
18 Ignatius of Antioch.
19 Huebsch, op. cit., p. 74
20 Ibid. p. 74
21 Markey, O.P., John J. Creating Communion. Hyde Park, N.Y., 2003, p. 16
22 Ibid., p. 17
23 Ibid.
24 McBrien, op. cit., p. 1302
25 Hebrew Bible. Habakkuk. Chapter 2, verse 3.

Chapter 7: Two Giants

1 Cohen, Leonard.
2 McBrien, Richard. Catholicism. Volume 1. Winston Press: Minneapolis, MN, (1980). p. 164
3 Ibid.
4 Ibid.
5 Ibid.
5 Ibid.
7 McBrien, Richard. Encyclopedia of Catholicism. Harper: San Francisco, CA. (1995). p. 1077
8 McCarthy, Timothy. The Catholic Tradition. Loyola Press: Chicago, IL. 1998.
9 Muller-Fahrenholz, op.cit. p. 36
10 McBrien, Richard, op. cit. p. 1254
11 McCarthy, Timothy, op.cit. p. 366
12 Ibid., p. 1007
13 O'Leary, Donal. "Begin With The Heart." The Furrow. Volume 4, (April 2007). p. 214
14 McCarthy, Timothy, op. cit. p. 29
15 John XXIII, Pope
16 Ibid.
17 McCarthy, Timothy G., op. cit., p. 98
18 Ibid.
19 Ibid.
20 Sullivan Ph.D., Jeremiah. Carroll College. Helena, Montana.
21 The Gospel of John, 20:20
22 Ibid., 20:22
23 McBrien, Richard, op. cit., p. 1255
24 John XXIII, Pope

Chapter 8: Harry Potter and Jesus

1 Galatians 5:1. The New Jerusalem Bible. Garden City, New York: Doubleday. 1985.
2 Ruiz S.D.S., Raul Gomez. "Liturgy and Ritual." New Theology Review: Volume 19, No. 4. Nov. 2006. p. 70
3 Keeler, Roger. "Liturgical Law." Celebrate. Volume 45, No. 6. (Nov.-Dec. 2007): p. 11
4 Johnson, Luke Timothy. Religious Experience in Earliest Christianity. Minneapolis: Fortress Press. 1998.
5 Cooke, Bernard. The Future of Eucharist. New York: Paulist Press. 1997.
6 Galatians 5:1. The New Jerusalem Bible. Garden City, New York: Doubleday. 1985.
7 Mick, Lawrence. "Christ Set Us Free". Celebration. Volume (July 2007): p. 19
8 Cooke, op. cit. p. 31
9 O'Loughlin, Thomas. "Preaching: Why We Bother." The Furrow: Volume 58, No. 9. Sept. 2007.
10 Johnson, op. cit., p. 1
11 Ibid, p. 1
12 The degree "On The Catholic Faith," quoted in Charles Williams, Arthurian Torso (Oxford: Oxford University Press, 1948) p. 19
13 Athans, B.V.M., Mary Christine. "Judaism and Catholic Prayer." New Theology Review. Volume 21, no. 4; (November 2008): p. 56
14 Gittins, Anthony J., C.C.Sp. "Can We Get Beyond Religion?" New Theology Review. Volume 20, No. 2; (May 2007): p. 11
15 Huebsch, Bill. The Council. Allen, Texas: Thomas More, 1997; p. 75

Chapter 9: It's About The Heart

1 Simon, Paul. "The Sounds of Silence."
2 Oregon Catholic Press; Portland, Oregon.
3 The Gospel of Mark 5: 34
4 Nolan, Albert. Jesus Today. Maryknoll, New York: Orbis Books. 2006. p. 87
5 Ibid, p. 88
6 Kaufman, Gordon D. Jesus and Christianity. Minneapolis: Fortress Press. 2006, p. 32
7 Julian of Norwich. 14th Century
8 Johnson, Elizabeth. Quest For The Living God. New York: Continuum, 2007.
9 Ibid.
10 Nolan, Albert. op. cit. p. 88
11 Ibid.

Chapter 10: The Wondrous Gift

1 "Celebration." November 2006.

Chapter 11: Return to What?

1 Karban, Roger V. "Our Eucharist." Celebration. (October 2007) p. 4
2 Hosea. 6:1-3
3 Daniel 12: 1-2

4 Flood, Edmund. The Resurrection. New York, NY: Paulist Press. (1973) p. 9
5 Diekmann, Godfrey, O.S.B.
6 Koernke, I.H.M., Theresa F. "Issues Around Eucharistic Practice." New Theology Review. Volume 17, No. 4. (November 2004): p. 41
7 Cooke, op. cit., p. 52
8 II Vatican Council. Constitution on the Sacred Liturgy. Rome, Italy (1963). No. 10.
9 I Corinthians 10:16-17
10 The Gospel of Luke 24: 16, 30, 35,
11 Bergant, Dianne. "Food! Glorious Food!" America. October 3, 2005. p. 31
12 Wills, op. cit., p. 133

Chapter 12: Creation Ever New

1 Genesis 1:1
2 Sheldrake, Rupert. "In the Presence of the Past: An Interview." http:twm,co.nz/shel-ints.html
3 America. (February 2008)
4 Ibid.
5 Ibid.
6 Garvey, John. "Become All Fire." Commonweal. Volume CXXXV, No. 4, (February 2008): p. 13
7 Gilkey, Langdon.
8 Spong, J. Shelby. A New Christianity For A New World. San Francisco: HarperCollins, 2001.
9 Otto, Rudolph. The Idea of the Holy. London: Oxford University Press, 1926.
10 Acts of The Apostles
11 Johnson, op. cit., p. 36
12 Wright, N.T., op. cit., p. 60
13 Wright, N.T., op. cit., p. 96
14 Hopkins, Gerard Manley

Chapter 13: Guru or Son of Man

1 St. Paul. 1 Corinthians: 11: 23-27.
2 Ibid. 15: 3-7
3 St. Paul. Letter to the Ephesians: 1: 22-23.
4 St. Paul. Letter to the Colossians 1: 15-20
5 Ibid. 15: 20-25.
6 St. Paul. Letter to the Romans: 8: 10-11
7 St. Paul. Letter to the Ephesians 2:5.
8 Borg, Marcus. Meeting Jesus Again For The First Time. Harper San Francisco, 1995. p. 9
9 Beier, Matthias. A Violent God-Image. New York: Continuum, 2004.
10 The Gospel of Matthew 12: 13-17.
11 Nolan, Albert. Jesus Before Christianity. Maryknoll, N. Y.: Orbis Books, 1978. p. 117
12 Wright, N.T. op. cit. p. 56
13 Genesis 3: 1-7
14 Matthew. op. cit. 26:50

15 Ibid. 26: 63
16 The Gospel of Luke 23: 34

Chapter 14: Children of God
1 Source Unknown.
2 Source Unknown.
3 Gomes, Peter J. The Good Book. New York, NY: Avon Books, 1996. p. 199
4 Ibid. p. 201
5 St. Paul. Letter to the Romans 8: 14-17
6 Rahner, Karl. Foundations of Christian Faith: An Introduction to the Idea of
    Christianity. New York: Seabury, 1978, p. 283

Chapter 15: Pray For Rain In A Time of Drought
1 Proverbs 29:18
2 Hybels, Bill. Courageous Leadership. p. 32
3 Wink, Walter. "Without a Vision the People Perish". April 14, 2002; All Saints
    Church, Pasadena, California.
4 The Gospel of Mark 12: 28-31
5 Washington, Irving. Tales of the Alhambra: The Legend of The Three Beautiful
    Princesses.
6 Wessels, OP, Cletus. The Holy Web. Maryknoll, NY. Orbis Books. 2003.
7 Pope Benedict XVI. Switzerland
8 Pope Benedict XVI. Vatican City.
9 Stafford, Betty. "Why U.S. Catholics Are Heading For The Exits." N.C.R. Volume
    44, #30. (Oct. 17, 2008) p. 16
10 Huck, Gabe. "Celebration," Volume 35; #5. (May 2007). p. 9
11 Marrin, Patrick. "Celebration." Volume 35; #5. (May 2007). p. 1
12 Heschel, Abraham. Source unknown.

Chapter 16: Ideals and Possibilities
1 The Gospel of John 1:39
2 The Gospel of John 14:6
3 America Magazine
4 St. Paul. Letter to the Romans 7: 15, 19
5 West, Stanley Gordon. Blind Your Ponies. Shakopee, Minnesota: Lexington-
    Marshall Pub., 2001 p. 539
6 "Fortune 500." Details unknown.

Chapter 17: Denise and Susan
1 Brink, Laurie, O.P. "A Marginal Life: Pursuing Holiness in the 21st Century."
    Kansas City, MO. LCWR Keynote Address. August 2, 2007.
2 Hahn, Thich Nhat. Quoted in Connect. Liturgical Publications, Inc. May 4, 2008
3 Hoge, Dean, (Dinges, Johnson, Gonzales). Young Adult Catholics. Religion in the
    Culture of Choice. Notre Dame, University of Notre Dame Press, 2001.

Chapter 18: Only One Body
1 Loxterkamp, David. "A Mutual Presence." Commonweal. Oct. 7, 2005. Volume
    CXXXII. No. 17. p. 17